PENGUIN BOOKS

Independence or Union

'The book offers a crisp and well-paced assessment of the Union'
Donald MacRaild, *Times Higher Education*

'An outstanding analysis of how Scotland changed from a Tory
stronghold to Nationalist redoubt'
Sunday Times

'Devine brings his usual acute historical critique to the question in hand . . . the
analysis of the changes that worked their way into Scottish society during
the last four decades of the twentieth century is convincing. The most
profound point in Devine's argument is that it was the Conservatives
who unwittingly undermined the Union'
Keith M. Brown, *The Times Literary Supplement*

'Thorough, readable and grounded in statistics'
Stuart Kelly, *Scotsman*

'Surefooted, balanced and reliable in analysis throughout'
Colin Kidd, *London Review of Books*

'A formidable historical overview with a regular flow of insights which challenge
many a pre-existing pre-conception. There is a very pronounced and
welcome international perspective which is highly illuminating'
Open House

'Its accessibility provides a very welcome service in opening up the
flowering of history to a wider audience'
Irish Times

D1059961

T. M. Devine has written three previous books for Penguin: *The Scottish Nation, Scotland's Empire* and *To the Ends of the Earth*. He is Sir William Fraser Professor Emeritus of Scottish History and Palaeography at the University of Edinburgh. In 2001 he was awarded the Royal Gold Medal and has won all three major prizes for Scottish historical research. He was knighted in 2014.

Independence or Union
Scotland's Past and Scotland's Present

T. M. DEVINE

PENGUIN BOOKS

PENGUIN BOOKS

UK | USA | Canada | Ireland | Australia
India | New Zealand | South Africa

Penguin Books is part of the Penguin Random House group of companies whose addresses can be found
at global.penguinrandomhouse.com

First published by Allen Lane 2016
Published in Penguin Books 2017

003

Copyright © T. M. Devine, 2016

The moral right of the author has been asserted

Set in 10.5/14 pt Sabon LT Std
Typeset by Palimpsest Book Production Limited, Falkirk, Stirlingshire
Printed in Great Britain by Clays Ltd, St Ives plc

A CIP catalogue record for this book is available from the British Library

978-0-141-98157-4

For Lady C; has always been a real lady

Contents

CONTENTS

Preface

As this is written in early summer 2015, conventional wisdom has it there is only one significant 'Scottish Question' in UK politics, namely whether or not Scotland will remain within the United Kingdom or become an independent sovereign state. This was the option put to the people of Scotland in the referendum of 18 September 2014. They answered by a majority of around 10 per cent of those who voted to remain within the Union. At the time, many expected that vote would settle the constitutional issue for at least a generation and possibly much longer. Analogies were drawn with the aftermath of the failed devolution referendum of 1979 when the home-rule movement of that time did not recover its confidence or sense of purpose for almost two decades.

Subsequent events, however, have suggested that the question put in 2014 had still to be given a decisive and lasting response which could be accepted by the Scottish nation as a whole. The aftershock of the referendum was not a repeat of 1979. The many groups supporting independence were not cowed for long and soon began to proclaim that the referendum was a battle only narrowly lost; the war could and should continue. This was accompanied by an enormous upsurge in support for the SNP and in its recorded membership, followed by the party's stunning success in the May 2015 general election. Scotland remains a restless nation.

Some commentators also suggest that September 2014 was at best but a pyrrhic victory for unionism. The commanding ascendancy of the Scottish National Party in the post-referendum polls, the historic humiliation of Labour in the last general election – the only credible unionist party left in Scotland – and the ongoing activities of the numerous and varied extra-parliamentary activists who had enthusiastically supported the independence cause before the referendum, hardly suggested that a return to a world of humdrum Scottish politics could be expected in the near future. There was a feeling in the land that a political Pandora's box had been fully opened in spectacular fashion and no one could yet be certain how or whether it would be closed again.

Self-evidently, therefore, the key question, and its elusive answer, about the constitutional future of Scotland remains of great significance both for the Scottish people and their fellow citizens in other parts of the UK. This book argues however that, while obviously by far the most important and most recent issue, it is but one of a series that have marked the history of the Union and the relations of England and Scotland over more than three centuries. Further, taking the long view back into history, as is attempted here, can help to give a context for understanding the persistence of the present post-referendum constitutional issues while providing a broader framework for determining how these developments came about and now sit within the longer narrative of Scottish and British history.

In this book, therefore, a number of related questions are considered, from the making of the Treaty of Union in 1707 until the political circumstances of 2015, which try to shed light on the past and on the background to present concerns:

- Why did the Union first come about between England and Scotland?
- Why, despite early turbulence between the two countries, did the Anglo-Scottish Union survive when unions between several other European states in similar close geographical proximity collapsed in failure?
- What factors over the long run helped to embed and cement this relationship?
- What happened to Scottish identity within the Union state when Scotland had to share the British bed with 'the English elephant'?
- How was the new hybrid identity of Scottishness and Britishness then constructed and perpetuated?
- Why, when Ireland and much of central Europe were in the throes of nationalist revolt and revolution in the nineteenth century, was

no 'Scottish Question' ever asked in any meaningful political sense until a century later in the 1960s?
- How can the rise of effective Scottish nationalism after that time be understood?
- What factors led to the opening of the Scottish Parliament in 1999?
- How is the electoral collapse of the two main unionist parties in Scotland, first the Conservatives and then Labour, more recently, to be explained?
- Why did a referendum on Scottish independence take place in 2014 and what were the consequences of the result?
- Why, in 2015, has the Scottish Question not yet been answered and resolved?

In trying to respond to these questions, I am fortunate to have gained from the vast outpouring of research and publication in Scottish history, sociology and political science over the last forty years or so. I argue later in the book that the public dissemination of this new and unprecedented understanding of the Scottish past and present has itself helped to shape national political discourse as well as adding significantly to academic scholarship. The key works that have proved most helpful are listed in the short bibliographies for each chapter as set out in the Selected Further Reading section. But these form only the peak of a veritable mountain of excellent academic and journalistic writing. Most of the texts listed also contain substantial suggestions for further reading that those interested can consult to explore issues in more detail. From time to time, I have also included some material from my own previous publications.

The final chapters could not have been written as they are had it not been for the referendum and its aftermath. The information in the British and foreign press, numerous websites and blogs, personal comments and recollections, opinion polls and some published diaries of the campaign – all proved fascinating and vital sources. Never before has a single political event in Scottish history left behind such a treasure trove of evidence to be worked on, analysed and argued over by scholars of the future. I am deeply grateful to all who contributed their views before, during and after the campaign, whether anonymous or named, together with senior politicians on both sides of the debate and the citizens of Scotland, for the richness and diversity of their opinions. Truly it was a time when democratic debate went into overdrive. Nevertheless, the conclusions of the near contemporary chapters must remain interim and provisional. Much material is already in the public domain. But scholars of the future will have even more evidence available, as well as the signal advantage of the perspective of time, to enable a fuller assessment of the most important period in Scottish political history since the passing of the Treaty of Union in 1707.

A personal comment is also required at this point. In the latter stages of the referendum campaign the press reported on my decision to vote 'Yes' on 18 September. My own preferred choice, like the majority of my fellow Scots at an earlier stage, would have been to support a more powerful Scottish Parliament via some form of enhanced devolution. That option was in the end not available in the wording of the referendum. Many of those who thought like me were effectively disenfranchised. My choice of vote in the most important political decision taken in Scotland for over three centuries is therefore in the public domain. It is only fair that readers of this volume know about that. They can be assured, however, that what follows is not intended to be a political tract, a manifesto or a polemic. Instead it is a history, written in the way I have always tried to write history since my first book was published in 1975 – with a commitment to impartiality, the use of representative evidence, and due respect for conflicting opinions. Whether the book lives up to these ideals in whole or in part or not at all is for readers to decide.

I am most grateful to all those who have made this book possible: my supportive and very capable agent, Andrew Lownie; my editor, Simon Winder of Penguin, for his customary acute insights and valuable comments, now extending over four books, on the first draft of this volume; and also his other colleagues at Penguin, particularly Richard Duguid and Pen Vogler, for their efficient work. Outside Penguin, I am very much in debt to Richard Mason, the most careful and scrupulous of copy-editors. One of my academic colleagues at Edinburgh, Professor Lindsay Paterson of the School of Social Science, kindly commented on the last few chapters of the book.

The University of Edinburgh is a wonderfully stimulating and supportive academic environment in which to teach, research and write history. The School of History, Classics and Archaeology has around seventy historians with expertise on all continents of the world and all periods of the human past, from the earliest times to the present day. History at Edinburgh was graded first in Scotland and third in the UK for the quality and volume of its research in the 2015 UK Research Excellence Framework. For scholarship in Scottish history, the School has no equal. In the related areas of sociology, politics and geography there is also a remarkable abundance of academic talent working on modern Scottish themes. That is the scholarly stable from which this study has emerged.

Once again I am indebted to Margaret Begbie, who, not for the first time, miraculously transformed my crabbed handwriting into clean typescript. My children, their spouses and partners were as always most supportive. I also wish to express warm thanks to my eight young grandchildren: in order of birth, Sean, Mia, Thomas, Erin, Cara, Rebecca, Lena and Evan Thomas. As the author struggled with his text, they were a joyful source of diversion, fun and mischief when they visited, and in the process enormously eased the challenges of composition.

The book is dedicated with love and deep affection to my wife, Catherine, for being there with me over more than four decades during which we have shared many great joys but also some sorrows.

Tom Devine
Scoor House
Isle of Mull
July 2015

PART ONE

Unionism Triumphant

I

The Context of Union

I

The Union of England and Scotland in 1707 was a marriage of convenience founded on pragmatism, expediency, competing national
patriotisms and realpolitik. Love and friendship for the other were
entirely notable by their absence during the negotiations. Nor, despite
the beliefs of unionist-minded Victorians at a later time, can the Union
be considered inevitable, some kind of providential gift from a caring
Protestant God. Even in the few years immediately before final agreement between Edinburgh and London, all was unpredictable and
outcomes were uncertain. It was this that explains the concessions
and compromises made by both parties during the discussions. At
the end of the day, most politicians on both sides of the border who
supported the Union experienced emotions of relief rather than
uninhibited joy. It was indeed a close-run thing. Nearly half a century
then passed before the new Anglo-Scottish association achieved some
stability and became properly embedded. During those decades ran-
corous divorce always remained a possibility.

When the Treaty of Union was written into the statute book on
May Day 1707, the historic decision was publicly recognized in London. Queen Anne and the Houses of Commons and Lords attended a
service of thanksgiving in St Paul's Cathedral while bonfires were lit
and church bells tolled throughout the land. Yet in Scotland the occasion was hardly marked at all. Indeed, the event is little mentioned in
both the public and private documentation of the time. Both protests
and celebrations were notable by their absence. The church bells of
Edinburgh did ring out, but sometimes with such plaintive dirges as

3

'Why should I be sad on my wedding day?' In general, the birth of Great Britain was greeted with muted indifference north of the border. It was not a happy portent for the future.

Nonetheless, historically the idea of union between two old enemies had a long pedigree in Scotland dating back to the sixteenth century. While the survival of the independent and sovereign kingdom was by far the dominant belief in the early modern period, some Scottish thinkers of the time did argue for a much closer association, not simply to ensure more peaceful relationships, but in order to provide an alternative to the historic English aspiration of achieving hegemony over the entire Britain Isles. The Reformation and the emergence of Protestantism in both countries, albeit in different forms, gave added impetus to this discourse, especially when the forces of Counter-Reformation in Catholic France and Spain presented such an existential threat to the religious revolution across Britain. When James VI of Scotland became monarch of both states in the Regal Union of 1603, he set out to develop a closer bond between the two nations that he likened symbolically to the consummation of a marriage between husband and wife. In due course, however, the English reaction to his proposals demonstrated the depth of the political opposition south of the border to such an arrangement and how far the two countries were from entering into even a modest association. James's plans collapsed amid a welter of anti-Scottish abusive racism in Westminster and the unyielding English determination to defend their exclusive rights over trade and commerce from the impecunious neighbour in the north.

A federal union was also mooted by the Scots Covenanters as the means of establishing a universal British Presbyterianism during the Wars of the Three Kingdoms, and the idea was incorporated in the treaty made by them with the Long Parliament in 1643 known as the Solemn League and Covenant. Significantly, however, the only real Anglo-Scottish union of the seventeenth century was achieved a few years later not by agreement but rather by coercion and brute force. Scots' support for the restoration of Charles II as their rightful king following the execution of his father in 1649 led to an invasion of Scotland by Oliver Cromwell and his formidable New Model Army. After comprehensively routing the Scottish forces at Dunbar in 1650, Cromwell annexed the country to the British Commonwealth, with himself as

Lord Protector, eliminated the independent sovereignty of Scotland and suppressed the Edinburgh parliament. This was an imperial union imposed by diktat and conquest and far from the ideas of those who had argued for a mutually agreed rapprochement in earlier times. It was predictably short-lived and ended with the restoration of the Stuart monarchy under Charles II in 1660. Nevertheless, the idea of closer relationships between the two kingdoms never quite disappeared, especially north of the border. The Scottish political class, casting envious eyes on England's growing wealth, continued to be very attracted by 'ane union of traid'. Some negotiations to this end took place in 1668, 1670 and again in 1688–9 but without any significant results.

The insurmountable obstacle was England's complete opposition to the surrender of any of its commercial privileges and advantages to a poor country that could offer precious little in return. The conventional wisdom in Europe at the time was the mercantilist concept that resources in the world were finite and that one state could only gain economic advantage over another either by making aggressive war or by passing tough protectionist legislation to safeguard its trade. For much of the later seventeenth century, therefore, far from ceding any trading rights to the Scots, England tightened up customs regulations even further and the Royal Navy became more proactive against the increased levels of Scottish smuggling and evasion in the Atlantic trades. When James II and VII succeeded his brother Charles II in 1685, it was eighty years and three regimes since James I and VI had first tried and failed for a closer association between his two kingdoms. The new king marked his own accession by inviting the Scottish Privy Council to negotiate with English representatives for 'the freedom and intercourse of trade between the two kingdoms of Great Britain'. Nothing came of the king's overtures and he himself was soon mired in deep crisis in England over his pro-Catholic religious policies. The possibility of any kind of union seemed further away than ever.

The reign of James II and VII began well with a supportive and loyal Tory majority in Westminster, strong state finances and effective authority in Scotland. Yet this early period of goodwill did not last. James's objectives of granting religious freedom and political rights to Catholics resurrected in both kingdoms the old fears of a papist restoration and absolute monarchy. He adopted an overt policy of 'catholicizing' appointments in Ireland after 1685, so that by 1688 a majority of the army officers there were papists. Anxieties were soon roused among elements of the ruling classes in both England and Scotland, in part because of fears that Catholic Ireland might become a base from which to launch armed Counter-Reformation on the British mainland. Militant Catholicism was once again seen to be on the march in Europe, where renewed persecution of the Protestant Huguenots in France culminated in their notorious expulsion from the country in 1685. James's policy of granting toleration and according civil and religious rights to dissenters and Catholics was therefore regarded by Protestant opinion as the thin end of a potentially sinister wedge. When his queen bore him a son, James Francis Edward Stuart, in June 1688, the continuation of a Catholic dynasty became certain. This was too much for some of the English governing classes. They invited the unambiguously Protestant Dutch prince, William of Orange, and his wife Mary, daughter of James, to assume the throne of England instead, a coup d'état that has gone down in history as the 'Glorious Revolution'.

At first, Scotland remained loyal to the Stuarts. Indeed, the Privy Council ordered Scottish troops under John Graham of Claverhouse, Viscount Dundee, to march south to London to provide support and succour to the beleaguered monarch. But James was not made of the stuff to stand and fight and, when much of his political and military support in and around the capital started to melt away, he fled into exile in France in December 1688. However, his fate in Scotland was still not sealed. All would depend on the reaction of the Convention of Estates, which met in Edinburgh in 1689 to consider the Scottish response to the events in England. Although proceedings were opened by a prayer led by the Bishop of Edinburgh that God should have compassion on James and restore him to the throne, the Stuart cause soon badly foundered when the assembly was presented with letters from the two rival claimants. William's was not only conciliatory but stressed above all his determination to ensure the security of the Protestant religion. James, on the other hand, was totally uncompromising and even threatened with retaliation those who might not be willing to submit to his rule. Through this approach the last Stuart king committed political suicide. The Convention's decision to invite William and Mary to accept the Crown of Scotland was by then almost a foregone conclusion. When it finally resolved that James had forfeited the Crown, there were only four opposing votes. Nevertheless, the momentous decision to overthrow a king soon provoked the first Jacobite rising under Graham of Claverhouse. The standard of King James was raised on Dundee Law in April 1689. In the same month, William and Mary were proclaimed king and queen in London.

II

William soon actively encouraged discussion of union and indeed would recommend on his deathbed that he wished it to happen. But the relationship between the Revolution of 1688–9 and the Union of 1707 did not hinge on royal advocacy alone. For a start, the Revolution had transformed the political authority of the Scottish parliament. William and Mary came to the throne of the kingdom not through divine hereditary right but by the invitation of the Scottish Convention of Estates. At a stroke, therefore, the balance of power between parliament and monarchy was irreversibly altered. The relationship was now contractual and no longer dependent.

As a result the Scottish parliament soon began to flex its muscles. In 1690 the Lords of the Articles, the key parliamentary committee for initiating and drafting legislation, and normally under executive control, was abolished. Royal influence and that of its representatives was immediately diluted. In the same year, the estate of bishops, another instrument of executive influence, was removed. The Articles were replaced by a number of ad hoc committees that were not as easily managed and, as a result, for the next several years the government of Scotland became increasingly volatile. After 1695 the king's main strategy was to try to build a stable ministry around such powerful noblemen as the Dukes of Queensberry, Argyll, Atholl and Hamilton. The theory was that only these mighty aristocrats could deliver a pro-government majority in parliament through their personal followings and networks of clientage. This, together with an effective system of 'management' – the promise of offices, pensions, fees and jobs in return for toeing the line – would ensure secure government. This hope proved illusory. The dukes were divided by bitter personal rivalries and a competitive craving for the spoils of office that were in practice far from stabilizing. Collaboration among such grandees for any length of time was a chimera. At the same time, however, no single great man could dominate parliament alone. To deliver power to one dynastic grouping was to risk alienating others, who might then promote destructive opposition in parliament itself. Not surprisingly, business was often in a state of paralysis for long periods and it was increasingly difficult to extract agreement on financial supply to carry on the daily administration of the country.

This volatility was aggravated by increasing friction between England and Scotland. From 1689 to 1697 William's wars with France had a serious impact on Scottish commerce, while the Royal Navy was now enforcing the Navigation Laws with full rigour against illicit Scottish trade with England's American colonies. Conflict in the economic sphere was intensified by the collapse of the Company of Scotland's ill-fated expedition to Darien in central America. This enterprise was launched in a mood of great national optimism in 1695, but by March 1700 the attempt to found a Scottish colony on the Isthmus of Panama to trade with the Pacific and Atlantic simultaneously had ended in complete disaster. The reasons for the catastrophe were many, ranging from poor planning to the lethal effects of tropical disease on the first settlers. But the political blame was laid squarely at England's door by revengeful Scots. English investment had been withdrawn from the original undertaking as a result of mercantile and political pressure from London. Meanwhile the possibility of bringing relief to the Scottish settlement in 1699 had come to naught, in large part because the London government, conscious of the vital diplomatic need to maintain Spanish support against France, refused to provide much-needed provisions or support. The Darien project may well have been doomed under any circumstances, but the exact conditions under which it failed were believed to have been substantially brought about by England. This disaster had a serious economic impact on the homeland because of the national treasure that had been invested in it, but the political fallout was just as significant. It directly hit the pockets of many noblemen, lairds and merchants represented in the Scottish parliament. It also happened precisely at the time when landowners were already suffering from a collapse of rental income from the calamitous harvest failures of the 1690s. Simmering discontent now erupted into strident criticism that Scotland's miseries were all rooted in the Regal Union of 1603. This alienation crystallized in a truculent opposition, shown during the parliamentary sessions of 1698 and 1700, so potent that only the lavish dispensation of patronage allowed the Scottish ministry to survive.

Parliamentary recalcitrance was not the only problem for the Crown. Equally crucial was the emergence in the 1690s of the enemy within. Jacobitism became a serious threat in Scotland to political stability after the Revolution, though the first Jacobite rising in support of the exiled House of Stuart led by Viscount Dundee proved to be a missed opportunity. His famous victory over government forces at the Pass of Killiecrankie was a notable feat of arms. But Dundee himself was killed in the moment of triumph and the attempt by his victorious army to break into the Lowlands was repulsed in vicious street-fighting in the town of Dunkeld. Finally, on May Day 1690 the Jacobite forces were comprehensively routed by government cavalry at the Haughs of Cromdale on Speyside.

Nevertheless, for nearly half a century afterwards Jacobitism remained a potent threat to the Protestant Revolution. In December 1688, James II and VII had been given succour by Louis XIV of France, with shelter for the exiled king and his court provided at the chateau of St Germain-en-Laye, situated near the palace of Versailles. For France, support for Jacobitism was obviously an effective means of encouraging internal instability in the kingdom of Louis's mortal enemy, William, and even perhaps the possibility of opening a second front against him from areas of Jacobite loyalty in the Scottish Highlands and Ireland.

Pro-James feeling also revived so quickly because of the decision by the Scots parliament to impose a radical Presbyterian settlement on the Church of Scotland in 1690 and abolish the estate of bishops. More than half the established clergy in Scotland refused to accept this resolution. These Episcopalians were also loathe to take the oath of allegiance to William and Mary and their successors, because to have done so would have been in direct conflict with their adherence to the sacred hereditary principle of kingship and, in consequence, the absolute requirement of submission to royal authority. Those who refused to swear the oaths became known as the non-jurors. In a typical response, for instance, Duncan MacRae, an Episcopalian minister from Wester Ross, utterly condemned the removal of James II and VII in 1689 as a heinous crime against God's fifth commandment.

The non-juring factor in the development of Jacobitism became of fundamental importance as the Episcopalian clergy provided the moral and ideological backbone of the Stuart cause and helped to ensure its survival even in times of extreme adversity. They refused to accept accommodation with the Presbyterian establishment in 1690, and even the toleration offered by the Hanoverian government in 1712. Areas of Episcopalian loyalty in Scotland therefore became vital to popular support for the series of Jacobite risings in the eighteenth century. An estimated 15 of the 26 Highland clans active on the Jacobite side in the Rising of 1715 were Episcopalian in sympathy, and a further five were of mixed denominations. It was a similar pattern in the Lowlands. Overwhelmingly, Jacobite support in that region came from the north-eastern shires of Angus, Aberdeen, Banff, Forfar and Kincardine, which, together with Perthshire, were all counties of Episcopalian tradition and affiliation. The tiny Catholic Church in Scotland, which had pockets of support in parts of the western Highlands, the north-east and the southern Hebrides, also developed a fierce loyalty to the Stuarts. During James VII's reign the Catholics had experienced a short period of formal toleration, which ended abruptly when the penal laws were again imposed in 1689. Catholics were inspired not only by James's sympathetic policies before 1688 but also by his uncompromising refusal afterwards to sacrifice his faith for reasons of political expediency as the price for recovering his Crown. The Catholic commitment to Jacobitism was important but, because the Church had few adherents (probably some 2 per cent of the Scottish population around 1750), it was less decisive than the contribution of episcopalianism. Indeed, the role of Catholicism in the Jacobite Risings has probably been exaggerated in the past. In the 1715 rising only six of the 26 clans actively involved were Catholic. Despite this, Catholic participation helped to shape the development of Jacobitism as an ideological crusade, founded on deep religious principles and not easily deflected by setback or misfortune. It also strengthened the connections with sympathetic Catholic powers in Europe such as France and Spain whose support was key to the movement's international credibility.

Because of this background of opposition, William now concluded that Scotland could no longer be governed effectively within the Union of the Crowns. A union of the Edinburgh and Westminster parliaments was believed to be vital to deliver national stability and the security of the Revolution of 1688–9. The king was obsessed with winning the great war against the France of Louis XIV and political volatility in Scotland threatened that fundamental objective. This was not only because Scotland was an important source of recruits for William's armies but also because support for the exiled House of Stuart was being encouraged by French money and promises of military aid. Nevertheless, while the union project may have had appeal for the king personally, it still failed to attract much support in Westminster. This was to change radically after the session of the Scots parliament that met in 1703 during the reign of William's successor, Queen Anne.

III

Overwhelmingly, Scotland remained a rural-based society in this period. Landowners formed the political and social elite. The produce of the land – skins, grain, wool and coal – were vital trading commodities. On the return of the annual harvest depended the health, prosperity and food supply of the nation. If the harvest partially failed, emergency provision would have to be acquired from Europe with scarce coin, which might force a collapse in credit and shrinkage of the cash base. The typical Scot was also a country dweller. One estimate suggests that in 1700 only just over 5 per cent of the population lived in towns with over 10,000 inhabitants. This proportion was a long way behind more urbanized societies such as those of England, the Low Countries, parts of Italy and even Spain and Portugal; it was on a par with the Scandinavian countries, Ireland and some of the German states. Even artisans, industrial workers and fishing communities had to have a small stake in the land in order to ensure their own subsistence.

But towns were becoming increasingly important, and changes were also under way in the pattern of Scottish urban development. Between 1500 and 1600 the proportion of the nation's population living in the larger towns nearly doubled, and it did so again by 1700. Edinburgh, the capital and biggest town, had a population of around 30,000 by the early eighteenth century. Aberdeen and Dundee had about 10,000 inhabitants each, while Glasgow emerged as the second burgh in the land by the later seventeenth century, with a population reckoned at 15,000 and growing. Relative to Edinburgh and Glasgow, however, Aberdeen and Dundee were experiencing stagnation in the second half of the seventeenth century. Edinburgh's predominance in Scottish urban life was long-standing, but Glasgow's new role reflected the growing importance of developing links to Ireland and the Atlantic economy, links that would prove so important to Scottish progress after 1700. The vast majority of other Scottish burghs were little more than villages in this period. Few, apart from Inverness, Stirling, Dumfries and Renfrew, even had more than 1,000 inhabitants each. Nevertheless, in some areas, most notably the coastlands of the River Forth, the sheer number and growth of small burghs created a regional urban network to rival any in western Europe in its density.

The growth in the number of town dwellers had major implications for rural society. Above all else, the new townsfolk had to be fed from the countryside. In the later sixteenth century this would have proved difficult, since between 1550 and 1600 there were around 24 years of dearth on a national and local scale. But harvests improved after about 1660. Between then and the devastating famines of the 1690s, food prices indicated serious scarcity only once, in 1674. Also in this period, several landed estates on the east coast were producing substantial quantities of grain for export. All this suggests that Scottish agriculture was not as inefficient as was sometimes suggested in this period. It may well be that the climate was also more favourable and the balance of food supply and demand was also helped by Scotland's demographic safety valve, the huge levels of emigration to Europe and Ulster that prevailed for much of the seventeenth century. From medieval times Scots had moved to continental Europe in large numbers as soldiers and traders, and there is some evidence that this exodus reached particularly high levels in the 1600s, especially when Ulster also started to attract farmers and cottars from the south-west Lowlands. All in all, it is reckoned that Scottish emigration reached levels estimated in total at between 78,000 and 127,000 in the second half of the seventeenth century.

Other influences help to account for the better times of the 1670s and 1680s. After the massive losses of blood and treasure in the Wars of the Covenant of the 1630s and 1640s, followed by the conquest and annexation of Scotland by Cromwell in the 1650s, there was a period of greater social and political stability. One illustration of the new order was the changing domestic architecture of the nobility and lairds as the tower house, designed mainly for defence, was gradually replaced by the country house. Some landowners were also showing greater interest in raising the revenue of their estates. Even in the Highlands full-scale clan warfare had become a thing of the past and most unrest was now confined to localized banditry and petty lawlessness. The reformed Church also contributed powerfully to the new stability in the Lowlands. Its kirk session, consisting of the minister and elected elders, acted as a local moral tribunal supervising the conduct of the parishioners and punishing them when they breached the Christian code. Already by 1620 most Lowland parishes and many Highland parishes had active kirk sessions and then became effective agencies for the development of group discipline. In the 1680s there was also an intellectual flowering that paralleled the greater economic stability of the time. This was the age of Viscount Stair in law, Sir William Bruce in architecture and Sir Robert Sibbald in medicine. Historians now consider these developments as critical to the origins of the Scottish Enlightenment in the following century.

But the better times proved to be short-lived. Scotland's economy was small, the range of exports limited mainly to foods and raw materials, and the nation's political position weak in relation to that of the great European powers. It was an era of rampant economic nationalism when the leading states tried to gain advantage at the expense of their trade rivals through the aggressive use of prohibitive tariffs. The problem was that Scotland was ill-equipped to fight a trade war not only because of the absence of any credible naval force but because Scottish merchants dealt in little that was regarded as either scarce or vital in overseas markets. Scotland could therefore be hit badly by high customs barriers erected by foreign powers but was unable to retaliate against them to any meaningful extent. The policy of the Scottish parliament when confronted by rising tariff walls in several of the nation's traditional markets came to depend on a strategy of industrial diversification at home to produce luxuries the raw materials for which were imported from abroad. Some of these manufactures did prosper, especially those producing high-quality textiles, but by and large this laudable attempt at self-help did little to prevent a deterioration in Scotland's international economic position. It was partly because of these difficulties that the nation embarked on the great gamble of the expeditions to Darien between 1695 and 1700 in the hope of escaping from a steadily contracting vice of economic misfortunes.

A second problem was with England as Anglo-Scottish relationships in this period were wholly anomalous. The difficulties were rooted in the Regal Union of 1603 when James VI of Scotland succeeded Elizabeth I to the Crowns of England and Ireland. James had been eager to go much further, as earlier suggested, and in 1604 commissioners from England and Scotland discussed a union of parliaments and a scheme of common citizenship. Despite James's keen support, the idea foundered. The Scottish nobility feared a loss of influence in a London Parliament, while the English were concerned that the Scots would be favoured in the new arrangement by their royal master. Within a few years the projected union was off the political agenda and the difficulties of ruling Scotland from Westminster soon became apparent in the latter stages of James's reign – and even more so during that of his son and successor, Charles I, when they were instrumental in provoking the crisis that led to the outbreak of the Civil War. Union was enforced between 1652 and 1660 by Oliver Cromwell, but at the Restoration of 1660 and the return of Charles II it was dissolved, to the relief of the majority of both countries.

But after 1603 Scotland was far from being an independent state. Scottish foreign policy had moved with James to London in 1603 and that led to the great grievance that it was now exclusively designed to suit English needs. Thus the three Dutch Wars of the later seventeenth century were fought against a nation that was England's deadliest commercial rival but one of Scotland's main trading partners. Similarly, the fact that the Scots and English shared the same monarch did not prevent the London Parliament levying punitive customs dues on such key Scottish exports as linen, cattle, salt and coal at a time when England was becoming the single most important external market for these Scots commodities. Increasingly, Scottish interests argued that the Regal Union had to be amended and reformed because of the damage being inflicted on the country. Westminster almost certainly viewed most of these concerns as windy rhetoric or special pleading. In the 1690s, however, a series of crises transformed the debate on Anglo-Scottish union and made it a much more pressing issue than it had been since Cromwell's armies had marched north in the early 1650s.

IV

Not only did the Darien venture fail spectacularly but in the 1690s Scotland was hit by two other consecutive disasters that triggered a domestic crisis unparalleled in most decades of the seventeenth century. The first was an unusual run of poor harvests caused by a marked fall in temperatures in northern and western Europe. Countries with many upland and marginal areas such as Scotland – even today two-thirds of its land is only suitable for rough grazing – were likely to be especially vulnerable. Meagre harvests were repeated in 1691–2, 1693, 1695 and again in 1698. The prices of grains soared, malnutrition increased, and the death rate started to climb. Mortality varied throughout the country, with the north-east, the Highlands and the northern isles suffering most. Overall, however, the national population may have fallen by around 13 per cent, causing a decline to just over one million souls in 1700. This catastrophe forced mass emigration from south-west Scotland to Ulster, with as many as 40,000 to 50,000 fleeing across the North Channel to escape the crisis.

To this natural disaster was added a second, war with France. In 1689, Scotland and England did not simply acquire a new monarch but also William's war with Louis XIV. This, known as the Nine Years War or War of the Grand Alliance, put Scottish trade to Europe at risk both from French privateers and Royal Navy vessels seeking to impose embargoes on commerce with the French enemy. Hostilities endured until 1697 but the peace of that year was short-lived. In 1701 the War of the Spanish Succession began with the same objective of trying to limit Louis IV's territorial ambitions in Europe. This was on an even greater scale than the previous conflict and lasted until 1713 when the Peace of Utrecht was finally agreed. The costs of supplying British forces in Europe grew exponentially, to which were added expenditures in support of continental allies in the war against France.

Inevitably, land, excise and cess taxes in both England and Scotland had to rise.

This background of economic crisis and international war is central to understanding the origins of union. The Scots may have been in denial about the intrinsic causes of the Darien disaster, but the national belief at the time was still that perfidious Albion was mainly to blame for the collapse of the scheme, and for two reasons: it prevented London and European investment in the venture, and English colonies in the West Indies refused help for the beleaguered Scots survivors. Indeed, Darien effectively served notice on the Union of the Crowns. The failure proved conclusively that when the vital interests of Scotland and England were in conflict, the monarch would opt in favour of the more powerful kingdom. At the same time the fiasco brought home brutally to thinking Scots that the nation was not simply in economic difficulties but was also running out of credible alternatives to solve them. Darien confirmed that going it alone in the transatlantic sphere in a world of more powerful enemies was no longer an option. This perception did not lead inevitably to the union of parliaments but did at least help to place the future of the relationship between England and Scotland more emphatically on the political agenda than ever before.

In the meantime, the Anglo-Scottish relationship deteriorated further as Westminster continued to remain indifferent to Scottish interests and sensitivities. The decision to go to war with France in 1701 was taken without consultation in Edinburgh and was only later rubber-stamped by the Scots parliament. Even more crucially, in the same year, Westminster unilaterally passed the Act of Succession, stating that in the absence of any natural heirs to the childless Queen Anne, the succession should pass to Sophia, Electress of Hanover, granddaughter of James I and VI. The measure was thought vital to safeguard the Protestant succession of 1688 after Anne's last surviving child, the Duke of Gloucester, died in July 1700. No attempt was made to consult with Scotland about who the country's future monarch should be. This was perceived not only as an attempt to ignore the Scottish interest but to brazenly ride roughshod over the separate parliamentary authority of the Scots within the Regal Union. It has been said that 'anti-English feeling in Scotland now became stronger than at any time since the Anglo-Scottish wars of the Middle Ages'.[1]

The resentments that had been building up north of the border boiled over with a vengeance in the Edinburgh parliament in the session of 1703. The assembly was beyond the control of the Duke of Queensberry, the queen's Commissioner, and his governing party. First, the assembly refused to vote on the financial supply necessary for the prosecution of the European war. Second, in open defiance of the queen's representatives, the Scottish parliament passed *The Act for the Security of the Kingdom* proclaiming that it had the constitutional right to decide on Queen Anne's successor and that England and Scotland would only have the same sovereign in the future if London granted the Scots 'free communication of trade ... and the liberty of the plantations'. Moreover, the Union of the Crowns would only be maintained if in the current parliamentary session 'there be such conditions of government settled and enacted as may secure ... the freedom, frequency and the power of Parliaments, and the religion, liberty and trade of the nation from English or any foreign influence'. This read like a manifesto for Scottish independence and was intended to be deliberately provocative. Not surprisingly, the queen initially refused to give her assent to the bill although she conceded, reluctantly, in the following year.

Third, the ministry was forced to accept the equally contentious *Act anent* (concerning) *Peace and War*, which gave the Scots parliament the right to declare war and make peace if the two nations continued to share a sovereign after Anne's death. In a vain attempt to extract financial supply in return for these concessions, Queensberry and his associates allowed this to pass, despite the fact that its whole emphasis suggested a separate and autonomous foreign policy. Fourth, another measure, the Wine Act, formally permitted trade with France during the war. The motive for this came from the governing party, which was keen to raise more revenue by boosting trade, but on the surface it also seemed to be another piece of legislation driven by economic nationalism. Certainly the Wool Act, passed during the Scottish parliamentary session the following year, was regarded as openly hostile by England because it allowed the export of wool but prohibited the import of the commodity. In the words of one historian, these four pieces of legislation 'had the appearances of being both militantly nationalist and anti-English'.[2]

2

Making the Union

I

For the English the hostile Acts passed by the Scottish Parliament in 1703 and 1704 were the catalyst for union. They convinced Westminster that Scotland could no longer be governed securely within the Regal Union at a critical moment in history when the entire revolutionary settlement of 1688–9 was under threat. The London Parliament had attempted to deal swiftly with the vexed issue of succession by settling the Crown on the Protestant House of Hanover. But the recalcitrant Scots had failed to follow suit and their truculence was now seen as a material threat to the Protestant succession. Moreover, the belligerence of the Edinburgh parliament had come at the worst possible time. Conflict with the arch-enemy France broke out again in 1702. Hostilities were at a critical stage and the final outcome was far from certain. It was not until August 1704 that the Duke of Marlborough finally laid to rest the legend of French military invincibility with his crushing victory at Blenheim. In the meantime, Louis XIV brazenly encouraged Scottish Jacobites by recognizing the young son of the dying James II and VII as the true heir to the thrones of England and Scotland. By doing so he now openly and directly connected the issue of the English and Scottish successions to that of the outcome of the great European war.

The Jacobites in Scotland had done well in the elections to the parliament of 1703 and their support in the country had grown because of the unpopularity of the Scottish administration. They were also sustained by the interest shown by Louis and some of his ministers in a possible invasion of Scotland. The continuing instability of the Scottish parliament therefore seemed only to be giving comfort to the mortal enemies of England both at home and abroad. The political sources of this insecurity had to be tackled urgently. It was certainly the threat from the French war that finally moved Sydney, Lord Godolphin, Queen Anne's Lord High Treasurer and Chief Minister, and Marlborough, her Captain-General, to opt for the union solution to the Scottish problem. Marlborough was personally concerned because many of the crack troops in his armies were recruited from Scotland. Since the need to safeguard national security was therefore the paramount motivating force for England, only an 'incorporating union', which would dissolve the Edinburgh parliament and create a new United Kingdom legislature, was ever acceptable to English negotiators. A federal solution, which might have perpetuated weak government and appealed to many Scottish politicians at the time, was never on offer from London.

The Westminster anxiety for union was now confirmed by legislation passed in the House of Commons in early 1705 as targeted retaliation for the unacceptable behaviour of the Edinburgh parliament. This was the *Act for the effectual securing of the Kingdom of England from the apparent dangers that might arise from several Acts lately passed by the Parliament of Scotland* (commonly known thereafter as the Aliens Act). It recommended to Queen Anne that commissioners be appointed to negotiate for union between the two countries. If the Scots refused to take part and discussions were not advanced by Christmas Day 1705, all Scots resident in England would forthwith be treated as aliens and the major Scottish exports to England of coal, linen and cattle would be banned. This naked piece of economic blackmail, designed to bring the Scottish parliament swiftly to the negotiating table, infuriated many across the border and caused rioting in Edinburgh and outrage in other parts of the country. In the event, the measure was repealed by the incoming Whig government in November 1705. But the Aliens Act served to demonstrate the unambiguous English volte-face on the principle of union and at the same time the capacity of London to brandish the big stick if that was deemed to be necessary. The decades' old English opposition to union had quickly collapsed. It was now seen to be vital in order to secure the Protestant Revolution of 1688–9 and the northern frontier of

England from the menace of the French and Jacobites. The final act in the drama of the making of the Union was about to unfold.

II

Tensions between the two countries persisted. Anti-English feeling among the Edinburgh populace over the Darien disaster reached a brutal climax in the spring of 1705 when Captain Thomas Green and two of the crew of the English ship *Worcester* were hanged before a braying mob on Leith Sands after being found guilty of a charge of piracy against a vessel of the Darien Company. It was alleged that Green and his crew boarded the ship, the ironically named *Speedy Return*, off the Malabar coast in India, massacred all on board, stole the cargo, and then sold the vessel. The evidence for the crime was thin in the extreme and the execution has ever since been regarded as an act of judicial murder. Green was ridiculed in a contemporary ballad:

> Of all the pirates I've heard and seen
> The basest and bloodiest is Captain Green

In the Edinburgh parliament, Sir John Clerk of Penicuik, an enthusiastic advocate for union, noted later, with some understatement, that in early 1706 there still remained 'a great backwardness ... for a union with England'.[1] Much scholarly ink has been expended in recent years in attempts to explain why the independent-minded and almost mutinous Edinburgh parliament of 1703 then voted itself out of existence three years later by a decisive majority. This can only really be understood through the political and party structure of the legislature.

The parliament was a single-chamber assembly with a total of 147 members in 1706 representing the nobility, barons (or shire members) and town burgesses. It was divided by a number of political groupings. These were not organized and structured parties in the modern sense, but composed of much looser alliances, affiliations and personal loyalties. The largest of these was the Court Party, which, as its name suggests, was the party of government. It helped to carry out the policies of London and controlled patronage, essential to the management of parliament since the abolition of the Lords of the Articles. It was the Court Party, under the queen's Commissioner, the Duke of Queensberry, which had the responsibility for ensuring that the Treaty of Union was passed by Parliament. The mere fact of holding office and patronage gave the Court Party a cohesion and stability that the Country Party, the main opposition, manifestly lacked. Essentially the latter was an uneasy confederation of different and sometimes conflicting interests, many of which had little in common except opposition to the ministry of the day. So volatile was the party that the Jacobites would sometimes see themselves allied to it and at other times functioned independently as the 'Cavaliers'. The potential of the Country Party to be an effective opposition in the crucial session of 1706 was also significantly weakened by the ambiguous leadership of the Duke of Hamilton, whose contradictory behaviour in 1706–7 will be explored in more detail below. Finally, the 'New Party', soon to be known by the exotic name of 'Squadrone Volante', had emerged out of the Country Party in 1704. As events were to prove, this group of around two dozen members was to have a key role in the outcome of the union vote.

The Court Party under Queensberry's leadership had the advantage from the beginning in two important ways. First, at the curious suggestion of the so-called leader of the opposition, the Duke of Hamilton, the Scottish representatives on the joint Anglo-Scottish parliamentary commission to discuss draft articles of union were to be chosen by the queen rather than by parliament. As a result most of the Scots commissioners were hand-picked followers of Queensberry and Argyll, both powerful grandees with considerable personal followings who were supporters of incorporated union. George Lockhart of Carnwath, a noted Jacobite sympathizer, was an isolated figure in the commission. Not surprisingly this arrangement ensured that a draft treaty for union with 25 articles for debate and decision within the two parliaments was quickly agreed.

Second, steps were taken to eliminate the most potent source of opposition to full union, the Presbyterian Church of Scotland. The Kirk feared the contamination of Anglican influence in a potentially diabolical pact with the non-jurors of Scottish episcopalianism. Ministers were loud in their denunciations from the pulpits at services on the Sabbath, passionately condemning the proposed union as a profane and terrible threat to the Scottish Protestant tradition. However, in November 1706 the Edinburgh parliament passed an Act of Security of the Church of Scotland, by which the historic rights of the Kirk and the Presbyterian system of government were to be guaranteed as fundamental conditions of union. This legislation was later to be incorporated in the treaty itself. Religious anxieties and suspicions did not suddenly evaporate, but the teeth of the political opposition of the Church had been effectively drawn. One pro-union sympathizer noted:

> in the churches, by and large, the trumpets of sedition began to fall silent. Ministers who had formerly meddled over-zealously in politics now learned to leave the direction of government to parliament. This greatly upset the Hamiltonians who saw themselves abandoned by those they most relied on to stir up anti-union sentiment.[2]

This was an over-optimistic view in hindsight as the more militant Presbyterians remained far from satisfied. Nonetheless, many of the public attacks from the Church on the union concept now began to die out.

When the Scottish parliament met in October 1706 at the start of the historic session to debate the draft Articles of Union, it was plain that opposition outside the House was still alive. Not all burghs and counties sent in petitions to parliament, but those that did so were virtually all vehemently anti-union. The Duke of Argyll dismissed these as mere paper kites, but it was significant that they were not balanced by pro-union addresses. From the unionist perspective, Sir John Clerk of Penicuik lamented the yawning gap that he recognized between the parliament and the people on the issue. He estimated that 'not even one per cent approved what the former was doing'.[3] In Edinburgh the Duke of Hamilton was cheered to the echo by crowds who then proceeded to attack the house of Sir Patrick Johnstone, a strong union supporter. The Duke of Queensberry, the queen's Commissioner, needed a personal military escort to Parliament House. From that point on, anti-union demonstrations were common in the capital. In November rioting also spread to the south-west, that historic citadel of strict Calvinist and covenanting tradition. The Glasgow mob rose against unionist sympathizers in disturbances that lasted intermittently for over a month, while in the burgh of Dumfries the proposed Articles of Union were ritually burnt before an angry gathering of several thousand townspeople.

It was rumoured that plans were being laid for an armed uprising to be led by the Cameronians, the militant Presbyterians from the western shires, in an unlikely alliance with the Jacobite Highlanders of the Duke of Atholl in Perthshire. It was said that a force of some 8,000 men might be mustered, more than enough to break up the parliamentary session and defeat any Scottish government army that might take the field against it. In the event, and not surprisingly, this great host never materialized. Nevertheless, the potential for armed opposition was clearly there; for example, the Jacobite conspiracy and threatened invasion of 1708, which was fuelled by strong anti-union feelings and much better supported than was once thought. The elaborate military precautions taken by the government in Edinburgh also confirm the level of anxiety about the threat of insurrection. While the city's mob was taking to the streets, Queensberry ensured that the small Scots standing army, 1,500 men in all, was encamped near the capital and troops were also quartered in Edinburgh itself. But the Privy Council feared that the Scottish forces at its disposal would not be enough if matters got out of hand. In late October, therefore, Lord Godolphin assured the Scottish commander-in-chief, the Earl of Leven, that a powerful force would be ordered to the border to be in readiness in case the 'ferment' should continue to give any further disturbance to the 'publick peace'. By December these infantry levies had been reinforced with 800 cavalry and were made available for action on orders from the government in Edinburgh. More ominously, troops were also sent to the north of Ireland, from where that major bastion of anti-union sentiment, the south-west counties of Scotland, could more easily be intimidated and, if necessary, attacked.

Within the Scottish parliament, however, the pro-unionists who seemed relatively weak outside parliament displayed much more muscle and purpose within it. Their cause was helped by the manifest political and organizational weaknesses of the opposing Country and Jacobite/Cavalier parties. It would not be an exaggeration to suggest that in the crucial session of 1706 they were in disarray and signally failed to capitalize on the noisy extraparliamentary hostility to union. If effectively led, this might have developed into a potent threat to the government. But the opposition was intellectually and conceptually bereft and failed to produce any coherent alternative vision to the union project. To this key weakness was added the fundamental ideological divide that split the Countrymen from the Cavaliers. They could always be relied upon to act together to make political mischief and embarrass the Court Party, but at a more fundamental level they were irreconcilable. The Cavaliers or Jacobites wanted the return of the Catholic Stuart Pretender, but such an aspiration was anathema to the Presbyterian nobility who led the Country Party. The 'leadership' of the Duke of Hamilton was supine and indecisive at key moments that the opposition might have exploited to advantage. Indeed, so ambiguous was his posturing that some questioned which side he really supported. The opposition tactic of formally withdrawing from parliament in January 1707 and in effect boycotting proceedings came to nothing because of Hamilton. He initially failed to turn up, complaining of being seized of the toothache, and, when he eventually appeared, declined to lead the proposed mass withdrawal.

The man who had been lionized by the Edinburgh crowds as the only hope for Scottish independence had again let his followers down. He had done so before, in September 1705, when parliament was deciding whether the commissioners to treat for union should be appointed by the queen or by parliament. As noted already, Hamilton amazingly suggested that they ought to be the queen's nominees, thus ensuring a pro-unionist majority on the commission. He was also later blamed for calling off the rising of Cameronians from the southwest and the Highlands in November 1706. Hamilton's behaviour demoralized the forces of opposition both in and outside parliament. Some have explained his hesitations as being the result of his personal position. Not only was he heavily in debt, but through marriage the duke had acquired large estates in Lancashire that he stood to lose if the union project collapsed in failure. His personal circumstances meant that he was also vulnerable to the promise of favours from government. James Johnstone, Lord Clerk Register and one of the Scottish officers of state, alleged that Hamilton was actively seeking assistance from London ministers with his debts in the winter of 1705.

Probably the only real hope for the anti-unionists lay in an alliance between the parliamentary opposition and the disaffected population in the country, given the numerical strength of the Court Party and its potential ally, the Squadrone. But whether the leadership of the Country Party had any real stomach for a popular uprising must be doubted, especially since the Kirk was no longer actively or publicly opposed to the treaty. A civil war could have given comfort only to the Jacobites, with the possibility of the Stuarts restored through an invasion from France. The 1688–9 Revolution (which the Country leaders strongly supported to a man) and the Protestant Succession itself could have been brought into clear and mortal danger.

Friction and dispute within the opposition was in clear contrast to the solid pro-union ranks of most of the Court Party. Recent research has demonstrated how the loyalty of many of its members to the government went back to the Revolution of 1688–9 and even before. They were a formidable phalanx of the committed who had no interest whatsoever in trimming or equivocation. Some had suffered exile in the Low Countries during the reigns of Charles II and James II and VII for their beliefs because they could not stomach the religious policies of those Stuart kings. They were principled and sturdy believers in Presbyterianism, in the Hanoverian succession and in union as the best ways to ensure Scotland was spared the threat of a Stuart counter-revolution. However, to make insurance doubly sure, Queensberry and his associates presided over an effective machine of political management during the final session of the Scottish parliament (3 October 1706–23 March 1707). The influential Duke of Argyll agreed to return from the armies in Flanders in order to support the Court Party. His personal rewards included promotion to the rank of major-general and an English peerage. Some £20,000 sterling (the equivalent of £240,000 Scots sterling, and £1.3 million in today's values) was secretly dispatched north from the English treasury. Whether it was disbursed to pay office-holders whose salaries were overdue or as straight money bribes, as some have suspected, is in a sense immaterial. Payment of arrears to selected individuals was just as much part and parcel of effective management as handing over direct cash inducements in both the Edinburgh and Westminster parliaments. The Squadrone benefited handsomely from the distributions. Modern research has also identified as beneficiaries former members of the opposition, such as William Seton of Pitmedden, Sir Kenneth Mackenzie and the

Earl of Glencairn, whose rewards may have encouraged a more favourable opinion of union. But not all parliamentarians were susceptible. The voting record of at least 13 members shows that they supported the union without either cash inducement or promise of office. But the loyalty of the Court Party as a whole could not be taken entirely for granted because allegations suggested that some, though enthusiastic for union, were not so enamoured of full incorporation. Support had therefore to be shored up by patronage. In this crucial final parliamentary session there was to be no repeat of the debacle of 1703.

Several Articles of the Treaty itself added to the growing momentum towards acceptance of union. Article XXII, which provided for Scotland to be represented in the new Parliament of Great Britain by a mere 16 Lords and 45 Members of the Commons (condemning as it did the Scots to being a perpetual and small minority in Westminster), was probably the most controversial at the time. For the rest, however, there is evidence that English ministers were so keen to achieve union that they were prepared to make concessions. The most popular measure by far, according to the voting record of the Edinburgh parliament, was Article IV, which gave the subjects of Great Britain freedom of trade and navigation within the kingdom and 'the Dominions and Plantations thereunto belonging'. An enormously significant historic Scottish aspiration was thereby satisfied. The measure was opposed by a mere 19 votes. Article XV dealt with the 'Equivalent'. A sum of £398,000 was allowed to compensate the Scots for their estimated share after a union in the repayment of England's large national debt, which had been swollen by war expenditure. In addition, however, a proportion was also to be employed to compensate shareholders of the ill-fated Darien venture in exchange for the formal winding up of the Company of Scotland. It used to be thought that members of the Squadrone were set to gain most from this inducement and voted accordingly. But modern historical opinion is less certain that the sweetener did much in the end to influence their votes.

For the rest, Articles IX, XX and XXI buttressed and safeguarded the vested interests of those who mattered in Scottish society. Issues of integration within the Union were to be confined to parliament, fiscal issues and public law. As well as the rights of the Kirk, already protected through the Act of Security, Scottish private law was maintained as were heritable offices, superiorities and heritable jurisdictions (or the private feudal courts of the landed classes). The existing privileges of the royal burghs were guaranteed. Such key Scottish institutions as the universities, schools and the poor law were left undisturbed and indeed were not even mentioned in the Treaty. In return, the ancient sovereignty of Scotland came to an end.

On 16 January 1707 the Edinburgh parliament voted itself out of existence in ratifying the Act of Union by a decisive majority of 110 votes to 67. The London Parliament soon followed suit. The Act of Union became law on 1 May 1707.

3

A Fragile Union

I

The first article of the Treaty of Union proclaimed in sonorous language 'THAT the Two Kingdoms of England and Scotland shall ... forever AFTER be United into One Kingdom by the name of GREAT BRITAIN'.

Very soon the new relationship threatened to collapse in acrimony, division and mutual hostility between the two nations. Yet at first all was peaceful. Lord Godolphin and his Whig coalition in London decided to tread carefully in the knowledge that the Scottish parliament had passed the union legislation in the teeth of much bitter opposition outside the House. He therefore left untouched almost all of the pre-union Scottish administration and added only new Boards of Commissioners to secure improved revenue yields in Scotland. The two existing Scottish secretaries, the Earl of Loudon and the Earl of Mar, kept their jobs. The strategy was intended to avoid any radical change and so keep the Scots quiet. Nevertheless, Godolphin in 1708 had to concede the abolition of the Scottish Privy Council, the main executive organ of government before the Union. This was not planned by Westminster but came about as a result of the machinations of the Squadrone Party in the House of Commons. The Squadrone had long been convinced that the Council was a loyal and partisan instrument of the Court Party which had used its influence to maximize electoral advantage. The Council had traditionally continued in session when the Edinburgh parliament was adjourned and so had key judicial as well as administrative functions. Its abolition meant one British Privy Council sitting in London with its membership extended to include the surviving Scottish officers of state, Lord

Justice General, Lord Clerk Register and Keeper of the Great Seal. Very soon, however, it became obvious that the loss of such administrative capability north of the border gravely weakened the ability of government to respond vigorously and decisively in times of crisis. Indeed, the vacuum left at the centre of power could only give comfort to the Jacobites, the implacable enemies of the Union.

The Jacobites saw the Union as a fundamental buttress of the Revolution of 1688–9, so ensuring the Stuart dynasty would never again return to claim its rightful inheritance. In Scotland they were able to count on the support of several of the most formidable Highland clans – it was reckoned that as many as 26 of them could be mobilized in support of the Stuarts at this time. The key Jacobite strategy was to seek help for their cause from the Catholic powers of France and Spain and then meld that with any military support they could attract within Britain. As the War of the Spanish Succession dragged on, France in particular could not resist the temptation to feed internal dissent and revolt across the Channel in order to force the withdrawal of regiments from the victorious armies of the Duke of Marlborough in the European theatre for purposes of French domestic security. Louis XIV and his ministers decided to play the specific Scottish card in 1708, so an expedition from France was mounted to link up with Jacobite forces in Scotland. In the event, the enterprise ended in disastrous failure. Faulty navigation and bad weather were blamed and the debacle was complete when the French fleet missed the rendezvous with its Scottish allies in the Firth of Forth.

Nonetheless, the episode served to illustrate the fragility of the Union a mere one year after its inception. There was considerable support for the rising in Scotland which, if the French had indeed landed, might have brought together a force much greater in number than the roughly 1,500 troops available to the government. Even after the end of the War of the Spanish Succession with the signing of the Treaty of Utrecht in 1713, the 'Old Pretender' (or Stuart claimant to the throne), 'James VIII', signed a secret treaty with the Catholic monarch, Philip V of Spain. In it, Philip agreed to support the restoration of the Catholic Church in Ireland and then in the rest of Britain.

In the years that followed the abortive 1708 attempt at counter-revolution, discontent with and then outright opposition to the Union increased in Scotland. An important catalyst for this was the election of a Tory government that replaced Godolphin and his Whig coalition in 1710. The policy of restraint and caution maintained by the previous regime towards Scotland was now swiftly abandoned, especially in the religious sphere. Scottish Presbyterians had long feared a London Parliament dominated by members of the Church of England. Now these concerns were realized. High Church Tories seemed bent on a strategy of removing the privileges of the Church of Scotland enshrined in the Treaty of Union as part of their broader campaign against dissenters in the country at large. Tensions rose in 1711 when James Greenshields, an Episcopalian minister, appealed to the House of Lords against his imprisonment by the magistrates of Edinburgh for using the English liturgy in defiance of the presbytery of the city. This sort of issue was always an inherent and unresolvable problem within any real union and now showed itself. The decision by the Lords to grant Greenshields' appeal to allow the Anglican prayer book for worship in an Episcopalian meeting house in the capital enraged the Kirk. The principle of Presbyterian worship was at the heart of its claim to have inherited the purest and most comprehensive reformation of any Protestant Church in Europe. This belief was central to the religious identity of Scots Presbyterians who saw themselves as the chosen people of God. Now this belief was being challenged in the nation's capital by an alien form of worship borrowed from the Church of England, an institution that pious Presbyterians thought had never been truly reformed.

Much worse, however, from the Presbyterian perspective was soon to follow. In 1712, Parliament passed two provocative measures, the Toleration Act and the Patronage Act, both viewed by the Kirk to be in overt violation of the Treaty of Union. The first granted freedom of worship to Episcopalians in Scotland as long as they agreed to pray for the reigning Hanoverian monarch. This law was seen to give comfort to the Jacobite cause since one of the heartlands of its support, the north-east Lowlands, was strongly Episcopalian in sympathy. The Patronage Act was even less acceptable to the Kirk. The Act restored the right of major landowners rather than local congregations to nominate parish ministers to vacant appointments. Patronage eventually proved to be the most contentious issue in relations between the

Kirk and the British state between 1712 and the middle decades of the nineteenth century. General Assemblies of the Church called for repeal of the Act year after year until 1784. Patronage was in direct conflict with the much-vaunted spiritual independence of Presbyterianism. The issue indeed helped to trigger the major secessions of the Associate Presbytery in 1733, the Relief Church in 1761, and, above all, and finally, the Disruption of 1843 that led to the formation of the Free Church of Scotland. Such anglicizing legislation also seemed to confirm that the Treaty of Union was not a fundamental and unalterable law but was in fact something that might be amended at the whim of the sovereign legislature in Westminster where the Scots had but meagre numeral representation. The guarantees given to the Church of Scotland in the Treaty were now apparently worthless.

Adding to growing disenchantment and then hardening opposition to the Union was the vexed issue of taxation. This impinged even more directly on the Scottish people than problems of Church governance. Tensions over tax and tax collection were almost inevitable. England had fought a very costly war that ended only in 1713 and had also expended much treasure in support of continental allies. More resources to pay off a hugely inflated national debt were urgently required. At the same time, Parliament started to shift the tax burden at the end of the conflict from land taxes to customs dues and excise payments on a whole range of commodities in common use and consumption, including ale, malting barley, salt, linen and soap. Home salt, not taxed before 1707, doubled in price when duties were imposed in 1713. The enraged reaction was predictable as salt was the universal food preservative of the day. The same year the House of Commons voted to apply the Malt Tax to Scotland, a decision that would have significantly pushed up the price of ale, the most popular drink in the country. Such was the furious response that the new tax was never properly enforced.

Most of the increased revenues from these new fiscal policies were actually retained in Scotland to cover the costs of civil administration and government. But this was not the perception at the time. It seemed on the contrary that increased taxes within the Union were a form of tribute levied on the Scots that was then channelled south to England. Overall, duties rose fivefold between 1707 and 1713. The fact that the much-vaunted post-union economic miracle, so beloved of pro-union pamphleteers, had signally failed to come about, also aggravated the burdens. The Scottish economy for the most part remained in the doldrums in the first decade of union, still suffering from the impact of the crises of the 1690s. It was no help either that Scotland's pre-union debts were now found to be greater than first assumed and rising. Some manufacturing industries, such as paper-making, candle-making and fine woollens, were also hit by higher duties. Worst affected was linen, the nation's premier industry, already under pressure because of poor quality, but now subject to new Westminster-imposed duties on exports. The printed-cloth sector almost vanished in these years.

What compounded the problems was the Westminster contention that the Scots were not simply undertaxed and not paying their way but were indulging in tax evasion on a massive scale. This intolerable behaviour now warranted vigorous intervention and reform from London. Smuggling had existed from time immemorial but the post-1707 black economy across the whole of Scotland was unprecedented in scale. London merchants, for instance, raged at the brazen levels of evasion in the Clyde tobacco trade with the Americas. Modern estimates suggest that from 1707 to 1722 the Scots paid duty on only around half of their imports from Virginia and Maryland. They had long been accustomed to low taxes and what can be described as 'relaxed' methods of gathering revenue. It therefore came as a rude shock to the populace when much more rigorous collecting regimes were established soon after 1707. By 1714 nearly 450 customs officers were in post north of the border, with a mandate to root out the chronic native diseases of revenue evasion and mass smuggling.

The people did not remain passive in the face of this onslaught by the British state. Armed resistance became common with violent mobs breaking open customs warehouses and absconding with impounded contraband. So widespread was the scale of the opposition to regulation that, although higher rates of excise were enforced after 1707, the revenue generated in Scotland between 1714 and 1717 was probably less than for the years before the Union. At the customs precincts of Ayr, Dumfries and Greenock the threat to life was such that officials could only carry out their daily duties with armed protection.

Elsewhere, a stream of reports came from across the country of officers stoned, assaulted or imprisoned and goods seized from ships and warehouses. Some even thought that Scotland was now becoming ungovernable. Certainly, these attacks on the Crown revenue represented the most serious popular protests against the Union state in the period apart from the Jacobite risings.

The Jacobite printer, Robert Freebairn, though predictably partial, nevertheless summarized many of the origins of the discontent in 1712:

> ... we have not only the Cess and Land tax, and Customs conform to the English Book of Rates, near the triple what we formerly pay'd, and Excise most rigorously exacted by a Parcel of Strangers sent down to us from England, but also the Malt-Tax, the Salt-Tax, the Leather-Tax, the Window-Tax, the Taxes upon Candles, Soap, Starch ... the Tax upon stamped Paper and Parchments ...[1]

Righteous indignation finally reached the mightiest in the land, including notable political figures who had voted enthusiastically in favour of the Union in 1706–7. Daniel Defoe, who had been a government agent during the union debates, thought in 1713 that 'not one man in Fifteen' in Scotland would now vote for the Union.[2] In that year Scots were hurt both in their pockets and their religious sensibilities. The imposition of the Malt Tax in 1713 was the final straw for many. Magnates such as the Duke of Argyll, the Earl of Islay (Argyll's younger brother), the Earl of Mar and others gathered and began to consider that the Union had failed and should be dissolved forthwith: Islay 'at a public entertainment, drunk a new kind of health, even to the speedy and legal dissolution of the Union'.[3]

They and other peers, both Scottish and English, now moved for a debate on the Union in the House of Lords with the intention of starting the process of dissolution. The Earl of Oxford commented caustically that the action of the Scots resembled a man with a toothache who was willing to cut off his head to end the pain. Their motion was presented in the Lords by the Earl of Seafield, a Scottish aristocrat who had been at the very heart of the pro-Union campaign in 1706 and became immortalized in history with the famous phrase at the end of the last session of the Scottish parliament, that it could now be seen as 'the end o' an auld sang'. Eventually no vote was taken on the issue itself but rather whether to delay the motion or not. The anti-unionists lost the division by a narrow majority and the measure never came before the Lords again.

But union was not yet secure. In 1715 another Jacobite rising broke out that in its scale and support was potentially more formidable than any other, including the more famous '45. Loyalty to the Stuarts had been originally founded on dynastic and religious principles, but now the Jacobites were able to pose as the champions of the Scottish nation and defenders of Scottish liberties against Westminister autocracy and imposition. At the outset of the rising the exiled House of Stuart issued proclamations publicly committing the restored monarchy to repeal of the Union and establishing once again an independent Scottish parliament. 'No union' now became a common motto on Jacobite banners. Lockhart of Carnwath, an ardent champion of the Stuart cause, was committed to the view that repeal of the Act of Union should be at the very heart of Jacobite strategy because of the popular appeal such a manifesto would now have in the country.

Not surprisingly, therefore, the rising of 1715 led by John, Earl of Mar, reflected a much greater range and depth of support for the Jacobite cause than that of Viscount Dundee in 1689. Mar was able to muster around 10,000 foot and horse, the strongest Jacobite host ever to take the field, against 4,000 troops in the government army, commanded by the Duke of Argyll. Even more significantly, considerable support now came from some of the greatest landed families of Lowland and especially north-east Scotland, which had been notable by its absence in the rising of 1689 to 1692. The list of sympathizers included such grandees as the Earls of Southesk, Panmure and Strathmore. Indeed, an estimated 40 per cent of Mar's army were recruited from Lowland Scotland. At the same time a Jacobite uprising in north-east England suggested the possibility of an effective military coalition between disaffected areas in each of the two kingdoms. From a Jacobite perspective, therefore, the prospect for the rising of 1715 was bright indeed. But when Mar, who as a general possessed a fatal combination of caution, timidity and indecision, failed to defeat the numerically inferior forces of the Crown in the inconclusive battle of Sherrifmuir in November 1715, the Jacobites completely lost the initiative. The failure of the rising was a crushing blow to their morale.

Opportunities for real progress were there, but they had literally been thrown away by inept leadership. Mar's indecisiveness cost the Stuarts dear and soon squandered their military superiority. His delay in marching south from the movement's strongholds in the southern Highlands was crucial: 'Mar waited and waited: he waited for French help, he waited for the Duke of Berwick, he waited for the King, he waited for yet more recruits to make his position impregnable.'[4]

So confident had the Jacobites been of success that James III and VIII himself had landed at Peterhead in December 1715, though he brought no help from France to augment the Scottish army. His triumphal entry into Dundee and then Perth was intended to be the prelude to a coronation at Scone. Instead, James was soon forced to beat a hasty retreat from Scotland via the port of Montrose. The fiasco of the '15 rising was then followed by the catastrophic failure of a Spanish invasion attempt in 1719, which was hoped would trigger a Jacobite revolt in both England and Scotland. The history of the main expedition was characteristically full of disasters. Severe storms in Spanish waters resulted in the scattering of the fleet and the cancellation of the main assault on the west of England. A smaller diversionary force pressed on to the Highlands, where it landed in Kintail, on the mainland off the Isle of Skye, only to be routed by government troops at the battle of Glen Shiel. It was indeed ominous that Jacobitism had been crushed in the very area where it claimed most military support.

The history of these years of post-union instability in Anglo-Scottish relations prompts two reflections. First, it demonstrates that neither Scots or English had yet embraced any concept of Britishness. Westminster policies demonstrated the failure to buy into the implications of union. They were founded on English nationalism and English priorities rather than those of the new union, even to the extent that formerly staunch and powerful supporters of union in Scotland in 1707 became profoundly alienated from a cause they had long supported. Tories in the House of Commons seem to have seen themselves above all else as the defenders of the rights and privileges of the Church of England, and saw Scottish Presbyterianism as a menace in the same way as they did all religious dissent. This explains their support for the Toleration and Patronage Acts that caused such outrage north of the border. England had entered into union to ensure its own national security. However, when Westminster peers enacted unpopular measures in both the religious and fiscal spheres in Scotland, they came close to destroying the Union itself in its very first years of existence. The feckless performance of the Jacobite command in 1715–16 gave the impression that that movement was little more than a paper tiger, but this was far from the truth, especially if the leadership had proved capable of marshalling the forces of popular anti-unionism, loyalty to the House of Stuart and France into even a temporary combined alliance.

Second, the leadership of the Church of Scotland was well aware of the potential threat of this instability, not only to the Union but to the Protestant Revolution of 1688–9 itself. As a result, Presbyterian ministers, despite their anger at anglicizing measures emanating from Westminster, were not in the end prepared to break or even undermine the Union. They would never support a campaign that might lead to the restoration of the Catholic pretender: 'their hostility to the Stuarts surpassed their hostility to the Union'.[5] Paradoxically, therefore, the very potency of the Jacobite threat at this time served in the final analysis to provide succour to the Union in hazardous times.

II

Nevertheless, the issues of revenue and taxation continued to be a running sore in Anglo-Scottish relations. This was confirmed by the events of 1724 when Robert Walpole's Whig government once again decided to apply the Malt Tax to Scotland. The tax passed easily in Parliament but when it came to be collected violent resistance rapidly spread across the country. A wave of popular fury was soon unleashed in the summer with rioting erupting in places as varied as Stirling, Dundee, Ayr, Elgin, Paisley and Glasgow. The disturbances in Glasgow were by far the most serious. The local Member of Parliament, Daniel Campbell of Shawfield, was suspected of supporting the hated tax, so the mob proceeded to exact revenge by burning and looting his impressive town house, engaged in a pitched battle with the local garrison, which resulted in eight fatalities, and then drove the retreating troops out of the city towards Dumbarton. It took the intervention of

General Wade with a force of 400 dragoons and accompanying foot to finally restore order and end a dangerous challenge to the Union state. With other towns apparently ready to join in, one scholar, perhaps over-enthusiastically, described the enraged reaction to the Malt Tax as 'a movement of national resistance'.[6]

The riots of 1725 finally concentrated the minds of Walpole's government on the Scottish problem. The insurrection itself was a serious matter, but of equal concern was the apparent impotence of the Scottish administration when confronted with such a major challenge to law and order. The Lord Advocate of Scotland, the country's senior law officer, Robert Dundas, had in fact opposed the Malt Tax and was dismissed as a result. The Secretary for Scotland, the Duke of Roxburgh, did little; and the vacuum in executive authority left by the abolition of the Privy Council was now laid bare for all to see. The Earl of Islay, who was sent to investigate the situation, reported to Walpole that there had been 'a long series of no administration' in Scotland and the 'mere letter of the law had little or no effect with the people'.[7] This was tantamount to saying that Scotland was ungovernable within the Union. It was not a situation that could be allowed to continue.

Walpole's solution was to sack the incompetent Roxburgh and appoint Islay to manage Scottish affairs. This was partly because the two men were close friends but also because the parliamentary votes of the great Argyll political interest were invaluable to Walpole's cause. The decision was a turning point in Anglo-Scottish relationships. Islay, later third Duke of Argyll from 1743, became the dominant political figure in Scotland between the 1720s and his death in 1761, excepting the brief few years between 1742 and 1746. Such was his power that he became known as the 'King of Scotland'. His influence rested on a solemn contract with Walpole: Islay would deliver political stability in Scotland and the votes of most Scottish MPs in return for the lion's share of patronage and the authority to govern personally north of the border.

The Walpole connection soon gave Islay immense influence, which he deployed with great skill in alliance with his two able principal agents, Andrew Fletcher, Lord Milton, and Duncan Forbes of Culloden, or 'King Duncan' as he was dubbed in the Highlands. The civil administration, law courts, army, Church and universities were all colonized as Islay relentlessly built up a formidable empire of clients and dependants. It was reckoned that two-thirds of the judges promoted to the Court of Session owed their position to his influence, and it was also paramount in the appointment of sheriffs who, it was alleged, were 'little more than a list of the sons, sons-in-law, and alliances' of Islay's clients.[8] By the 1730s his power was such that even King George II himself could describe Islay as 'Vice Roy in Scotland'.

Islay's effective management of Scotland gave a new stability to the Union. He was a skilled politician who had done much in 1725 to defuse the dangerous crisis over the Malt Tax. But he then ensured that order was maintained and recalcitrance diminished by trying to respond positively to Scottish concerns. Out of this came the foundation in 1727 of the Board of Trustees for Manufactures and Fisheries with a mandate to improve the Scottish economy. The sum of £6,000 per annum was to be devoted to the development of linen, wool and fisheries. In intent at least this was the practical implementation of Article XV of the Treaty of Union, though not to the full extent actually agreed in 1707. But the law was also rigorously enforced against the Glasgow Malt Tax rioters. The town was fined to compensate Campbell of Shawfield, and several of those involved in the disturbances were sentenced to transportation to the colonies. This approach showed that Islay was able to placate Scottish opinion but at the same time satisfy London that Scotland was being effectively governed. As his system of patronage became more sophisticated in the next several years, so Islay's expertise in reconciling conflicting interest groups became ever more refined. In consequence, Walpole trusted him to run Scotland with hardly any reference to Westminster. Indeed, not until 1737 did the government in London interfere in Scotland again in any direct fashion.

This occurred in response to the Porteous Riot in Edinburgh in 1736, when the mob lynched the Captain of the Town Guard, John Porteous, who had ordered his men to fire on the crowd at a smuggler's execution in April of that year. Porteous was under sentence in the city tollbooth because several had been killed as a result of the Guard's actions. But the mob, inflamed that he had been given a brief reprieve, forcibly removed the unfortunate from gaol and hanged him. This brutal lynching incensed Westminster. Not only was the government appalled at such an outrageous incident but angered also that the mob was suspected of being aided and abetted by the Edinburgh authorities. A bill was therefore prepared that proposed draconian punishments for the capital. The extreme measure was diluted in part only because of the determined opposition of the Duke of Argyll, Islay's older brother, and resistance to the imposition of heavy penalties on the nation's capital by Scottish political opinion.

The Porteous incident briefly damaged Islay's reputation as the man on whom Walpole and the London ministers could depend to run Scotland with minimal supervision from London. However, for over a decade Islay's regime had done much to accommodate Scotland to the Union. There was little additional pressure during that time for assimilation of the kind that had seriously jeopardized the union settlement in 1712–13. The cement of patronage had created loyalty to his rule in virtually all the key areas of Scottish civic life by the 1730s and this in turn allowed Scotland to be governed almost as a separate polity within the Union. Westminster was sovereign in theory but in practice the real business of running Scotland remained the responsibility of Scots and institutions inherited from the period before 1707.

The Treaty of Union itself had protected the Church and the law from radical change, and now an essentially Scottish form of national and local government was re-established. Edinburgh, despite the loss of its parliament, survived as a centre of law and administration. The major Scottish courts of Justiciary, Session and Exchequer, together with the Admiralty and Commissary Courts, met there, as did the General Assembly of the Church of Scotland, the Convention of Royal Burghs, the Board of Excise, the Post Office and the Scottish Board of Customs. The system of justice at the local level, consisting of the sheriffs and justices of the peace, was also inherited from before the Union, while the two key social functions at parish level, those of education and poor relief, were the joint responsibility of the pre-1707 kirk sessions and local landowners. All of this represented a remarkable degree of legal, religious and administrative autonomy and continuity, which meant that most of the political decisions that really mattered continued to be made in Scotland itself. As long as

Westminster kept a low profile, which in most years after 1725 it did, skilled managers such as Islay were able to defuse possible sources of friction and Scotland's semi-independent status was assured. This in turn helped to mollify anti-union opinion and promote acceptance of the new relationship with England. By 1740, therefore, the Union seemed on a much more stable basis than at any time since the passage of the legislation in 1706–7. This was, however, but the quiet before yet another storm.

4

Union Embedded

The Act of Union was a legislative measure agreed in Scotland by a tiny patrician elite against some internal parliamentary opposition and much external popular hostility. As already described, the future of the new association remained unpredictable in its first decades as the Scots came to terms with the English constitutional principle of 'the Crown-in-Parliament', a dictum that was potentially the most lethal threat to the Union. The old royal tradition of the Divine Right of Kings to rule without constitutional limit was inherited after the Revolution of 1688–9 by the Westminster Parliament and later the British Parliament after 1707. From that date, the amount of parliamentary representation between the two nations, whether based on relative taxation or property levels, was imbalanced to the detriment of the junior partner. The concept of the Crown-in-Parliament soon allowed the new authority in London to impose unacceptable policies on Scotland in areas of revenue and religion. Above all, these revealed in explicit terms that the Treaty of Union was not a fundamental, supreme or inviolable law but rather one that could be altered and amended by an electoral majority in the Westminster Parliament.

This revelation and its effect in practice led to turbulence in the Union relationship and could easily have led to its speedy disintegration. The history of Europe was littered with failed unions between countries in close geographical proximity, such as Spain/Portugal and Norway/Sweden. It was by no means inevitable that the Anglo-Scottish union would prevail. That it did so was not simply because of the clauses in the Treaty of Union itself but the history of Scotland and England, their relations in the four decades after 1707 and again in the half century from around 1750.

I

The relationship between Scottish Jacobitism and the survival of the Union was contradictory. On the one hand, some of the negative short-term results of 1707 helped to swell the ranks of Jacobite sympathizers. On the other, the threat of a possible return of the Catholic Stuarts and the monarchical absolutism associated with that dynasty ensured that Presbyterian Scots, who formed the overwhelming majority of the nation, were prepared to endure the provocation of some odious post-Union policies. The more menacing the possibility of a Jacobite counter-revolution became, the more these fears were reinforced. Nevertheless, a final elimination of the Jacobite threat could only help to cement the stability of the Anglo-Scottish association in the longer run.

The last and most famous Jacobite rising came to an end soon after the final rout of the army of Prince Charles Edward Stuart at the battle of Culloden on 16 April 1746. The territories of Jacobite loyalty in several parts of the Highlands and the north-eastern Episcopalian Lowlands were now at the mercy of the vengeful forces of the Duke of Cumberland, reinforced by men o' war of the Royal Navy. A huge regular army had been drawn into the very heart of the Highlands as it pursued the Jacobites north to the outskirts of Inverness before the fateful day. Effectively, disaffected areas could now come under military occupation. The missed opportunity by the London government after the 1715 rebellion to discount wholesale punishment of the rebel areas and the policy of leniency of that period were not to be repeated. The clans had to be broken once and for all because it was their martial elan and loyalty to the Stuarts that had brought Charles so close to success during the '45. An estimated 2,000 clansmen had been slaughtered during the carnage of the battle of Culloden itself and in the immediate aftermath. But even this military catastrophe had not apparently shattered the Jacobite spirit. The fact that so many of the defeated army were prepared to muster once again at nearby Ruthven and carry on the struggle suggested to Cumberland that only extreme and radical action would finally root out their intolerable spirit of disaffection, stubbornness and recalcitrance.

At first the duke favoured a strategy of wholesale transportation of the clans to the colonies and would indeed have pressed ahead with this policy of ethnic cleansing but for the unacceptable level of the costs involved. So instead he opted for a scorched-earth policy of burning, clearance and pillage in the Highlands. In May 1746 Cumberland moved his troops to Fort Augustus in the Great Glen and from there unleashed a reign of terror on some of the most loyal Jacobite areas in the surrounding region. His explicit intention was to teach the people of these districts a terrible lesson that they would never forget. Thus numerous settlements throughout Glenelg, Kintail, Lochaber and Morvern were burnt out, plundered and laid waste by four independent raiding parties, supported offshore by the Royal Navy. Even clans loyal to the Crown were not immune from the relentless depredations that lasted for nearly a year after Culloden. Cattle, the main source of wealth in this pastoral society and the means of buying in grain from more favoured areas, were confiscated on a massive scale. Fort Augustus, supplied from the booty plundered from the people of the surrounding districts, became for a time the largest cattle mart in Scotland, reckoned to have sold in one year alone nearly 20,000 head of cattle as well as numerous sheep, oxen, horses and goats. Long after the exactions had come to an end the Union state remained committed to a strategy of rigorous military control. The road system begun by General Wade and others was extended until a network of around 1,000 miles had been built by 1767. Even more significant was the construction between 1748 and 1769 of Fort George at Ardersier, east of Inverness, the most formidable bastion artillery fortress in Europe at the time and a permanent physical demonstration of the Hanoverian government's absolute determination that the clans would never again rise to threaten the Protestant succession.

When the military onslaught ended, the legislative attack on clanship began. Highland dress was proscribed as the sartorial symbol of rebel militarism. It was a measure for punishing and 'undressing those rascals'. A Disarming Act stiffened previous legislation to prohibit the carrying of weapons of war. The abolition of heritable jurisdiction (the private courts of landowners) and military land tenures was supposed to destroy the legal basis of the power of the chiefs. In reality, clan loyalties were primarily influenced by the mind, the heart and generations of traditional affiliation rather than by the law. Military tenures such as wardship were anyway already becoming obsolete because of the first fruits of commercialization in Gaeldom. The act to suppress non-juring Episcopalian meeting houses (one of the government army's main targets during the months after Culloden in the north-east counties as well as in the Highlands) was more significant since it was a recognition that Episcopalian ministers were one of the key ideological supports of Jacobitism. Estates of rebel landowners were forfeited to the Crown. The majority were sold off to pay creditors, but 13 were inalienably annexed and managed from 1752 to 1784 by a Commission to promote 'the Protestant Religion, good Government, Industry and Manufactures and the Principles of Duty and Loyalty to his Majesty'. The thinking was that Protestantism would induce ideological conformity while prosperity would remove the poverty on which disaffection was supposed to thrive.

The truth was, however, that Scottish Jacobitism was not simply destroyed amid the carnage of the field of Culloden and the punitive legislation and enforcement which followed that catastrophic defeat. In 1715 there had indeed been a real chance of Stuart counter-revolution, but this was less likely by 1745. Jacobitism was unpopular throughout most of the Lowlands south of the River Tay; the central Lowlands in particular was mostly hostile and Glasgow and the western towns were resolutely opposed. In 1715 opposition to the Union of 1707 had been a major factor strengthening Jacobite support. By the 1740s, however, there was much greater acceptance of the relationship with England. Many Scottish merchants and landowners were now obtaining significant material rewards through the Clyde's expanding transatlantic trades and the impact of English markets on demand for linen, cattle, coal and grain, though some east coast ports, traditionally linked to Europe, were less favoured. In addition, a fundamental barrier to the Stuarts' restoration was their Catholicism. They were not prepared to sacrifice their faith for political ambition and inevitably they paid the price. Thus, by far the most effective propaganda agents for the London government were the Presbyterian clergy of the west, central and south-east Lowlands, effectively the economic heart of Scotland. They stoked up fears that the return of the House of Stuart would bring in its train an autocratic papist regime that would threaten both the 'liberty' and 'true religion' of the Scots. Whig propaganda relentlessly identified Charles Edward Stuart as a foreigner who had come from Italy (the home of popery), and every attempt was made to exploit the anti-Catholic prejudices of the population in order to encourage opposition to him and his cause. As one Whig diatribe had it:

> From Rome a limb of Antichrist [the Pope]
> Joined with a Hellish Band of Highland Thieves,
> Came here in haste
> God's Laws for to withstand.

Culloden was therefore for many Scots a happy deliverance from the threatened dominion of the Antichrist. The *Glasgow Journal* brought out a special large-print edition to celebrate the defeat of 'Chevalier de St George's eldest son' and also to record 'the greatest rejoicings that have been known' in the city. All the heartlands of Presbyterian Scotland indeed greeted the news from Culloden with heartfelt relief and celebration. The Duke of Cumberland was feted, elected Chancellor of St Andrews University, and became the recipient of other honours from a grateful nation. Only much later was he to achieve lasting notoriety as 'Butcher Cumberland' when the lost cause of Jacobitism came to be memorialized and sentimentalized in song and story.

During the '45 rising it was noted that only a small minority of the Scottish landed classes came out for the Stuarts. Even in traditionally Jacobite areas the elites of some clans, such as the Macintoshes and Chisholms, were terminally split in their loyalties by the 1740s. Influential Hebridean chiefs like Sir Alexander MacDonald of Sleat, Kenneth MacKenzie, Earl of Seaforth, and Macleod of Macleod in Skye took no part. Indeed, Scottish backing for the Stuarts during the rising was remarkably thin on the ground long before the crushing defeat of Culloden; it was this fact, together with the virtual disappearance of support in the north of England and the disinterest of France, rather than force of arms alone, that ultimately killed off the dynasty's hopes of restoration.

So decisively had the threat of counter-revolution been crushed that Jacobitism could become sentimentalized by the end of the eighteenth century. With the rebels tamed and their martial power destroyed, the scene was set for their metamorphosis from faithless traitors to national heroes who had shown immense and commendable loyalty and courage, albeit in an unworthy cause. The rehabilitation of Jacobitism was also helped when the strategy of the Secretary of State, William Pitt the Elder, during the Seven Years War (1756–63) of channelling the military prowess of the clans into imperial service proved so successful. Then the spectre of republicanism emanating from the French Revolution made the old conflict between Hanoverian and Stuart obsolete at a stroke. Jacobitism now became redefined as an ideology committed to monarchy in the abstract sense at a time when the institution in Britain was threatened by radicalism at home and the spirit of revolution abroad. The mythology of Jacobitism was even embraced by the House of Hanover, above all with enthusiasm and affection by Queen Victoria as part of her love affair with the Scottish Highlands in the nineteenth century.

II

In the 1740s, the same decade that Jacobitism met its final defeat, the long-hoped-for economic benefits of union were finally beginning to become apparent. Linen was Scotland's premier industry and one that experienced unprecedented expansion between about 1740 and 1780, with the output of cloth recorded for public sale rising fourfold over these decades. In addition, linen manufacture was to play a key role in the early stages of Scottish industrialization as the most important source of capital, labour and business skills for cotton, the 'leading sector' of the Industrial Revolution. Linen's success seemed to rest to a large extent on the common market created by the Union. In the 1760s, for instance, as much as two-thirds of stamped linen output was sold in the English home market or those of the American and Caribbean colonies. But for the Union, this core manufacture would very likely have been confronted with an English tariff wall in competition with aggressive Dutch and German rivals. The Scots instead received protection within the Union and were also aided from 1742 by a series of bounties to encourage exports. These, rather than native initiatives to improve efficiency, seem to have been the decisive influences on growth. Linen, therefore, was one case where the record shows a direct and positive benefit from the Union.

It was a similar story with the 'golden age' of Glasgow's tobacco trade with the American colonies. Scottish tobacco imports had reached greater volume than those of London and all the English outports combined by the late 1750s. In 1771 the highest-ever amount of tobacco was landed, a staggering 47 million pounds. Glasgow had become the tobacco metropolis of western Europe, and in the west of Scotland the profits of the trade started to feed into a very wide range of industries, several banks and agricultural improvements. The transatlantic trades played a key role in the development of the Glasgow area, the region that was to become the engine of Scottish industrialization. The legitimacy afforded by the Union was crucial to this dazzling story of commercial success. As already noted, Scots traders had been active in the tobacco colonies before 1707, though on a relatively small scale, and much of it was clandestine in nature. But no London government would have permitted such an enormous illegal growth in Scottish tobacco imports of the post-1740 dimensions to take place outside the Union. Indeed, it was English protests against the boom in Scottish smuggling *within* the Union that had led to the wholesale reorganization of the customs service in 1723 and the formation of a more professional customs bureaucracy. This reflected the great political sensitivity of the issue, since it was widely recognized that much of the Scottish success was at the expense of English merchants.

Smuggling before 1707 clearly had its limitations; the Union was therefore a necessary condition for the phenomenal Glaswegian performance in the American trades. Yet those successes were not inevitable. In the final analysis they were won by the Scottish merchant houses pursuing more efficient business methods than many of their rivals. The big Glasgow firms were able to drive down their costs by a number of innovations in purchasing, marketing and shipping that made them formidable competitors in American and European markets. So the Union did not *cause* growth in the Atlantic trades; it simply provided a necessary context in which growth might or might not take place. Ultimately the decisive factor was the Scottish response.

Scots had been migrating to the (then) English empire before 1707, but the Union soon opened up new opportunities. Indeed, by the time of the American War of Independence (1775–83) several parts of British North America and the West Indies had become virtually surrogate Scottish colonies. By then around 15,000 Gaels had settled in Georgia and the Carolinas, while it is reckoned that over 60,000 Lowland emigrants had made their way to the Chesapeake, the Carolinas and Boston, and perhaps another 15,000 to the sugar plantations of the Caribbean. Even more crucially for the future, middle-class Scottish adventurers, merchants, mariners, military officers and colonial officials were exploiting imperial opportunities not only in the western hemisphere but in the provinces of India:

> Even the rawest frontiers of the empire attracted men of first-rate ability from the Celtic fringe because they were usually poorer than their English counterparts with fewer prospects on the British mainland. Having more to win and less to lose, Celtic adventurers were more willing to venture themselves in primitive conditions.[1]

Their story is told in more detail in Chapter 5.

England had no economic ambitions in Scotland. As already discussed, its motivation for union was to secure the northern border. But the Union in the long term enabled ideas, technical innovations and skilled labour to flow north from the more advanced south. Indeed, the early phase of Scottish industrialization was overwhelmingly based on borrowed expertise from Holland, France and, above all, England. Technology transfer on a remarkable scale took place from south to north, reflecting Scotland's relative backwardness and also the strategy of English businessmen on the lookout for cheaper labour and low-rent factory sites. The spinning revolution in cotton was entirely based on the seminal inventions of the Englishmen John Kay, James Hargreaves, Richard Arkwright and Samuel Crompton. Men with experience of English mill practice often became the managers of early Scottish factories. The best known of them was Archibald Buchanan, who, after serving an apprenticeship at Cromford in Derbyshire, became the technical genius behind the rise of the great Scottish cotton empire of James Finlay and Company. The manufacture of sulphuric acid was pioneered at Prestonpans in 1749 by John Roebuck and Samuel Garbett after their earlier venture in Birmingham. The blast furnace and the coke process of smelting were both introduced from England, as was the coal-fired reverberating furnace, which was central to technical progress in the brewing, chemical, pottery and glass industries. Perhaps the most famous example of the penetration of English know-how came with the foundation in 1759 of Carron Company, Scotland's largest manufacturing plant of the day, based on the coke-smelting techniques pioneered at Coalbrookdale in Shropshire. The speed of Scotland's economic transformation also created technical bottlenecks and recurrent shortages of skilled labour, which were often relieved by a steady trickle from England of experienced smelters, moulders, spinners and ironworkers.

This is far from being a definitive list but it is enough to demonstrate that Scottish economic progress would surely have been impeded without English technical expertise and skills and, to a lesser extent, those of other countries. But these new processes were assimilated swiftly, confirming that Scotland itself had the appropriate social, cultural and economic environment in which to become rapidly industrialized. Like a latter-day Japan, having borrowed ideas from other countries on a grand scale, Scotland soon moved swiftly to the cutting edge of the new technology itself. A stream of key inventions soon started to emanate from Scotland: James Watt's refinement of the separate condenser for the steam engine (perhaps the fundamental technological breakthrough of the age); Neil Snodgrass's scutching machine, enabling wool to be processed effectively before being spun; the aforementioned Archibald Buchanan's construction of the first truly integrated cotton mill in Britain in 1807, where all the key processes were carried out by steam power within a single complex; Henry Bell's *Comet* of 1812, which pioneered steam propulsion for ships; and J. B. Neilson's invention in 1829 of the 'hot-blast process', which helped to transform iron manufacture by radically reducing the costs of production.

Several historians have done much to revise and clarify the overarching influence of the Union on Scottish development. They have shown that the pre-1707 economy, though stricken with the disasters of the 1690s, was not quite as backward as was once believed. The decades after the Union were not an entirely new dawn following centuries of darkness and poverty. Moreover, there is broad historiographical agreement today that union was a necessary precondition for Scottish economic growth but not in itself sufficient to guarantee that it would happen. Critics point to Ireland, also after 1801 a part of the Union, which almost became an economic satellite of England and eventually suffered the horrors of the worst human catastrophe in nineteenth-century Europe during the Great Famine (1845–9). Indigenous Scottish advantages making for development have therefore to be added to the formula for growth. These included the business enterprise of the merchant classes; a commitment (often ruthless) to agrarian capitalism by the landed elite; high levels of literacy and education; a favourable natural endowment of plentiful coal, water and ironstone. Yet little reference to these indigenous resources and advantages was made from the early nineteenth century. In Victorian times it was simply assumed that the Union was the unquestioned sheet anchor of the Scottish economic miracle. This belief in turn provided rock-like stability and resilience to the Union state.

III

As the Jacobite army marched into the very heart of England during the '45 rising, the Westminster government had been shaken to its very foundations. The rooting out of disaffection in Scotland after the Hanoverian triumphs now led to massive English military and political intervention north of the border. Indeed, some felt in London that disloyalty ran through Scottish society from top to bottom and was not confined to those who were 'out' in the rising itself. Even the Duke of Argyll was suspected by some to be a closet Jacobite as a wave of paranoia and Scotophobia swept across governing circles in London. After 1747 the ministry in Westminster was led by Henry Pelham, First Lord of the Treasury, while his brother the Duke of Newcastle as Secretary of State handled Scottish business and foreign affairs. Neither entirely trusted Argyll and believed he was trying to protect Jacobite sympathizers from the punishment that they so richly deserved.

Gradually, however, the Duke of Argyll re-established his power as ministers in London needed the support of the Scots MPs that only his political machine could deliver effectively. Crucially, direct rule from Westminster after the '45, which could very well have damaged the Union relationship in the long run, soon came to an end after 1752 as Argyll restored his own control in Scotland. Several of his policies became emphatically pro-Scottish as he sought to heal the wounds opened up both by Jacobite disaffection and the effects of the punitive policies of the Westminster government. The important export bounty on Scots linen, which as already indicated was so critical to the nation's leading manufacture, had lapsed in 1754, causing widespread unemployment among the workforce. Argyll's influence helped the measure to be fully reinstated by the summer of 1756, so helping the industry to flourish again. He was also instrumental in the implementation of proposals for raising the Highland regiments during the Seven Years War. By 1761 the duke had named and nominated no less than 40 per cent of the commissioned officers in these formations. Their reputation as hardy mobile light infantry in the American campaigns did much to assuage suspicions in London about lingering disloyalty in Scotland.

The duke's long tenure therefore did a great deal to manage the integration of Scotland and England within the Union while at the same time safeguarding the autonomy of Scottish interests and institutions. In return for delivering the votes of Scots MPs to the ministry of the day, he was once again given the authority to govern Scotland autonomously, ensure stability, and hold the strings of patronage to appointments. Westminster was sovereign in law, but in practical terms Scotland was Argyll's domain.

Henry Dundas at a later date could be regarded as Argyll's heir after the death of the duke in 1761. When the Argyll hegemony came to an end there was no obvious replacement to fill the gap that had been left, in order to maintain the link between London and Scotland as the source and distributor of patronage and effectively to manage the Scottish administration. The problem of government was also compounded by the increasing absenteeism in England of several of the greater Scottish magnates, the traditional leaders of Scottish society, and the Cabinet's indifference to issues north of the border as long as the country remained politically conformist and quiescent. Henry Dundas seized the opportunity created by this vacuum to make his mark. He was not of noble birth but a scion of the lairds of Arniston in the Lothians, a family with strong legal connections and traditions. His rise was meteoric. He became Solicitor General in 1766 and Lord Advocate in 1775. Crucially, these posts were not simply confined to the law but extended into a whole range of other political and administrative duties. Essentially, it was the senior law officers who actually ran Scotland in the later eighteenth century.

However, control over patronage was the real key to power for Dundas, as it had been for his predecessor. From 1779, as sole Keeper of the Signet, he became the decisive influence over appointments to government posts in Scotland and systematically used his position to build up a complex network of clients, voters and local interests who depended on Dundas for favours, places, promotions and pensions. His ascendancy was further confirmed by appointment as a commissioner of the Board of Control of the East India Company in 1784 and later its president from 1793 to 1801. Although Scots were finding Indian appointments in significant numbers long before Dundas came on the scene, access to the Company's vast circle of patronage could only strengthen his position even further. He was capable of serving many masters for his own ends and indeed in 1782–3 had been a member of three governments, each of a different political hue. But thereafter his loyal and close relationship with the younger Pitt (which included sharing in many heroic drinking sessions together) put the seal on Dundas's rise to pre-eminence. Yet his position in the final analysis rested not so much on a shared commitment to conviviality as on his ability to deliver what William Ferguson called 'the well-drilled phalanx in the north' for Pitt's interest. In 1780 Dundas personally controlled 12 of the 41 Scottish constituencies contested in the general election; by 1784 this number had risen to 22, and in 1790 to 34. 'King Harry the Ninth' was coming close to the zenith of his personal power in Scotland.

Dundas's game was to maximize the number of loyal supporters in the House of Commons, by so doing to make himself indispensable to the government of the day and to consolidate and, if possible, expand his sources of patronage. In this last respect he was a past master. The number of places and sinecures in the navy, army, colonial, excise and government service taken by Scots increased substantially during his period of influence. By 1800, Scotland had obtained more than a quarter of all official pensions and one-third of state sinecures, a much higher proportion than was warranted by the country's population (one sixth of England's) or national wealth. Success on this scale eventually provoked outrage in London, and Parliament determined that the volume of patronage to the greedy Scots had to be drastically curbed. But the number of requests for posts was still far in excess of the supply. For the years 1784–90 alone there survives in the National Library of Scotland a bundle of almost 600 petitions for everything from university professorships to peerages, and these are not by any means all of those received by Dundas during those years. As a result he was able to pick and choose, not simply ensuring rewards to political clients and associates, but also selecting on the basis of talent, ability and potential. This gravy train was vital to the careers and family prospects of many in the Scottish landed and professional classes, and few were likely to risk preferment by being found guilty of needlessly disturbing the status quo.

The short-lived radical movement of the early 1790s in Scotland for a time did challenge the emerging unionist consensus. Although some in the leadership of the reform organization, the Friends of the People, were committed unionists, many others, led by the young advocate Thomas Muir, were much more critical of the close relationship with England. Lord Daer, another leading light in the reform movement, asserted that 'the Friends of Liberty in Scotland' were in the majority enemies of the Union. Muir himself strongly opposed any increased integration with England, stressing that Scotland was a nation with its own distinctive laws, courts, judges and juries. But such thinking was not typical of the times. Radicalism in Scotland collapsed in 1792–3 as the Reign of Terror in France brought the propertied classes of Britain together in collective defence amid fears of anarchy and revolution spreading from across the Channel. In a series of state trials Muir and several of his supporters were sentenced to Botany Bay in Australia by a vengeful judiciary. The Friends of the People were crushed. The ensuing war with the old enemy, France, effectively put an end to all public talk of anti-unionism. Instead, an

enhanced loyalty to the British state soon became the dominant commitment of the nation's political and social elites.

IV

By the late 1750s some of the tensions that surfaced within the Union
in the aftermath of the '45 were still alive despite the developing
economic benefits to Scotland and the final destruction of Jacobitism.
National pride was offended by the Militia Act of 1757, which created a volunteer force for defence of the realm against foreign attack
in England and Wales but not in Scotland. It seemed that the treacher-
ous Scots could not yet be trusted with the bearing of arms.
Scotophobia then reared its ugly head in the early 1760s, during the
short-term office of John, Earl of Bute, the first Scots-born Prime Minister after the Union. Bute's tenure in this exalted position was brief
– ending in 1763 – but his influence was said to endure beyond that
through interest, networks and clientage; so also did the relentless
attacks both on him personally – his family name, Stuart, did not help
– and on Scots in general. During the 1760s the number of his fellow
countrymen holding state office had risen dramatically and it was
suspected that Bute was favouring his own kind. As one scholar has
noted, 'With the sole exception of the French, no other nationality
[other than the Scots] was so despised and derided in the vast array of
caricatures turned out by the London press.'[2] These cartoons were
savagely racist in tone, portraying Scots as greedy mendicants growing rich on England's rich pastures. Bute himself was satirized in one
ribald print after another as the well-endowed seducer of the mother
of George III, explicit sexual symbolism for the intolerable penetration of England and the empire by ragged swarms of Scots crossing
the border in desperate search of places and pensions:

> Friend and favourite of France-a,
> Ev'ry day may you advance-a.
> And when dead by tomb be writ on,
> 'Here lies one whom all must sh-t-on,
> Oh, the Great, the Great North Briton'.

It has to be said, of course, that at root this violent hostility reflected ethnic jealousy about the remarkable Scottish success in securing careers in both the empire and London.

Probably the turning point in these strained relations came during the American War of Independence and then, finally and even more emphatically, during the French Revolution and Napoleonic Wars. The vital contrast here was with Ireland, by this time becoming the much more awkward neighbour. Between 1776 and 1783 the Scots would be enthusiastically loyal to the British Crown. Even in the colonies more loyalist settlers had apparently been born in Scotland than in any other country. They became the hated enemies of the American Patriot Party, denounced as natural supporters of tyranny, confirmed by Scottish support for the exiled Stuarts in 1745, a dynasty viewed as the very incarnation of absolute monarchy and Catholic autocracy by many Protestant colonists. At the same time, however, Irish politicians were seen to be behaving badly and attempting to extract advantage from England's travails.

That contrast between Scotland and Ireland became much more clear-cut during the Napoleonic Wars, a conflict that finally ended the epic 'second Hundred Years War' with France for global imperial hegemony. Britain was comprehensively victorious and the foundation of *Pax Britannica* across the oceans of the world was established. But at the time it was a close-run thing. From 1798 to 1805 Napoleon's all-conquering armies were encamped a few miles across the Channel preparing for invasion. It was at this critical juncture that the Irish committed the ultimate betrayal. The major uprising of 1798, led by the United Irishmen, offered the French the real chance of an effective flank attack and invasion at the hour of England's greatest peril. They attempted to land troops on three occasions on the Irish coast before that year was out. Two years earlier, in 1796, the French General Hoche, accompanied by Wolfe Tone, had also come very close to successfully bringing 15,000 troops ashore at Bantry Bay.

The contrast with the loyalty of the Scots could not have been more apparent. Already over-represented among the officer class in the field armies, 52,000 Scots also joined the ranks of the volunteers. With around 15 per cent of the British population, Scots accounted for 36 per cent of all the volunteer soldiery in 1797, 22 per cent in 1801 and

17 per cent in 1804. Scottish loyalty and the Scottish contribution in blood to final victory over France had cemented the Union by 1815. If contemporary English caricatures and cartoons are any guide, the 'venomous contempt' of the mid-eighteenth century became the 'innocent humour' of the Victorian era.

Scholars rightly point out that nothing promotes common patriotism so effectively as a common enemy. In Scotland the enemy within, Jacobitism, had long been eliminated by the time of the Napoleonic Wars. This was not so in Ireland, because there Jacobitism had been but one element in Irish opposition to the British states. The history of Ireland and Scotland in their relations with England since medieval times had differed profoundly. Ireland had long been a colony of England in a process that had its roots in the twelfth century but was then imposed much more brutally in the seventeenth century. Ireland did have its own legislature and executive before the Union of 1801 but in essence the country was a subject province of England. Attempts were made to impose Protestantism on the Irish but the strategy ended in failure and the faithful allegiance to Catholicism became not only a badge of religious identity in most of Ireland but of national identity as well. This made England very vulnerable when its main continental enemies from the sixteenth century were the leading Catholic powers of France and Spain. It was fear of Ireland becoming the proverbial backdoor into England that prompted three violent waves of colonization in the seventeenth century: first in the reign of James I and VI with the formation of the Ulster plantation; second, and with much more force, by Oliver Cromwell; and finally by William of Orange at the end of the century. Draconian measures against the Catholic population made the post-Culloden exactions in Scotland at a later date pale into relative insignificance by comparison. Soon a Protestant minority of English and Scottish origin held a monopoly of both landownership and political office. Other statutes proscribed the Catholic religion and the bearing of arms. All of this was hardly likely to inspire amity in the long run between Ireland and England.

The differences in the Anglo-Scottish relationship before the eighteenth century were stark and became the basic historical foundations of the closer association achieved in the wars of the eighteenth century between the two countries. Scotland had never been an English colony but an historic independent state with its own monarchy and civil institutions before 1707. At the time of the Union, Scotland was also already overwhelmingly Protestant. There were differences between the reformed traditions in both countries but nonetheless a shared Protestantism in the face of hostile Catholic powers became a powerful ideological bond between them. The Scots were also able to strike a good bargain in 1707, gaining free access to the English domestic market (more than ten times the size of their own) and the opportunities for even greater profit as the British empire began to expand across the globe. Ireland, on the other hand, was treated like a foreign country for customs purposes and did not achieve freedom of trade with the rest of Britain until its union in 1801. The rapid expansion of the Scottish economy eventually occurred in response to these commercial privileges and was probably the most important single factor facilitating the making of a Scottish/British identity in the country. At the same time, while Ireland was garrisoned by a standing army and governed by a colonial bureaucracy, the Scots ruled themselves within the Union for most of the eighteenth century even if Westminster remained sovereign in theory. The mutual amity between Scotland and England that developed during the European wars flowed naturally from these shared advantages.

Especially important both in fact and symbolism in this alliance of blood between England and Scotland was the Highlands, formerly the very heart of many of the campaigns against the House of Hanover and the Union. The raising of imperial regiments from Gaeldom, which began during the Seven Years War, expanded further during the American War of Independence and even more significantly in the French Revolutionary and Napoleonic Wars. Around 12,000 Scottish rank and file were recruited during the Seven Years War, almost as many as those who had taken part in the most supported Jacobite rising in 1715 and more than twice the size of Prince Charles Edward Stuart's forces in the '45. Indeed, Gaeldom became more militarized between the early 1760s and 1815 than at any period in its recent past. Estimates of recruits suggest 37,000 to 48,000 men in regular, volunteer and fencible regiments (the last raised for the purposes of home defence against invasion), a remarkable figure given that the population of the Highlands did not exceed 300,000 in the later eighteenth century. From the island of Skye alone between 1792 and the 1830s came 21 lieutenant or major generals, 48 lieutenant colonels, 600 other officers, 120 pipers and numerous rank and file. The west coast parish of Gairloch was virtually stripped of its menfolk. A survey concluded in 1799 that the population of the parish then mainly consisted of children, women and old men. Fort George near Inverness, constructed to intimidate the clans after Culloden, now had a new role as the great drill square to prepare Highland levies for overseas service.

The Highland regiments that had seen action against Napoleon's armies at Waterloo in 1815 were feted on their return to Scotland as national heroes, the proud inheritors of the ancient martial traditions of the Scots. Their fame not only lived on but grew even more spectacularly in Victorian times. They symbolized a new, closer bond within the Union. On the one hand, these elite soldiers were unambiguously Scottish, clad in tartan, kilt and sporran. On the other, they were also British warriors, destined to be memorialized in song and story as the military spearheads of empire. Their hybrid nature was a metaphor for the new identities being fashioned more generally within the Union state by the time of Waterloo.

5

Early Fruits of Empire

By the middle decades of the eighteenth century, Scotland was at a crossroads between the old world and the new. From the 1760s and 1770s the social and economic structures of the nation went through a process of transformation unparalleled among contemporary European societies in its speed, scale and intensity. Indeed, no other area of the Continent achieved such rapid revolution in its economy until the state-initiated and forced industrialization of Soviet Russia in the 1920s and early 1930s. The great Scottish leap forward towards an urban and industrial society was without precedent. England was, of course, in the vanguard of modernity, but it took around two hundred years to achieve what its northern neighbour managed in a couple of generations. Scottish industrialization was explosive; that of England, cumulative, protracted and, for the most part during the seventeenth and eighteenth centuries, evolutionary in character.

Economic historians are able to show that a range of factors helped to establish this new economic order. They included growing markets, the natural advantages of water, coal and iron-ore resources, relatively low-cost labour and fertile sources of enterprise, among other causes. But most accounts fail to address convincingly or sometimes even fail to mention a major puzzle at the core of Scotland's progress to modernity. In earlier centuries the country had been recognized as one of the poorest in Europe with high levels of emigration and low standards of living. As already seen, in the 1690s Scots had suffered several years of famine and serious economic crises triggered by the failure of the Darien expeditions and acute difficulties in overseas trade. Also, as late as 1738–41, Scotland went through one of the worst economic depressions of the eighteenth century. Two consecutive harvest failures led to price inflation, a fall in agricultural output, and a marked decline in average incomes. The transformational process, especially in its early stages from the 1760s before internal productive gains came through, therefore required investment and a lot of it. From where did the new financial resources come?

Again, a comparison with England is worth making. Historians there spend little time pondering over sources of capital for eighteenth-century trade, agriculture and industry. This is hardly surprising because England far exceeded Scotland in national wealth. It was a country with the resources not only to make war on a global scale but also to fund existing economic expansion, primarily through the reploughing of earlier profits into new investment. Scotland differed in three key respects: it was a much poorer country, the economic revolution took place rapidly over a few decades, and unprecedented levels of investment were needed simultaneously not only in industry, towns and the transport infrastructure of roads, harbours and canals, but also crucially in agriculture. Significant injections of capital were required not only in niche developments or the sectors of industry and infrastructure but across the whole range of the economic system.

The evidence from the revolution in agriculture is compelling in this respect. In its first phase at least, the process of innovation was led and managed by the landed classes and their agents. Only by the 1790s were there clear signs that the tenant farmers were coming into their own as the primary driving force. This top-down approach involved lavish expenditure from the elites either as loans to their tenants or in outright expenditure on the provision of huge tonnages of lime to improve acidic soils, on roads, enclosures, ditching, timber plantations, walls, dykes, drains and village development. Three examples from many illustrate the magnitude of the investment. Over a five-year period from 1771 to 1776, the Earl of Strathmore laid out £22,223 in a large-scale programme of improvement on his Angus lands, while over six months in 1803, Richard Oswald's expenditure on Auchencruive in Ayrshire was of the order of £2,600. On the Crawford estate in South Lanarkshire in 1772 the annual spend was over £4,700. In addition, it was reckoned that from 1780 to 1815 between £2.5 and £3 million was paid out by the new turnpike trusts on the construction of roads and bridges in Scotland, a scale of investment that revolutionized the country's formerly primitive system of communications. It must be remembered, too, that much of the nation's industries of textiles, mining, printing and quarrying were rural-based in this period and were capitalized by collective partnerships of landowners and entrepreneurs.

All of this improvement does not take into account the rise in the levels of conspicuous consumption among the Scottish aristocracy and gentry classes that was simultaneously occurring in this new age of agrarian capitalism. The costs of landownership spiralled in the eighteenth century. These were the decades of competitive display when social standing became defined by material status designed to impress and embed personal prestige. Magnificent country houses, opulent furnishings, and the adornment of estate policies were not only fashionable but essential in order to maintain and demonstrate high positions in the social hierarchy of the day. It is noteworthy how many of the great houses of Scotland were either built or significantly renovated during this period: Inverary, Culzean, Hopeton and Mellerstain were only the most famous examples. This was the era when the remarkable Adam family of architects did their best work, much of which involved the comprehensive remodelling of the old castellated houses and fortified dwellings of an earlier and more turbulent age. In the later eighteenth century the number of aristocratic and laird houses built from scratch also multiplied. Nearly twice as many were constructed in the 1790s (over sixty) as between 1700 and 1720. Most of Robert Adam's commissions were for the laird classes even though his best-known work was for the nobility. Also driving up costs was the revolution in interior design. At the time of the Union the domestic furnishings of a typical landowner's house were simple in the extreme. Less than fifty years later the Scottish aristocracy was aspiring to standards of unprecedented splendour with gilded ornamentation, framed paintings, lavish fabrics and elaborate ceiling mouldings. Mahogany furnishings based on the designs of Chippendale, Sheraton and Hepplethwaite enjoyed remarkable popularity.

Over time the resources for elite spending on the grand scale would increasingly derive from fatter rent rolls generated by improved agricultural methods and booming markets. But this explanation still leaves out of account the problem of the crucial pioneering decades of the 1760s to the 1780s when modern agrarian capitalism first evolved in Scotland. It is the case that a prime source of the new wealth was the profits of empire, founded on the Union, and trade with the Americas, the Caribbean and India, together with the impact of 'sojourners' returning with fortunes made overseas in merchanting, plantation ownership, the professions and colonial administration.

II

An empire of transoceanic Scottish trade would not have existed on such a scale but for the Union of 1707. It enabled the inclusion of Scotland within the English system of tariff protection and protected by the military power of the Royal Navy in the long series of wars fought against France in North America, the West Indies and India for territorial and commercial hegemony. In the final analysis, the British markets in the Americas and India rested on the deployment of force backed by the financial resources of the state. One contention has it that there was a definable difference between the 'Scottish' and 'English' empires. The latter, it is suggested, was driven by the urge to conquer, while the former was more benign and concerned with making money and settling emigrants. The supposed distinction is illusory. Even if the Scots were dedicated to profit rather than conquest (itself a highly questionable proposition), the colonies where they traded only remained British, and hence markets open to them, because of the muskets of the army and the firepower of the navy.

The governing assumption among all eighteenth-century European states was that global wealth was finite. Any increase in the share of one nation could only take place at the expense of another. Aggression, predatory behaviour, and an obsession with protection of national interests by commercial regulation and armed force were inevitably built into these beliefs. Scottish trading communities were therefore usually enthusiastic about colonial wars if they brought real commercial gains – hence the open letter of gratitude sent to the dying George II by the Scottish Convention of Royal Burghs in 1760. Praise was heaped on the monarch for the military successes in the West Indies and British North America culminating in the triumphant capture of Quebec from the French in 1759. Scottish interests were quick to spot the opportunities that opened up as a consequence of these victorious campaigns. As early as 1760–61, Edinburgh publishers were already selling maps of Guadeloupe, Louisburg, Quebec and Montreal, all areas soon to attract Scottish adventurers when the Seven Years War came to an end in 1763. They would have agreed with the famous aphorism that 'Trade is the source of finance and finance is the vital nerve of war.'[1]

Equally, the only effective guarantor of Scottish colonial commerce in such a hostile environment was the Royal Navy. That protection in turn depended on the Treaty of Union of 1707. A year before it was signed the pro-unionist William Seton of Pitmedden, calling to mind the bitter lesson of the Darien disaster, recognized the harsh realities of an international world riven by mercantilist jealousies and mighty rivalries. The 'Course of Commerce' could only be exploited, he asserted, 'where there's force to protect it'. That force could not come from Scotland. The country was possessed of only tiny naval forces. Therefore, only 'the Protection of some powerful Neighbour Nation' could provide the support necessary in a world of expansionist and aggressive maritime powers.[2]

These arguments soon became a reality in the years after union. Scottish Atlantic traders by then enjoyed the protection of a navy, expanded by the fiscal-military resources of the British state, against foraging wolf-packs of enemy privateers. Coastal shipping was also better safeguarded by the 12 cruisers despatched to 'North Britain' under the Cruiser and Convoy Act of 1708. However, it was only during the Seven Years War that the naval presence in home waters really became vital, as before then enemy privateers tended mainly to infest the English Channel and the Southern Approaches where there were richer pickings. But in 1759 and early 1760 the famous French commodore Thurot sailed north into Scottish waters with three heavily armed frigates, two corvettes and 1,300 troops. Such a force might have created mayhem. However, thanks to the arrival of a substantial Royal Navy squadron, Thurot's expedition ended in disarray. The whole affair was a striking demonstration of British naval power and it was this factor that underpinned the doubling of the Scottish merchant marine from a tonnage of 47,751 in 1759 to 91,330 on the eve of the American War of Independence in 1775.

Maritime security also provided the safety net for success in the colonial trades. By 1762 just under 50 per cent of Scottish imports and 52 per cent of the country's exports consisted of colonial tobacco. Even when that lucrative trade declined after the American War of Independence, imperial markets remained fundamental. The sugar and cotton trades from the West Indies now became the new money-spinners. As late as 1814 nearly half of all the vessels leaving Clyde ports sailed for the Caribbean islands of Jamaica, Grenada and Barbados; the remaining British North American territories (later Canada) also took double the Glasgow exports destined for the USA in that year. The West Indian connection was a key element in the development of Scottish cotton manufacture in the early decades of its expansion. Until near the end of the eighteenth century, the Caribbean was the great source of cheap and abundant 'sea-island' raw cotton for the industry. Imports rose from 2.7 to 8.4 million pounds in weight between 1790 and 1805 to supply the needs of the numerous spinning mills springing up across the western Lowlands.

Fortunes made from tobacco, sugar and cotton had a direct impact on the agricultural revolution, especially in the counties around Glasgow. Money poured from the Atlantic trades into land purchases as wealthy merchants bought up properties. A little under half of the Glaswegian merchant aristocracy owned at least one landed estate and the really rich managed to acquire a number of properties spread across several counties. Huge sums were often involved. Partners of the giant West India house of Alexander Houston and Company had bought up several estates to the value of £287,000 by 1800. Alexander Spiers, the so-called 'mercantile god of Glasgow', who headed one of the three great syndicates in the tobacco trade, had by his death in 1783 secured estates in Renfrewshire and Stirlingshire worth over £174,000. James Dunlop, another famous Virginia tycoon, held £130,000 of property in land by 1793.

It may have been that some of this opulent breed of merchant gentry were content to live out their lives at leisure, engaging in hunting, building mansions, entertaining, and beautifying the grounds of their estates. But many more were gripped by the contemporary mania for 'improvement' and keen to see their lands as assets to be exploited for profit as effectively as the shares they possessed in cotton mills or trading ventures. As observed by Adam Smith in *The Wealth of Nations*, merchants were 'generally the best of all improvers', being 'not afraid to lay out at once a large capital upon the improvement of [their] land' when there was 'a probable prospect of raising the value of it in proportion to the expense'.[3] Sir John Sinclair, the most knowledgeable commentator on matters agricultural in Scotland, was equally impressed: 'employing part of their capital in the purchase of land, and the improvement of the soil, [merchants and manufacturers] become most spirited cultivators'.[4] Sustained developments took place in some areas. The Monklands parishes in Lanarkshire were said to be 'in a high degree of cultivation' in the 1790s because '[w]hen a merchant has been successful, he purchases a piece of land, builds an elegant villa, and improves his property at the dearest rate'.[5] Other enthusiastic comments came from Renfrewshire, where the McDowall and Spiers families were very active. In Ayrshire and Kirkcudbright the very wealthy tycoon, Richard Oswald, who had made an immense fortune in arms contracting as well as slave-trading in Africa and merchanting in the Caribbean and Europe, poured many thousands of pounds into his estates of Auchencruive in Ayrshire and Cavens in the border country. But he was only the most prominent of a number of merchant princes who were doing the same thing throughout the country. The record also shows that few merchants gave up their commercial activities entirely after purchasing estates. The profits from the colonial trades continued to be pumped into schemes of landed improvement as well as the coal-mining ventures and factory villages that were also often established on country properties.

Nevertheless, one should take care not to be too Clydecentric when the eighteenth-century imperial economy is considered. Linen rather than cotton was far and away Scotland's greatest manufacture of the period. By 1813–17 the industry was producing 27 million yards annually. A few decades earlier it was reckoned that full- and part-employment in linen occupied almost a quarter of a million men, women and children. John Naismith in 1790 thought it 'the most universal source of wealth and happiness introduced into Scotland'.[6]

Most Scots producers concentrated on the cheaper and coarser lines, with Fife, Angus and Perthshire the dominant centres where the cloth was primarily destined for overseas markets.

The home population in Scotland grew only slowly in the later eighteenth century, at a rate of under 1 per cent per annum and well below the increases for Ireland and England. The total of 1.25 million in 1755 had only reached 1.6 million by 1801. Compare this with the massive increases across the Atlantic, of 2.3 million in 1770 in the North American colonies from 265,000 in 1707, and 877,000 in 1815 in the British Caribbean in contrast to 145,000 at the start of the century. Of that 1815 total, 85 per cent of the population in the West Indies were black slaves.

Scottish linen producers eagerly fed these booming markets. From 1745, linen bounties to support the manufacture were extended to low-priced cloth, which generated a dramatic increase in linen exports to the plantations across the Atlantic in the years that followed. Throughout the eighteenth century 80 to 90 per cent of these exports were supported by the bounty. The colonial markets were critical to growth. European consumption was marginal and Ireland was of minor significance. Nine-tenths of all Scottish linen exported from Scotland went to North America and the West Indies. Thus, after the American War of Independence, the Caribbean became even more fundamental as a market. In the last quarter of the eighteenth century, the standards of living of numerous working-class families in the eastern Lowlands of Scotland came to depend on the huge markets for cheap linen clothing among the teeming slave populations of Jamaica and the Leeward Islands.

III

In 1707 the Scots joined in parliamentary union with a bellicose nation that in the later seventeenth century was building the fiscal, political and military foundations for global imperial expansion. This 'fiscal-military state' has been convincingly described as 'the most important transformation in English government between the domestic reforms of the Tudors and the major administrative changes in the first half of the nineteenth century'.[7] Like most European governments of the time, the English state spent most of its resources in waging war or in preparation for future wars. It was reckoned that over most of the eighteenth century between 75 and 80 per cent of annual British government expenditure went on current military needs or to service debt accruing from previous wars. For Britain, far and away the biggest outlay was on the navy, the 'senior service', vital for the home defence of an island people and for the prosecution of a 'blue water' strategy around the world, safeguarding trade routes and establishing secure overseas bases for the protection of colonies. Sir Walter Raleigh's dictum of over a century before still rang true: 'Whosoever commands the sea, commands the trade of the world; whosoever commands the riches of the world, and consequently the world itself.'[8] The problem was, however, that navies were fearsomely expensive. Wooden ships rotted fast, maintenance costs were enormous, and the huge dockyards and shipyards required for repair and construction inevitably became a major drain on the public purse. It was no surprise that abundant finance rather than military force per se was reckoned to be the crucial sinew of war.

The English state had been pursuing a policy of expanding economic and military resources since around 1650. The process was virtually complete by the time of the Union of 1707 and it made available to the army and navy vast sums for the prosecution of war. The key components included a huge extension of the national debt, sharp increases in taxation, a government bank (the Bank of England) and the flotation of long-term loans on the London capital market that also attracted funds from the Continent. No other state in Europe – apart perhaps from the United Provinces (the Netherlands), which did not link its mercantile prowess as effectively to war strategy as England – was quite as successful in this financial transformation. The costs of the economic revolution were borne mainly by taxes, especially customs and excise on imported and home-produced goods. This was the main reason that Scotland was faced with an increased tax burden after 1707, as already described in Chapter 3.

Scottish taxes rose on consumer items, most notoriously the taxes on salt and linen of 1711 and the Malt Tax of 1725. Nevertheless, the revenue burden on a per-capita basis was still lighter in both Scotland

and Wales than in the richer counties of southern England. In addition, the Scots customs service was less effective in collecting revenue in the first few decades after union than its counterpart in the south. As indicated in Chapter 3, underpayment and smuggling were endemic. A black economy ran through Scottish society from top to bottom. Tax evasion on such a scale could not disguise the fact that union with England now presented the Scottish elites in particular with a golden opportunity.

A historic anxiety for the Scottish aristocracy and lairds was the challenge of ensuring gainful employment for younger sons, which would provide them not only with income but also an acceptably genteel position in broader society. Landed estates in Scotland, whether great or small, descended to the eldest male child. His siblings had to make their way in the world, either by the family acquiring some landed property for their remaining progeny or by younger sons achieving army or naval commissions, entering the law or the Church, or being apprenticed to a merchant house. This was the basic social dynamic that for centuries had impelled the offspring of the Scottish gentry to seek careers and fortunes in Europe. But the European connection was fading in the later seventeenth century and there is evidence that the decline of career opportunities there was beginning to stoke up anxieties among the laird classes. This was apparent in the plans for the Scottish colony in East New Jersey in the 1680s. The project was dominated by landowners from the eastern counties of Scotland, especially the north-east region, formerly a major supplier of Scots army officers and merchants to Scandinavia. The promoters envisaged a colony of landed estates and among those who eventually emigrated to the New World were a very high proportion of younger sons of the north-east gentry. Thus, three members of the Gordons of Straloch purchased proprietary shares, but only the two younger brothers actually travelled to the colony. Several other emigrants can be identified as sons of minor, cadet branches of landed families. Robert Gordon of Cluny probably spoke for many of his fellow proprietors when he stated that his own reason for being attracted to the project of colonization was to provide land for his younger son, 'since I had not estate whereby to make him a Scotch laird'.[9]

But perhaps even more intense pressures were building up by the early eighteenth century. Scottish landed families were simply having more surviving adult children as infant mortality levels started to fall rapidly. No exact figures exist to prove the point conclusively from a specifically Scottish perspective. However, research on the demography of British ducal families for the period can provide a useful surrogate source of information on changing patterns of population growth among the nation's governing classes. Family size among this elite was relatively stable until the later seventeenth century, but then after a few decades families of the British aristocracy started to grow at a rate considerably higher than in the general population. The percentage of children of the British nobility dying under the age of 16 was 31.1 between 1480 and 1679; from 1680 to 1779 the figure fell to 25.9 per cent and declined further to 21.1 per cent between 1780 and 1829. There were now many more sons surviving into adulthood. If this pattern was replicated across the Scottish landed classes, the concerns for placing younger sons in employment that was both gainful and socially acceptable must have become increasingly more acute.

But this was not all. Changes in the landed structure of Scotland added to the challenge. In 1700 there were around 9,500 landowners in Scotland, only about half of whom had the right to inherit or sell the land they possessed. The pattern of ownership was dominated by the great aristocratic landlords and their associated kinship groups. This elite was expanding its territorial control at the expense of lesser lairds between the later seventeenth century and the 1770s. Thus, the number of proprietors in Aberdeenshire fell by a third between about 1670 and 1770 (621 to 250), and the steepest decline of all occurred among the smallest group of landowners. This trend was repeated all over Scotland. The total of 9,500 landowners at the beginning of the eighteenth century had fallen to 8,500 by the 1750s, and it declined further to around 8,000 at the start of the nineteenth century. Manifestly, the minor lairds were under considerable economic pressure before the 1750s. Rental income was relatively stagnant until the 1760s and increases in farm productivity did not really take hold in most of Scottish agriculture until that decade and later. At the same time, as the number of estates possessed by this class was squeezed, one traditional option exercised to solve the problem of young sons, namely the purchasing of properties in their name, became more challenging.

In an important sense, then, imperial employment after 1707 in the armed forces, colonial administration, trade and the professions came as a godsend. In the decades after the Union, streams of eager Caledonians from genteel but impoverished backgrounds poured into the British empire at every point from the Arctic wastes of Canada to the teeming cities and plains of Bengal. The bureaucratic growth of the fiscal-military state ensured that career openings were now much more abundant than before. Therefore, a form of resource transfer developed from the metropolis to Scotland, a kind of eighteenth-century variant of the Barnett formula of later vintage, with the prime beneficiaries, however, being the landed, professional and merchant classes of the nation.

IV

What one writer has described as the 'luscious opportunity' of empire became even more enticing in the second half of the eighteenth century.[10] Especially after the end of the Seven Years War in 1763, huge British territorial gains accrued as a result of conquest, annexation and victory over the French. By around 1770 the population of the North American colonies had grown to around 2.3 million. Georgia, East and West Florida, Quebec and Nova Scotia had all been won from France and Spain. Then came the American Revolution in 1775 and the emergence of an independent United States, born out of the 13 British colonies. Their departure left only a rump of underpopulated territories in the north of the American mainland. Known as British North America they would in due course become the Dominion of Canada in 1867. Elsewhere, however, the momentum of territorial expansion seemed unstoppable. In the West Indies the Ceded Islands and Trinidad were acquired in 1763, while the most spectacular gains were achieved in India, where the whole of the eastern subcontinent and a large part of the Ganges valley came under the administration of the English East India Company by 1815. At that date, it was reckoned that 40 million Indians were living under British rule, which was also fast extending into Ceylon and Mauritius. The Company at the same time was raising some £18 million in taxation within its territories, a sum amounting to around one-third of peace-time revenue in Britain itself. Exploration was also being pursued in the vastness of the Pacific Ocean by the voyages of such famous navigators as Captain James Cook. A permanent British colony was established for the first time in Australia when the First Fleet arrived in New South Wales in 1788. By 1815, therefore, Britain ruled over a global population in America, the Caribbean, Asia and the Antipodes of around 41.4 million people. In 1820, British dominion already encompassed a fifth of the world's population. Contemporaries, such as Sir George Macartney in 1773, revelled in the scale of 'this vast empire on which the sun never sets and whose bounds nature has not yet ascertained'.[11] Patrick Colquhoun's *Treatise on the Wealth, Power and Resources of the British Empire* of 1814 had the revealing subtitle 'in every Quarter of the World'.

This extraordinary development hugely increased the demand for soldiers, arms, store contractors and colonial bureaucracies ranging from governors of huge territories at the top to humble clerks at the bottom of the administrative hierarchies. The numbers of men in British military service rose from around 113,000 during the War of the Austrian Succession of 1739–48 to 190,000 in the American War of Independence, while the cost of hostilities, standing at £8.75 million per annum in the 1740s, spiralled to over £20 million in the 1770s. The British state had never held out more alluring prospects for ambitious officers, traders and colonial administrators.

Moreover, in India, the victories at Plassey (1757) and Buxar (1763) became the military foundations for a veritable bonanza of pillage. The years from around 1757 to 1770 were those when the subcontinent became notorious as the place where easy riches could be made quickly. Mortality rates among servants of the East India Company were horrendous, but there were compensations. As one historian has noted, 'these twelve years were the only time during the eighteenth century when survival in Bengal virtually guaranteed that a man would return home with a fortune'.[12] It was not company salaries alone that mainly fuelled the rapacity but rather returns from private trade, prize money and tax revenues extracted from the newly conquered Indian territories. Edmund Burke summed it up as 'the annual plunder of Bengal'.[13]

The Scots par excellence were to the fore in the exploitation of this

Table 1. Scottish Ratios in the
Eighteenth-Century Imperial Elite

Period	Territory
1680–1780	American Colonies: One-third of university-educated men from Europe trained in Scotland
1707–75	Antigua: 60 per cent of planter elite
1707–1800	North America: Thirty Scottish-born governors and lieutenant governors
1740	India: One in three of colonel rank in the East India Company (EIC) army
c.1750	Antigua: 60 per cent of doctors
c.1760	North America: One in four of British army officer corps
1763	Ceded Islands (West Indies): Three governors appointed, all Scots
1771–5	Jamaica: 45 per cent of inventories at death above £1,000
1774–85	Bengal: 47 per cent of writers; 50 per cent of surgeon recruits (EIC)
c.1775	Bengal: One in three of the EIC army's officer corps
1776–85	Bengal, Calcutta, Madras: 60 per cent of 'free' merchants
1799	British North America: 78 per cent of staff (Hudson Bay Company) from Orkney
1800	British North America: 62 per cent of staff (North West Company) from counties of Inverness, Banff and Aberdeen
1813	Calcutta: 37 per cent of private merchant houses

Source: T. M. Devine, *Scotland's Empire, 1600–1815* (London, 2003), passim.

new imperial bounty. They were outnumbered as a nation by the English in the ratio 5:1 but, as the figures confirm (Tables 1 and 2), Scots achieved a much greater share of the imperial spoils than their population size within the United Kingdom might have justified.

The reasons for what one writer has termed these 'absurdly high proportions' of imperial Scots have been explored in detail by the present author elsewhere and the interested reader is therefore directed to the sources listed in the references for this chapter.[14] Here the focus is

Table 2. Scottish Ratios in Indian Service, 1720–1813

Territory	Period	Occupation	Scottish Percentage (%)
Bengal	1774–85	Writer	47
Bengal	1750	Writer	38
Calcutta	1813	Private Merchant Houses	37
EIC provinces	1754–84	Officer Class, EIC Service	62
Madras	1720–57	Principal Medical Officer	100
Madras	1800	Physician and Surgeon	40
East India	1740–60	Sea Captains	39

Source: T. M. Devine, *Scotland's Empire, 1600–1815* (London, 2003), pp. 250–70.

primarily on the impact that the spoils of empire had on Scotland, especially in helping to provide much of the capital for the great transformation of the country that accelerated from the 1760s, which in turn anchored the long-term stability of the Union.

Repatriation of the profits of empire from the Caribbean and India was likely since most Scots who went there to make their fortunes were transients, 'sojourners in the sun', who had no intention of settling and were committed to return as soon as their ambitions were achieved. They were temporary exiles whose roots remained in the mother country. Return, of course, did not always mean to Scotland because some retired to London, Bristol and elsewhere in England. Moreover, both the West Indies and Bengal, for all their allure for getting rich, were also the grave-yards of the white man. One East India Company officer in 1780 wrote that he had not yet made enough to come back home but still intended to leave rather than die 'in this vile country', while another admitted 'I'd almost as soon live in Hell as in India.'[15] Over the period 1707 to 1775, 57 per cent of the Company's servants succumbed to fatal diseases.

As seen earlier in this chapter, some of the tobacco and sugar princes of Glasgow's transatlantic trading empire had made great fortunes, but even these could not compare to the colossal riches repatriated, some to relatives after death, by the Indian 'nabobs'. Thus John Johnstone of Westerhall returned to Scotland in 1765 with an estimated fortune of £300,000, which helped him acquire three landed estates and a parliamentary interest. It was said of him that he pursued wealth with an enterprise and a dedicated ruthlessness second only to the victor of

Plassey, the mighty Robert Clive himself. Equally celebrated was William Hamilton, arguably the most famous and successful doctor to serve in India during the whole three centuries of the empire. A cadet of the family of Hamilton of Dalziel in Lanarkshire, he first came to the East as a naval surgeon in 1711. His major claim to fame was his successful treatment of the Mogul emperor for venereal disease. Hamilton was afterwards showered with gifts, including an elephant, five thousand rifles, two diamond rings, a set of gold buttons, and a presentation set of all his own surgical instruments fashioned in gold. He also brought untold benefits to the East India Company when its rights to free trade in Bengal, Bihar and Orissa were confirmed in consequence of Hamilton's cure of the royal patient.

John Farquhar outdid both Johnstone and Hamilton in rapacity. At his death in 1826 Farquhar was worth £1.5 million, making him one of the richest Britons of the nineteenth century. Farquhar's business ruthlessness was matched only by his eccentricity. On his return from India he was said to have offered to endow one of the Scottish universities with a sum of £100,000 to establish a Chair of Atheism, only to be disappointed when his generosity was summarily rejected. A stay of only one year in India for General Hector Munro, the victor of Buxar, yielded around £20,000, a sum reckoned to be equal in value to 38 years of income from his estate in the north of Scotland.

It is reckoned that between 1720 and 1780 at least 1,660 Scots were in East India Company service as naval and military officers, surgeons and civil servants. From those and other groups, 124 are reckoned to have returned as affluent gentlemen, 37 with 'large' fortunes (£40,000+), 65 with medium fortunes (£20,000–£40,000) and 21 with small to middling ones (£10,000–£20,000). All the returns will probably never be known in precise terms. Nevertheless, it was the chances of achieving such riches in India and elsewhere in the empire that went a long way to committing the loyalty of the Scottish elite to union long before the end of the eighteenth century.

6

Auld Scotia or North Britain?

In 1759, William Robertson, distinguished historian, strong supporter of the Union, Principal of Edinburgh University and a Moderator of the General Assembly of the Church of Scotland, made a bold prediction. He asserted that the Union of 1707 would eventually make one people of the English and the Scots. It was a statement based on his personal political hopes as well as considered opinion. By the early nineteenth century some other well-known Scottish commentators, such as Sir Walter Scott, Sir John Sinclair and Lord Cockburn, would have partially agreed with him. Yet they were more concerned not simply with the amicable fusion of the two peoples but with the threat of the anglicization of Scotland by the more powerful partner. There was a recognition that union had brought many material benefits north of the border but also that these advantages might have come at too high a cost. It was feared that Scotland faced the loss of nationhood within the Union state and its possible transformation into 'North Britain', a mere province of Great Britain. As Scott, though himself a unionist, put it: 'What makes Scotland Scotland is fast disappearing.' For Henry, Lord Cockburn, the eminent jurist, the Scots were steadily becoming invisible as a distinctive people as their ancient traditions, identities and institutions were gradually corroded by the effects of an ever closer association with what by 1815 had become the world's most powerful state. 'This,' he argued in consequence, 'is the last truly Scotch age.'[1] For some, such an outcome would be met with regret; for others, it could be seen as the inevitable and very desirable result of 'compleating the union'.

These thinkers had both facts and arguments to support their views. The Scottish aristocracy and many laird families had for some time been sending their sons to England to be educated in order to maximize their career opportunities in later life within the British state and empire. One result was that many Scottish Members of Parliament were now the products of English public schools such as Eton and Rugby. They also went on to attend Oxford and Cambridge and serve in elite English regiments such as the Life Guards and Coldstream Guards. Even some merchants and other businessmen who increasingly represented the Scottish burghs had a similar educational background in the south as well as trading or military experience in the empire. Those who made their fortune in the Americas, the Caribbean or Asia did not always return to spend leisured retirements in their homeland but rather chose to do so in London or the spa towns of southern England. The business and professional class of the west of Scotland, the nation's economic engine, was becoming ever more eager for further integration with England, as shown in their enthusiastic support of the movement to bring the Scottish legal system closer to English commercial law. The Glasgow Law Amendment Society argued that there were important aspects of Scots law which were no longer applicable in the new conditions of Anglo-Scottish rapprochement, a view strongly endorsed and supported by the Chamber of Commerce, Merchants House and the main Glasgow newspapers.

If members of the Scottish elites did not seek careers in London and the south, they did so in the empire in increasingly large numbers. As shown in Chapter 5, they were over-represented in almost every area of imperial employment from merchanting to administration, from soldiering to the professions of teaching and medicine. Rectorial speeches made in Scottish universities during the Victorian era assumed as axiomatic that most graduates would find posts in the empire rather than in Scotland itself. In Europe during the nineteenth century, many nations looked to their scholars, writers and other men of letters to fortify national identity. Their influence has often been regarded as catalytic in the great national revolutions that broke out across the Continent in 1848. The stunning achievements in the eighteenth century of what later became known as the Scottish Enlightenment might also have been expected to breed a similar sense of national pride and so a platform for an even stronger sense of national identity. But the literati were all committed unionists who saw 1707 and its effects as crucial to curing the old Scotland of the seventeenth century and before of the maladies of obscurantism, faction, poverty and religious fanaticism.

In addition, through their commitment to rational discourse and attachment to the broad stream of European culture, the men of the Scottish Enlightenment were internationalists in intellectual outlook. They not only denounced but also undermined many of the antique parochial myths of the origins of Scottish kingship and nationhood that had helped to mould a sense of Scottish identity since early medieval times. Mythology is a core building block of any nation because it serves to develop collective consciousness and belief in a glorious inheritance from the past. The history of Scotland also received a critical pounding as a subject unworthy of serious study. The country's experience of economic backwardness and political turbulence was seen in negative terms and in stark contrast to the so-called constitutional road of progress from feudalism to 'civilized' development regarded as the central attribute of the history of England. The only 'usable past' in many scholarly circles, therefore, was often that of English constitutional history. The English parliamentary experience was the template against which all other British political developments should be judged and measured. Whig Anglo-British history therefore became the favoured subject for instruction and study. For many Scottish intellectuals of the eighteenth century, the history of their country may have been picturesque and intriguing, but as scholarly citizens of the world they often regarded it to be of limited cerebral interest. Some of those writers who eventually did write Scottish history in the nineteenth century were nonetheless often uncritical apologists for union and even more anglicization. George Chalmers in his monumental *Caledonia* of 1807–24 typically saw 1707 as a year of liberation for the Scots, the sine qua non for their moral and material progress from superstition and poverty. Major histories written at a later time by authors such as John Hill Burton and P. F. Tytler tended to take a broadly similar approach.

The admiration of members of the Scottish academic and legal establishment for the constitutional history of England was a commonplace in the mid-Victorian era. Not surprisingly, therefore, when the first Chairs of History were established in Scottish universities in the later nineteenth century, no Scottish-born appointees were made. The professorship at Glasgow went to an Oxford man and Edinburgh's to a scholar from Cambridge:

> Thus the two chairs of history in Scotland were filled by Oxbridge candidates. Academic history was [for them] the corporate worship of the origins and development of the contemporary parliamentary establishment at Westminster which both the Scottish and English middle classes venerated as the supreme embodiment of their national class and communal interests.[2]

Not until 1901 was there created an established professorship specifically of Scottish history in a Scottish university when, in that year, the Sir William Fraser Chair of Scottish History and Palaeography was endowed at Edinburgh.

In addition to this unsympathetic intellectual environment, traditional Scottish identities were threatened by the enormous social and economic changes that the nation experienced from the later eighteenth century and some argued were likely to cause profound cultural discontinuity. As already described in Chapter 4, the extent and speed of the development of capitalism in Scotland was virtually unique in Europe at the time. It was a true revolution, not simply limited to manufacturing industry but encompassing also the profound transformation of ancient rural structures in both the Highlands and Lowlands and a remarkably rapid rate of urbanization that ran in parallel with those massive changes. Not surprisingly, it was suggested that in consequence Scotland was bound to be severed from its national past. Modernity was creating a quite different world, not simply materially but also in the realm of ideas, technologies, family structure, living environments, working relationships and social connections. By the early nineteenth century, unionism also seemed everywhere triumphant. The public buildings and streets of the new townscapes recorded names, memorials and statues commemorating British union, British empire, British heroes and British wars. Nowhere was this pattern more apparent than in Scotland's capital. Edinburgh's New Town featured George Street, Queen Street, Hanover Street,

Frederick Street, Royal Terrace, Charlotte Square and the colossal pillar dedicated to the arch-unionist Henry Dundas. Glasgow's thoroughfares of Virginia, Jamaica and Tobago Streets were redolent also of the success of Scotland's other major city in imperial commerce long before it became known as the 'Second City of the Empire'.

II

The cultural pessimists and also those who advocated full-blooded anglicization were in the event both proved wrong. Auld Scotia did not die in this period but survived, albeit by adjustment to the new realities of a cultural, economic and political nature, and especially to the implications of the Union relationship with England. A clue to the background of the Scottish response to the threats and challenges was given by a distinguished Frenchman many years later in a public presentation in Paris, which said much about nationhood and its origins and survival. The great historian Ernest Renan delivered a celebrated lecture at the Sorbonne in 1882. In it he asked the question, 'What is a nation?' His conclusions differed profoundly from the conventional wisdom of his day, which usually considered a nation to be based on ethnic and linguistic foundations. Rather, Renan argued, the identity of a nation depended ultimately on collective sentiment, which itself was based on a remembrance, real or mythical, of times past. A nation's sense of itself rested on the glories of its history, heroism and tales of great men. Much of this historical memory also derived from stories of war and conquest. It is against such a background that the resilience of Scottish identity in this period can be understood. From Renan's perspective, if Scotland ceased to feel like a nation, it would no longer be one.

Scotland was an ancient kingdom that had had an independent collective existence for several centuries before the Union. Indeed, it had emerged as a nation much earlier than most other countries in Europe. Even in the eighteenth century, principalities, electorates and duchies were much more common than nation states on the Continent. The independent Scottish state on the other hand had a long national monarchical line with established systems of administration and law, rich literary and musical cultures, four universities, a developed tradition of schooling, and a strong religiosity that both before and after the Reformation supported a distinctive Christian witness. The medieval epics, John Barbour's *Bruce*, composed in the late fourteenth century, and the fifteenth-century *Wallace*, ascribed to Blind Harry, the minstrel, told the epic tales of Scotland's hard-won struggle to preserve its independence against all the odds and the legendary deeds of the two great heroes, Bruce and Wallace, during those times of long ago. Post-union intellectual elites might have scorned much of the mythology of old Scotland but it lived on for ordinary folk in the oft-told tales of Bruce and Wallace in wars against the English 'other', the Protestant reformers of the sixteenth century in their struggle against popery, and the Covenanters of the seventeenth century, who fought and died for freedom of worship. This heritage and more was presented through the medium of books, broadsheets, oral tradition, song and poetry.

But the symbols of identity were not only those that had come down from a real or imagined memory of a distant past. Some also might take root in the near present, shaped by the changing cycle of contemporary ideas and interests. Often such markers weakened after an initial impact, declined in influence, and eventually were lost to history. In Scotland, for instance, the saga of the Covenanters of the seventeenth century resonated powerfully with many Victorian Scots, but today it is virtually forgotten. Yet, as some vanished, other stories and myths came to the fore to become embedded as fresh symbols of identity reinforcing the nation's continuing sense of itself.

Indeed, rapid modernization from the later eighteenth century in Scotland, as elsewhere in Europe, formed even more fertile ground for old mythologies and their reinvention to suit present conditions. Both the French and the Industrial Revolutions failed to erase the past as some suspected, but rather by leading to enormous cultural, political and economic discontinuities they triggered a search for new emotional anchors from history. Far from wiping out the past, therefore, modernity with its multiple threats and challenges led in several countries to a boom in nostalgia. Pre-modern ancestors, indigenous languages, folk songs and culture came into romantic vogue. Heroic epics were rediscovered, forged or imagined, and national folklore quickly gained a new allure. In Scotland, such influential figures as Robert Burns, James Hogg and Walter Scott became inveterate collectors of tales, songs and poetry in order to ensure that they did not disappear from the national consciousness. Scott's later success as the world's first best-selling historical novelist was built on this widespread yearning to experience what had gone before.

The collective myth of national origins was given a boost in Scotland and then elsewhere in Europe by the publications of *Fingal* (1761) and *Temora* (1763), which their editor James Macpherson (1739–96) attributed to Ossian, a blind bard of the ancient Caledonian people of the third century AD. *Fingal* was indebted to genuine materials from the fifteenth and sixteenth centuries, not from early times, but much also came from Macpherson's own fertile mind. His idealized world of a Scottish golden age in the third century brought wide international interest and acclaim, as well as some withering criticism, and was quickly translated into several languages:

> The poems of Ossian played a central foundational role in the making of modern European nationalism ... it is arguable that these poems constitute one of the canonical Ur-texts of the romantic nationalisms which spread across the Continent in the century after the sensational discovery of Ossian in the early 1760s.[3]

Ossian soon spurred a search for national epics of their own by scholars in countries such as Russia and Poland, and did much to place the Scottish Highlands on the European map and then later in the American mind as the very epicentre of romance. Sceptics among the literati at home, such as the great philosopher David Hume, were less impressed. He asserted that he could not bring himself to believe in the authenticity of Ossian even if 'fifty bare-arsed Highlanders' should testify on its behalf. Dr Samuel Johnson found in the affair 'yet another proof of Scotch conspiracy in national falsehood'. Nevertheless, Ossian came to be a key factor in the growth of a Highlandism that helped cement a new hybrid identity of Scottishness and Britishness within the Union state.

In 1804, Sir John Sinclair had argued that Scotland was in danger of being 'completely confounded in England'.[4] The Highlandization of Scotland was one influence that did much to prevent the danger of this happening. The sartorial nationalism of kilt and tartan provided a distinctive but inoffensive mode of differentiation from England without in any way threatening or compromising the Union. In the words of one scholar, 'As Lowland Scotland becomes more and more like England, it turns to the Highlands for symbols to maximise its difference.'[5] At the same time, the indissoluble link between tartanry, the Highland soldier, British patriotism and imperial service helped to lend a new cultural and emotional cohesion to union. The Highland warrior clad in tartan and plaid was recognizably Scottish but at the same time an imperial warrior of the British state. But for the threat of anglicization in this period within the Union, it is doubtful whether Highlandism would have generated as much general appeal as eventually it did in Scottish culture. The anti-Gael racist hysteria of the Jacobite era in Lowland Scotland and England was abandoned and replaced by the adoption of Highland symbolism and aesthetics. But that sentimentalization was only made possible by the destruction of the Stuart cause and the emasculation of the menace of clanship after the '45.

Two other influences worked to the same end. First, and in part due to the fame of the Ossian controversies, the Highlands became the focus of a growing romantic interest in wild and allegedly primitive peoples whose histories might disappear as urbanization and industrialization generated a new and different world order. The Highlander was seen to represent an authentic version of the Scottish past surviving into the present. His homeland of rugged and untamed wilderness was a perfect environment for 'the primitive society' publicized in works such as *Fingal*. The Highlands were therefore transformed in the romantic vision from a barren and threatening desert of bleak hills and boglands into a landscape of sublime and compelling beauty that seemed not to have altered much since the time of Ossian himself. It appeared not to matter that at the same time as these myths were constructed the people of the real Highlands were enduring the harsh realities of clearance, mass emigration and famine.

Second, the growing cult of sentimental Jacobitism – a safely lost cause – encouraged even Hanoverian monarchs to be seduced by the tartan and the kilt. In 1788, the year that Charles Edward Stuart, the Young Pretender (Bonnie Prince Charlie), died of alcoholism and depression in Rome, three of the king's sons, the Prince of Wales (later George IV) and his brothers William Henry and Frederick, were provided with complete Highland dress. They were instructed by Colonel John Small in the wearing of 'tartan plaid, philabeg, purse and other appendages', and the future king then wore the kilt to a masquerade in London. A royal love affair with the '45 and the personalities of the rising had begun. Eventually, after their purchase of Balmoral at a later date, Albert and Victoria were wont to enjoy a Jacobite tableau, with Albert starring as the transvestite prince in the heather, and Victoria as the faithful Flora MacDonald.

Jacobite tradition entered the Scottish romantic consciousness through song and story. Scotland's bard, Robert Burns, was a prolific writer of Jacobite ballads, including such standards as 'Charlie's my darling' and 'The White Cockade'. Then there was the alchemy of Sir Walter Scott, who in his Waverley novels gave the Jacobite risings a magical appeal not only in Scotland but internationally. He skilfully presented the Highlanders, though following the wrong cause, as nevertheless brave, loyal and true, and all against a vivid romantic backcloth of chieftains, clans and tartans. By the 1820s, Jacobite songs had become the most common in the Scottish canon after love songs.

The reputation of the Highland regiments, especially during the Napoleonic Wars, inevitably lent a new prestige and glamour to the tartan. These battalions had been specifically exempted from the general ban on Highland dress in the Disarming Act of 1746, and thereafter the kilt came to be forever associated with the heroic deeds of the Scottish soldier. During the phase of intense patriotism in the wars with France, some of the Scottish volunteer corps and fencible regiments that were mustered for a short time all over the country adopted tartan and the kilt as their uniforms. By the end of 1803, more than 52,000 Scots were serving in these forces, in addition to the even greater numbers enlisted in the regular army. The military tradition had long been an important part of the Scottish identity; now that was being decked out in Highland colours and the kilted battalions were depicted as the direct descendants of the clans. Crucially, however, they now represented the martial spirit of the Scottish nation as a whole rather than a formerly despised part of it.

The recollections of Corporal John Dickson, who served with the Royal Scots Greys under the Duke of Wellington at the battle of Waterloo on 18 June 1815, vividly encapsulated the sturdy spirit of Scottishness that coexisted alongside loyal service to the British Crown on that fateful day. Narrating the story of the legendary charge of the Scots Greys against Napoleon's infantry, in which he took part, Dickson recounted:

> [The order came], 'Now then, Scots Greys, charge!' . . . All of us were greatly excited and began crying, 'Hurrah! Ninety-Second! Scotland for ever!' as we crossed the road . . . we heard the Highland pipers playing . . . and I clearly saw my old friend Pipe-Major Cameron standing apart on a hillock coolly playing 'Johnny Cope, are you wauking yet?' in all the din [a famous song celebrating the victory of the Jacobite army over British forces south of Edinburgh during the '45; Sir John Cope commanded the British army on that day] . . . I rode in the second rank. As we tightened our grip to descend the hillside among the corn, we could make out the feather bonnets of the Highlanders, and heard the officers crying out to them to wheel back by sections. A moment more and we were among them. Poor fellows! Some of them had not time to get clear of us, and were knocked down . . . They were all Gordons, and as we passed through them they shouted, 'Go at them, the Greys! Scotland for ever!' My blood thrilled at this, and I clutched my sabre tighter. Many of the Highlanders grasped our stirrups, and in the fiercest excitement dashed with us into the fight.[6]

The apotheosis of this transformation came in 1822 with the remarkable celebration of the visit of George IV to Edinburgh in August of that year. He was the first monarch to set foot in Scotland since Charles II in 1651. King George spent two weeks in the Scottish capital and a series of extraordinary pageants, all with a Celtic and Highland flavour, were stage-managed by Sir Walter Scott for his delectation. What ensued was a 'plaided panorama' based on fake Highland regalia and the mythical customs and traditions of the clans. Scott had determined that Highlanders were what the king would most like to see and he therefore urged clan chiefs to bring 'followers' to Edinburgh suitably dressed for the occasion. Several bodies of 'clansmen', MacGregors, Glengarry MacDonnels, Sutherlands and Campbells, paraded during the visit, and His Majesty's generous figure was clad in kilt, plaid, bonnet and tartan coat for the occasion. The climax came with the procession from Holyroodhouse to Edinburgh Castle when the Honours of Scotland – crown, sceptre and sword of state – were solemnly paraded before the monarch with an escort led by the once-outlawed Clan Gregor. At the banquet in Parliament Hall, the king called for a toast to the clans and chieftains of Scotland, to which Sir Ewan MacGregor solemnly replied with one to 'The Chief of Chief – the King'.

The great ball during the royal visit in which full Highland regalia was worn has been seen as a seminal event in the acceptance of the kilt as the national dress of Scotland. The monarch had now himself given it a bogus legitimacy. The entire Scottish ruling class, much of it urban or Lowland, was addressed as 'the chieftains and clans of Scotland' during the public events. More sceptical voices at the time were less impressed than the 'enthusiasts for the philabeg'. J. G. Lockhart, Scott's son-in-law and biographer, regarded the pageantry as a 'hallucination' in which the glorious traditions of Scotland were identified with a people that 'always constituted a small and almost always an unimportant part of the Scottish population'.[7] Even more appalled was Lord Macaulay. Looking back from the 1850s, he found it incredible that the monarch should show his respect for the historic Scottish nation 'by disguising himself in what, before the Union, was considered by nine Scotchmen out of ten as the dress of a thief'.[8]

Such voices were rare at the time. Only in the twentieth century did Highlandism become a target for contempt and criticism:

> Since all causes deemed progressive were firmly hitched to the British star, the forms of [Scottish] cultural nationalism took on a studied antiquarian air, as the cult of Highlandism descended on a Lowlands majority hitherto scornful of all things clannish and Celtic-sounding. Compulsory Celtification was adopted as the polar opposite of Anglican [sic] gentility, and as a fantasy foil to the starchy servility of native professional elites. This fake Gaelicism, entirely foreign to most Scots, brought on a plague of tartan kitsch for which there has existed no known antidote until recent times.[9]

III

In the final analysis, the cultural pessimists of the early nineteenth century were probably guilty of exaggerating the direct threat of assimilation by England. As noted in previous chapters, the primary, nay the exclusive concern of the English governing class, was to ensure Scotland's continuing loyalty to the Union state and the security of the northern border. Both were taken for granted during the Victorian era. Indeed, in a hypothetical sense, if any direct assault on Scottish civil and religious liberties had ever been contemplated it would probably have broken the Union. The controversy over Church patronage that reached a climax in the Disruption of 1843 and led to the founding of the Free Church of Scotland yet again demonstrated the sensitivities concerning Scottish rights. The episode showed that resentments might be stirred even if minimal interference by Westminster was suspected in a specific Scottish area of responsibility and tradition. Indeed, any threat that came from the big neighbour was bound to be cultural, subtle and indirect, the result of the enormous demographic and economic preponderance of England, a normally benign elephant occupying much of the British bed.

It was important therefore that for almost all of the nineteenth century, de facto Scottish political and administrative autonomy continued, with Westminster de jure sovereign but government delegated to Scottish institutions run by Scots. Only after the passing of the Education Acts of 1870 in England and 1872 in Scotland, the extension of the franchise to the working class on a larger scale and the creation of the Scottish Office in 1885, was there a decisive movement towards a more centralized state. Until then the United Kingdom was probably more decentralized than most European states. As in the eighteenth century, therefore, Parliament in London rarely intervened on Scottish issues unless invited to do so and the Lord Advocate in Edinburgh continued to control such key areas as law enforcement and policing. In the early twenty-first century the enormous influence of the state, in education, health, welfare and economic management, is taken for granted. During the nineteenth century, government intervention was, however, limited in the extreme, and most state expenditure was devoted to defence and support of the armed forces.

Below the parliamentary level the routine of government and administration remained devolved to town councils and the supervisory boards that emerged from the 1840s. The Scottish Board of Supervision ran the Poor Law from 1845 while a Prisons Board was set up in 1838. These two boards were then followed in due course by others for lunatic asylums (1857) and education (1872). Scots lawyers usually staffed this new bureaucracy and its inspectors were Scots doctors, surveyors and architects. The Scottish Burgh Reform Act of 1833 vested the management of the towns in the broad middle class. It was a crucial piece of legislation that, taken together with the administrative changes mentioned above, created a more powerful *local state* run by the Scottish bourgeoisie and reflecting their political and religious values. It was this local state, rather than a distant and usually indifferent Westminster authority, that in effect routinely governed Scotland. The absence of any form of political nationalism in Victorian Scotland is often remarked upon, especially in contrast to the history of Ireland and the European Continent at the time. But there would have been little reason for the Scots to adopt a nationalism hostile to the British state. They certainly sympathized with and enthusiastically supported nationalists such as Kossuth in Hungary and Garibaldi in Italy in their struggles for national unity, but they did not feel similarly oppressed or in need of a national Parliament to achieve what the middle classes in Scotland already possessed in full: liberty, economic prosperity and cultural independence, the very benefits for which European nationalists had yearned for so long. The Scots on the other hand had the best of both worlds: access to the opportunities of empire and also an unoppressive union with a hugely powerful state, but at the same time the maintenance of a Scottish polity that they mainly led and governed and that retained most of the traditional trappings of an ancient nation except for ultimate sovereignty.

Presbyterianism, made secure within the Treaty of Union, was also central to national identity within the Union state. It is sometimes argued that the Disruption of 1843 weakened the reformed religion by dividing the national Church into two ecclesiastical entities.

Certainly after it the Church of Scotland could no longer speak for the majority of Scottish Protestants. But the birth of the Free Church released an enormous evangelical religious energy that fed into the building of new churches, philanthropic endeavours and missionary work throughout the empire and beyond. The traditions of the Free Church shaped the values of thrift, independence, sobriety, the work ethic and education, which were the foundations of middle-class and 'respectable' working-class culture. These values were propagated in such seminal texts as *Self-Help* by Samuel Smiles from Haddington and were given political expression in the enduring loyalty shown to the Liberal Party by the Scottish electorate for virtually the whole of the second half of the nineteenth century. One of the reasons why William Gladstone was given a hero's welcome during his famous Midlothian campaign in 1879 was not simply because he was of Scottish parentage but also because he was the great leader of Liberalism, the political gospel of the vast majority of the Scottish electorate at the time.

The influence of Presbyterianism as the source and defender of Scottish values was also brought into sharper focus by mid-century with the marked increase in Irish Catholic immigration during and after the Great Famine. By the 1851 census, there were 207,367 first-generation Irish immigrants in Scotland, with most of them settled in Glasgow and the western Lowlands. At least two-thirds of these immigrants were Roman Catholic. Anti-popery organizations, such as the Scottish Reformation Society and Scottish Protestant Association, and the journals, *The Scottish Protestant* and *The Bulwark*, were established in the 1850s in response to the new popish presence in Scottish society. They were not simply defenders of the 'true' religion but also saw themselves as protectors of the Protestant Scottish nation from the dangers of association with an 'inferior' race which, they claimed, threatened to bring disease, crime and degradation to the country in their wake.

The cult of national heroes also remained an important link between the new Scotland and its national past. Indeed, the celebrity of great men could now be more effectively conveyed to the nation than ever before because of the communications revolution brought about by the new networks of roads, coastal shipping and, even more importantly, by the coming of the railways. The number of cheaper books, newspapers and pamphlets now published as a result of advances in printing created a new working-class readership. The very popular *People's Journal* alone could claim a circulation of 130,000 copies a week in the 1870s, and on the eve of the Great War its circulation reached an astonishing quarter of a million copies. It became a veritable treasure trove of tales from Scottish history and literature for the masses.

The fame of Robert Burns, the national bard, and William Wallace and Robert the Bruce, was even more widely disseminated. In the period after about 1840, Burns became a Scottish cultural icon and was celebrated as never before. In one Burns Festival, in 1844, an estimated 80,000 people were in attendance, and of this multitude 2,000 sat down to eat lunch, accompanied by numerous toasts to the poet. The remarkable influence of the bard was confirmed by the countless attempts at imitations of his verse that dominated the 'poetry corners' of local newspapers throughout Scotland. But the historic Burns and his literary achievement were also now moulded to suit the political tastes of Victorian middle-class readership. He was now depicted as anti-aristocratic, and a man of the people who had succeeded by his own individual talents rather than through inherited privilege, connections or noble birth. Burns became the apotheosis of 'the lad o' pairts', a key element in one of the most influential of Victorian Scottish myths, that personal merit was alone sufficient to achieve success in life. But he was also praised because he linked the Scots with their rural past – it was often said that the blood of the Ayrshire Covenanters flowed in his veins – and had preserved the ancient vernacular language by his genius. The remarkable popularity of Burns was shown in the number of copies of his works that were taken overseas by emigrants leaving Scotland for all corners of the world. To this day an astonishing number of statues to him stand in North America, Australasia and South Africa. In a similar manner to Sir Walter Scott's historical novels, but in a quite different genre, the works of Burns connected nineteenth-century Scots to a world that had disappeared, the old milieu of the ferm touns swept away by agricultural capitalism. Both authors responded to the thirst of nostalgia in a period of unprecedented social change.

The cult of William Wallace in the nineteenth century, on the other hand, was complex and certainly bore little relation to the raw nationalism of Hollywood's *Braveheart* in the 1990s. Wallace was lauded as one of the supreme Victorian icons. Statues to the hero of the Wars of Independence were erected overlooking the Tweed and in Lanark. But these paled before the magnificence of the 220-foot high tower, the National Wallace Monument, built near Stirling between 1859 and 1869. This colossal edifice overlooked the country where the Scots at Stirling Bridge and Bannockburn had fought their most decisive battles against the English in the late thirteenth and early fourteenth centuries. Wallace was not only remembered in stone. Blind Harry's fifteenth-century tale, *The Wallace*, which was vehemently anti-English in language and tone, maintained its popularity, while histories of Bruce and Wallace were always familiar features in the local press.

But the Wallace cult was not designed to threaten the Union or inspire political nationalism. Rather, it reminded Victorian Scots of their own history in which the Union was won *because* of Wallace's struggle for freedom. The Wars of Independence had ensured that the Scottish people had not been conquered. As a result of their own courageous fight for independence in medieval times, a fruitful union between two equal partners had become possible in 1707. Wallace also appealed to an industrialized Scotland profoundly divided across class lines. To middle-class Liberals, he had saved the nation when it had been betrayed by the aristocracy, a class that still retained formidable power and influence in the nineteenth century. Big landowners were seen as the reactionary enemies of the Liberal urban bourgeoisie throughout the Victorian era. For working-class Chartists, who often passionately sang 'Scots wha hae wi' Wallace bled' at their meetings, Wallace represented the spirit of the common man striving for freedom against oppression. Such hero worship of a medieval warrior, several centuries after his death, confirmed that pride in ancient Scottish nationhood could be reconciled with loyalty to union and empire.

When the distinguished medievalist, biographer of Robert the Bruce and nationalist sympathizer G. W. S. Barrow gave his inaugural lecture as the new Sir William Fraser Professor of Scottish History and Palaeography in 1980 at Edinburgh University, he gave it the title 'The Extinction of Scotland'. This chapter has taken a different approach and argued that the survival of a strong Scottish identity within the Union was crucial to what Scots at least regarded as a partnership of equals with England. The pessimism of those in the early nineteenth century who had predicted the death of Scotland were proven wrong. Inherited myth and story combined with new real or invented markers and symbols to maintain national identity as a living and vibrant force. Even later in the Victorian era, new beliefs continued to surface to add to the mix. The Scots then increasingly saw themselves also as a born race of 'empire builders' through their role as governors, officials, soldiers, merchants, engineers, professors and physicians in the four corners of the earth. The triumph of industrialism also changed the national economic persona. Now Scotland was a workshop of the world, a nation that made things – the great ships, locomotives, bridges, iron and steel products delivered to countries across the globe.

This analysis in fact is more in tune with that of another Edinburgh historian of older vintage than Professor Barrow. In 1907, Professor Sir Richard Lodge pondered the longevity of the Union: 'at its origin [it was] illogical, and will probably be illogical at the end. It may well be that this is the secret of its success . . . [for] the Union has satisfied Scotland only because it has permitted the conservation of Scottish nationality'.[10]

7

No 'Scottish Question'

The sociologist Michael Billig once coined the term 'banal nationalism' to describe a nationalism that is so dominant and deep-rooted
that it does not need to be publicly articulated or proven in explicit
terms, a nationalism that is simply taken for granted. The historian
Colin Kidd has adapted the concept in the Scottish context, with reference not to nationalism but to unionism in the period from the
1750s to the rise of nationalism in the 1970s. As he notes:

> The Union, indeed, was part of the wallpaper of Scottish political life
> ... there was no credible, sustained or widely supported Scottish cri-
> tique of the Anglo-Scottish Union, and as such no call for an articulate
> ideology of Anglo-Scottish unionism.[1]

When the Liberal Unionists merged with the Conservatives in 1912 to
form the 'Scottish Unionists', the union specified was between Britain
and Ireland not the Anglo-Scottish Union of 1707. The Union with
England required no such political defence in Scotland.

The dominance of banal unionism meant that there was virtually no
serious 'Scottish question' for over a century from the 1860s. When the
1848 revolutions rocked several countries in Europe, Scotland remained
quiet. The Irish question became the great issue of late Victorian and
Edwardian politics, leading eventually to a partial resolution with the
emergence of the Free State in 1922. Scottish problems were rarely
mentioned or debated in Westminster until the idea of home rule
within the Union was first floated in the later nineteenth century,
largely in reaction to the constitutional changes being considered for
Ireland. The period between the middle decades of the nineteenth
century and the Second World War was one of momentous social,

political and economic change: the continued acceleration of industrialization and urbanization; the growing powers of a more centralized and powerful state; full democratization with the achievement of universal suffrage; the war to end all wars after 1914; structural unemployment and economic recession for several years in the 1920s and 1930s. But none of these historic developments threatened the Union. Frictions and discontents sometimes surfaced but these were usually defused without too much difficulty.

I

In 1871 the Scottish aristocrat and politician Lord Rosebery reflected, 'Now indeed the jealousies and mistrust which once separated the two countries divide them no more than does the Roman wall.'[2] England and Scotland had indeed become even closer by the time of Rosebery's comment. There were four Scottish-born Prime Ministers in the nineteenth century, compared to only one in the previous century. Scots also regularly filled senior Cabinet posts. In most general elections, the same issues were contested in both countries. The creation of an effective working-class political party in the late nineteenth century began in Scotland with the Independent Labour Party and then spread throughout the UK. For a time the movement was led by three Scots, Keir Hardie, Ramsay Macdonald and Bruce Glasier. Many of their fellow countrymen sat for English constituencies while on the eve of the Great War nearly a fifth of all Scottish seats were held by English MPs.

The norm for British governments until at least the 1880s was to look for a consensus in Scottish civil society before legislating on Scottish issues. As the constitutional expert A. V. Dicey put it in 1867, 'Few governments would dare to legislate for Scotland and Ireland in the face of the united opposition of the Scotch or Irish members.'[3] In addition, the number of Scots who regularly sat in Cabinet meant that an understanding of Scottish issues was usually available at the highest levels of government. The British state continued to remain detached from routine Scottish governance in striking contrast to the large resident bureaucracies and military forces in Ireland. Significantly, from

1827 until 1885 there was no minister or government department with a specified brief of responsibility for Scotland. The old tradition of non-intervention from Westminster lived on. As before, Scotland enjoyed a high degree of informal self-government. However, a more powerful centralized state based in London was beginning to develop from the 1880s. It remained to be seen whether this would cause tensions between the centre and its peripheries.

The growth of centralization coupled with mounting resentment at the government's treatment of Ireland did result in some friction. A veritable litany of Scottish complaints was repeated year after year: Scotland was under-represented in Parliament compared to Ireland; more government funding was spent in Ireland; the time taken over Irish legislation in Westminster meant that Scottish issues were ignored or marginalized. The feeling was that peaceful and loyal Scots were losing out against the turbulent and potentially disloyal Irish. The discontent culminated in the demand for a form of a Scottish home rule from the mid-1880s. This was not meant to confront the Union. Rather, the objective was to make the operation of union more efficient and fairer. In essence, it was a political backlash against the alleged favouritism shown to Ireland rather than a bid for autonomy. Scottish interest in devolution tended to ebb and flow down to the Great War according to whether Irish home rule was reaching a significant stage in the debates in the House of Commons, which suggests an essentially reflexive response to the Irish question. Westminster tried to appease Scottish opinion with the creation of the Scottish Office in 1885, though some argued that this could be seen as a step towards even more control from the centre.

The threat of anglicized assimilation was also sometimes considered a threat in the spheres of law, education and the universities. By around 1900, English commercial law applied throughout Britain, though the Scottish system still remained inviolate in other areas. The major Scottish Education Act of 1872 was seen by some as too heavily influenced by the English legislation that had been passed two years earlier. Concerns were also voiced about the new Scottish Education Board being located in London. But the Scottish Act was in practice more innovative than that south of the border as it made schooling compulsory, giving school boards more power than their counterparts in England and ensuring the removal of direct religious controls. Most controversy, however, has focused on the perceived imposition of a specialized English model of higher education on the traditional Scottish generalist tradition. In fact, it was Scottish opinion which decided that more specialization to Honours level was now required if Scots graduates were to continue to compete in the field of imperial employment against the products of Oxford and Cambridge with their more advanced knowledge in a smaller number of specific subjects. Moreover, for many years to come, most graduates from Scottish universities continued to take the general Ordinary degree, especially if they intended to enter the teaching profession, as so many did.

II

The old protectionist structures within the Union that had laid the basis for the development of the Scottish economy in the eighteenth and early nineteenth centuries were abandoned in the Victorian era of free trade and British dominance of global commerce. Nevertheless, the Union and empire were still assumed to be the sheet anchors of Scotland's remarkable story of economic success. By 1913, Glasgow and its satellite towns in the surrounding region of intensive industrialization produced one-half of the British marine-engine horsepower, one-third of the railway locomotives and rolling stock, one-third of the shipping tonnage and about a fifth of the steel. On the eve of the First World War the Clyde not only built one-third of British output but almost a fifth of the world's tonnage, a record that was greater at the time by a considerable margin than all the German yards combined. At the heart of the heavy industrial complex with its worldwide markets was the huge range of engineering specialisms in engines, pumps, hydraulic equipment, railway rolling stock, and a host of other products. Three of the four greatest firms building locomotives were in Glasgow; in 1903 they came together to form the North British Locomotive Works, 'the Titan of its trade', with a capacity to produce no fewer than 800 locomotives every year. This made the city the biggest locomotive-manufacturing centre in Europe, with engines being produced in large numbers for the empire, South America and continental countries. In civil engineering, too, the west of Scotland was a famous centre of excellence, symbolized by the career of Sir William Arrol (1839–1913), the builder of the Forth Bridge, the Tay Bridge, Tower Bridge in London, and numerous other projects in many parts of the world.

When Coats of Paisley joined with Patons in 1896, the world's biggest thread-making producer was created. Archibald Coats (1840–1912) became known as the Napoleon of the thread trade and his business was so profitable that 11 members of the family became millionaires. When faced with American tariffs, Coats relocated to the USA and soon dominated the market in thread there. The firm eventually controlled no less than 80 per cent of the global thread-making capacity.

Just as significant was the development of jute manufacture in the coarse-linen areas of Dundee and the surrounding districts. Jute was a fibre used in bagging and carpeting and was imported from Bengal in India. Dundee soon became 'Juteopolis', with the Cox Brothers' Camperdown Works in Lochee in the 1880s employing 14,000 (mainly women) workers, making it the biggest single jute complex in the world. Again, the product was sold throughout the globe, with booming markets in the United States and the British colonies. Other Scottish town and cities had their own textile specializations: Kirkcaldy in floor coverings and linoleum; Galashiels, Hawick and Selkirk in the Borders, in tartans, tweeds and high-quality knitted goods; Kilmarnock and Glasgow in carpets (in Glasgow, Templetons was the largest carpet manufacturer in Britain by 1914); Darvel and Galston in Ayrshire, in fine lace-curtain manufacture, which employed around 8,000 people just before the First World War.

Diversity was not confined to the textile sector. James 'Paraffin' Young (1811–83) pioneered the exploitation of the shale oil deposits of West Lothian through a series of inventions that led to the growth of a substantial industry extracting 2 million tons of shale annually by the 1900s. Whisky distillation was, of course, a Scottish specialization, with over 20 million gallons charged for duty in 1884. At Clydebank, the American Singer Company had developed the world's largest complex for the manufacture of sewing machines, with a labour force that numbered over 10,000. Further evidence that heavy industry did not have a complete monopoly was the Barr and Stroud optical factory, the Acme wringer factory, and the experiments in new ventures such as automobile and aircraft making on the vast 45-acre site of the engineering giant, William Beardmore and Company.

Blackwood's Edinburgh Magazine marvelled in 1884, 'In the course of the first half of the present century Scotland was changed from one of the poorest to one of the most prosperous countries in Europe.'[4] Some estimates suggest that the total wealth of the nation was around £120 million in 1798. By 1910 the figure was thought to be more than £1,451 million, a twelvefold increase in crude terms without taking into account inflationary factors. But this economic bonanza was very unequally divided. In its global heyday, Scotland was a low-wage economy where deep poverty was an omnipresent fact of life for many. Dudley Baxter's calculations of 1867 suggested that 0.33 per cent of productive persons possessed a quarter of Scottish national income while just over 8 per cent controlled a bit less than half (47 per cent) of it. Not far from the magnificent new public buildings in the great cities and towns were situated some of the worst slums in Europe. The Royal Commission on Housing in 1918 concluded in its investigations that Scotland, compared to England and Wales, was on the brink of a housing catastrophe if urgent action were not taken.

This maldistribution of wealth coupled with the massive increase in the productive resources of the economy ensured that by the later nineteenth century the Scottish business and professional classes were able to accumulate savings and surpluses on an unprecedented scale. Much of this then flowed into further profitable investments in the homeland and eventually across the world. By 1887 Scottish railway companies had attracted over £101 million in stocks. The railway boom was followed by another in overseas investment. This grew spectacularly from an estimated £60 million in 1870 to £500 million by 1914, equivalent to an average of £110 per Scot in that year compared to £90 for the UK as a whole. Other estimates vary between £390 million at a minimum to £520 million at a maximum in 1914. Whatever the precise figures, the magnitude of these sums confirmed that the propertied and professional cadres of the country were doing rather well for themselves in the decades before the Great War. Their happy condition meant there was no reason for them to even contemplate questioning a union that was assumed to be the source of all these advantages.

III

So intense was the Scottish engagement with empire in this period that almost every nook and cranny of national life from economy to identity, religion to politics and consumerism to demography were affected. Glasgow arrogated to itself the description 'Second City of the Empire' (a term first used as early as 1824) while the broader west of Scotland region was later celebrated as 'The Workshop of the British Empire'. Scottish society more generally had the strongest of ties to empire. As already described in Chapter 4, throughout the eighteenth and for much of the nineteenth century, Scottish educators, physicians, soldiers, administrators, missionaries, engineers, scientists and merchants emigrated to every corner of the empire and beyond, so that when the statistical record for virtually any area of professional or business employment is examined, the Scots were over-represented.

This elite emigration was but one element in a greater mass diaspora from Scotland. Between 1825 and 1938 over 2.3 million Scots left their homeland for overseas destinations. This placed the country with Ireland and Norway in the top three of European countries with the highest levels of net emigration per capita throughout that period. The emigrants had three main destinations – the USA (after 1783), British North America (Canada) and Australia. After around 1840 the USA was the choice of most who left Scotland, but Canada predominated in the early twentieth century. Also in the 1850s Australia, for a period, was taking more Scots than each of the two North American countries considered individually. These levels of emigration generated a vast network of family and individual connections with the colonies and later the dominions, which were consolidated by return migration (in one estimate averaging more than 40 per cent of the total exodus in the 1890s), chain migration, correspondence and widespread coverage of the emigrant experience in the Scottish popular press and periodical literature.

The British empire also had a potent influence on Scottish national consciousness and identity. In the years before 1914 Scottish patriotism was not in conflict with the Union but rather was closely integrated within it. The empire was regarded as a primary means by which the Scots asserted their equal partnership with England in that joint enterprise of the Union state. In the Victorian era it was commonplace to assert that substantial imperial expansion only occurred *after* the Union and hence was a mutual endeavour, driven by both nationalities, in which the Scots had played a full and indeed often a leading part. This was no empty boast. Publicists, through such works as John Hill Burton's *The Scots Abroad* (2 vols, 1864) and W. J. Rattray's monumental four-volume magnum opus, *The Scot in British North America* (1880), were easily able to demonstrate the deep mark that Scottish education (especially at college and university level), Presbyterianism, medicine, trading networks and philosophical inquiry had had on the colonies. Pride in the Scottish achievement was taken even further by those who asserted that the Scottish people were a race of natural empire-builders. Thus Andrew Dewar Gibb of Glasgow University declared in 1930:

> the position of Scotland as a Mother-nation of the Empire is at all costs to be preserved to her. England and Scotland occupy a unique position as the begetters and the defenders of the Empire. They alone of all the Aryan peoples in it have never been otherwise than sovereign and independent. Ireland and Wales, mere satrapies of England, can claim no comparable place. Scotsmen to-day are occupying positions both eminent and humble throughout that Empire, and Scottish interests are bound up with every colony in it.[5]

Exposure to the imperial experience started early in Scotland. In 1907 the Scottish Education Department in its memorandum on the teaching of history in schools directed that the curriculum should develop from the study of Scotland to British and then to international themes but always throughout by stressing the nation's role in the empire. Textbooks embodying this approach were soon available in schools. The most popular was *Cormack's Caledonia Readers*, which placed very considerable emphasis on the imperial project. The British empire had a key part to play in late nineteenth-century history teaching because it provided the kind of blend of British and Scottish history that reflected Scotland's hybrid position in the Union. The 1900s also saw the widespread celebration of Empire Day when flags were exchanged between Scottish schools and those elsewhere in the empire. The stories of such Scots imperial heroes as General Gordon, Sir Colin Campbell (of Indian Mutiny fame), the missionary Mary Slessor and, above all, David Livingstone, would all have been very well known to Scottish schoolchildren. Biographies of Livingstone, the 'Protestant Saint' and the most famous and venerated Scotsman of the nineteenth century, were widely read and awarded as prizes in schools and Sunday Schools, a practice that continued unabated through to the 1960s. Of course it was not simply children who were taught to respond to these imperial heroes. They were also celebrated by the trade union movement, working mens' clubs and Labour politicians, such as Keir Hardie, as models of Scottish virtue and great exemplars for the nation. Knowledge of and loyalty to empire was also communicated by such organizations as the Junior Empire League, with around 20,000 members, and above all by the Boys' Brigade, which not only promoted Christian values but also inculcated fidelity to the imperial ideal within its membership. The 'BBs' were enormously popular among Protestant Scots lads until well into the twentieth century.

For the mass of the population, however, perhaps the main symbols of empire were often the Scottish regiments. Recognized as the famous spearheads of imperial expansion, and widely celebrated in music, stories, paintings and public monuments as the tartan-clad icons of the Scottish nation, they enjoyed a supreme status as symbols of the nation's hybrid Scottish and British identity. Ironically, however, despite the fame of the Highland soldier, the kilted battalions were by this time mainly recruited during the Victorian age from the working classes of the Scottish cities, not from the depopulated hills and glens of Gaeldom. Nonetheless, their exploits were widely reported in books, pamphlets and the popular press, and memorialized in such famous paintings of their heroic actions as *The Thin Red Line* by Robert Gibb. The regiments had a remarkable impact on Scottish consciousness. Seen as the heirs of a national martial tradition that

stretched back to medieval times, they also acted as important cata-
lysts for the wide diffusion of the military ethic throughout the
country. One major spin-off was the Volunteer movement, the ances-
tor of the Territorial Army, which developed into a permanent reserve
force for the forces and attracted many thousands of young Scotsmen.
The Volunteers were a focus for local pride but they also strongly
identified with the British empire. Both the Volunteers and the Boys'
Brigade adopted army ranks and nomenclature, undertook military
drill, and were regularly inspected by army officers. The important
influence of both organizations goes a long way to explaining the
exceptional scale of voluntary recruitment into the British armies
from Scotland in the first months of war in 1914.

IV

In the nineteenth century the institution of monarchy came to play a
much more influential symbolic role in defining Britain and its imperial identity than it had ever done in any period since 1707. This was
especially so during the long reign of Victoria, the queen-empress. Her
predecessor George IV had come to Scotland in the famous 'King's
Jaunt' of 1822. But it was a brief visit and was confined to Edinburgh.
Victoria, on the other hand, took Scotland to her heart and spent a
good deal of time in the country. The queen and Albert, her Prince
Consort, purchased the Balmoral estate on Deeside in 1852 and
embarked on a rebuilding programme of the castle there in 'Scotch
baronial' style. It is reckoned she spent over eighty months in Scotland during her lifetime, a much longer period by far than her visits to
Ireland. For Victoria it was a true love affair. She once told her children's governess, 'Scotch air, Scotch people, Scotch hills, Scotch rivers,
Scotch woods are all preferable to those of any other nation in the
world.'[6]

The expansion of the railway network throughout the country
made Victoria's tours to several locations even more possible. Royal
visits became common and the old royal palace at Holyrood in the
Scottish capital was lived in again by the monarch and her family
from time to time. Soon, 'the route from Stirling to Aberdeenshire

became littered with monuments, statues and fountains opened by or commemorating a visit by Victoria who was seen more in the area than any major politician'.[7]

Even more fundamental from the standpoint of the cohesion of union, however, was Victoria's emphasis on presenting a distinctive cult and style of *Scottish* monarchy as well as that of her role as British head of state and queen-empress. She published two popular journals about her Highland travels that achieved best-seller status. Great play was also made of her legitimate succession stretching back to the lineage of pre-union Scottish monarchs, noting as well that the blood of the Stuarts ran through her veins. Victoria was much moved by the romantic story of Bonnie Prince Charlie when she visited Glenfinnan on Loch Shiel in 1873 where the Jacobite standard was raised by the clans at the start of the '45. She even chose to worship in the Presbyterian Church when in Scotland, and especially while in residence at Balmoral, a tradition maintained by her successors to the present day. For many Scots it seemed the monarchy had finally come home. Victoria did much to give an honoured place to the Scots within the Union, which was further fortified as a result.

V

When war broke out in 1914, several thousand young Scots flocked to join the colours. The nation provided more voluntary recruits in proportion to population than any other part of the United Kingdom before conscription was established in 1916. Of the 157 battalions that comprised the British Expeditionary Force, 22 were Scottish regiments. However, the volunteering euphoria was short-lived. The terrible carnage on the Western Front and the endless list of casualties soon changed the collective mood to one of national grief. The human losses were enormous and unprecedented. Of the 557,000 Scots who enlisted in all services, some suggest that 26.4 per cent lost their lives in the First World War. The main reason for this terrible casualty rate among many Scottish formations was that they were often regarded as excellent, aggressive shock troops who could be depended upon to lead the line in the first hours of battle. The impact of the ensuing slaughter was made more devastating by the method of recruitment, which often concentrated soldiers from the same village, district and occupation in the same unit. During major engagements, such as the battle of the Somme in 1916, the columns of local newspapers back home became crammed with the names of the dead and wounded.

After 1914 Scottish industry became a vast military arsenal for the greatest conflict in human history and developed as a vital part of the British war economy. Unrestricted submarine warfare later in the war destroyed the equivalent of nearly a third of the pre-war merchant fleet and created a prodigious new source of demand for the shipbuilding yards of the Clyde. Engineering and metal production was diverted to the mass production of guns and shells. The linen and woollen districts of Scotland supplied huge amounts of canvas for tenting and clothing for troops. Trench warfare, the enduring image of the Great War, would have been impossible without sandbags made from Dundee jute. By 1918 one thousand million had been shipped to the fronts in Europe. In the same year the Clyde valley had become the location of the single most important concentration of munitions production in the United Kingdom with the great heavy industries of the region under government control, regulation or direction. Some areas of mining and manufacturing activity did lose out. The Border tweed industry, for instance, was hit when its sources of yarn in occupied Belgium were cut off. The eastern coalfield, which had been enjoying dynamic growth before 1914, suffered through the loss of the German and Baltic markets and the Admiralty's decision to requisition the River Forth ports. Overall, however, the Great War intensified Scottish reliance on a narrow range of great industries that were often interdependent and potentially very vulnerable in the long run to international competition.

This was especially so after the ephemeral distortion of war was also exaggerated by the boom of 1919–22. The crucially important UK industry of shipbuilding expanded capacity throughout Britain by nearly 40 per cent during this period in relation to the position in 1914, in expectation of the release of a huge pent-up demand to replace wartime losses. The problem was, however, that every other shipbuilding nation – the United States, Japan, Scandinavia and Holland – was actively pursuing the same strategy. After 1923 the latent danger of over-capacity in what had been the key factor in the heavy industrial economy quickly became a reality.

It is now fashionable to stress the economic complexity of the inter-war period in Britain. Scholars of the period argue that the experience of misery varied regionally and over time. Those who managed to keep a job did well as real incomes rose. This explains the housing boom, which did much to trigger high consumer expenditure in the south of England and the Midlands. Over Britain as a whole, national income per head rose by nearly a quarter between 1913 and 1937, a significantly faster rate than in the decades before the First World War. The traditional image of the period is one of depression, unemployment and decline, but across the UK it was also a time of significant economic change when a more modern structure of motorcar, bicycle, aircraft, electrical goods and light-engineering manufacture was born.

There were some traces of this revolution in Scotland. Middle-class employment held up well, with rarely more than 5 per cent in this group without a job. Partly for this reason, retailing giants such as Hugh Fraser and Isaac Wolfson were able to expand their business empire, while large English-based stores such as Lewis's, Marks & Spencer, Boots and Montague Burton moved into Scotland. Clearly those who were in work were able to afford to buy more. Neverthe-less, while Scotland did not suffer as much as Wales, Ulster or the north-east of England, conditions were different in two key respects from those in the Midlands, London and the south of England. First, Scotland depended heavily on a small number of exporting industries that were badly hit by the slump in international trade. As a result, throughout the interwar period unemployment was always above the UK average. In 1932, for instance, the UK figure was 22.1 per cent and that for Scotland 27.7 per cent. In the industrial heartland of the western Lowlands, over a quarter of the entire labour force, nearly 200,000 people, were out of work in the early 1930s. But even in the more prosperous Lothians the unemployment rate remained above that for the south of England. It is also important to remember that the numbers recorded as 'out of work' would have been even greater but for the great safety valve of emigration. Scotland had always been near the top of the European emigration league, but in the 1920s this traditional exodus of people rose to unprecedented levels. An average of 137,000 had left in each decade from 1801 to 1911. This figure more than doubled between 1921 and 1931. For the first time since census records began the population of the country actually fell in absolute terms.

Second, the healthy economic indicators that characterized the Midlands and the south were less common in Scotland. Gross industrial output contracted annually by 2.89 per cent between 1924 and 1935. Even more significantly, Census of Production data plainly demonstrate that the 'old' staple industries of the Victorian era were still dominant, while the 'new' industries made little headway. This was not just a failure to establish new specialist industries. Pre-1914 developments, new specialisms such as motorcar manufacture, did not survive for long in the 1920s. Even furniture-making, a classic consumer industry, was not based on modern mass-production techniques. In the booming electrical goods sector the Scots had only a toehold, contributing merely 2 per cent of British output – and this mainly in heavy machinery. The industrial structure of Scotland seemed to ossify. In 1939 it was not significantly different from the manufacturing economy inherited from Victorian and Edwardian times, a failure to achieve transition that was to cost the country dear in later decades.

Between 1924 and the 1930s Scottish politics were determined above all by these economic crises. But the response did not feed into any significant nationalist challenge. John Wheatley, MP, a leading figure among the 'Red Clydesiders' of the early 1920s, did once proclaim with some hyperbole that 'there was no subject in Scotland that arouses as much enthusiasm as home rule'.[8] By the mid-1920s, however, any pro-devolution sympathies in the Labour Party were crumbling. It abandoned the historic commitment to home rule, as did the Scottish Trades Union Congress (STUC) in 1931. Wheatley himself no longer thought devolution to Scotland was the answer. He now argued that only the power of the British state could protect the working classes from predatory international capitalism. The STUC agreed. The harsh economic climate meant that the formation of larger British unions with industrial muscle was the way forward and the means of helping the labour movement recover from the defeat of the General Strike of 1926. Wheatley's colleague Tom Johnston, a future Secretary of State for Scotland during the Second World War, shared his diagnosis. Scottish problems were so acute and profound that the resources of the Britain state as a whole were needed to tackle them effectively. As he put it, memorably, 'What purpose would there be in our getting a Scottish Parliament in Edinburgh if it only has to administer an emigration system, a glorified poor law and a desert?'[9]

It was the marginalization of home rule by the existing parties that helped trigger the formation of the National Party of Scotland in 1928. At first its main aim was to demonstrate that home rule was popular with the electorate and by so doing convince Labour that it neglected the national cause at its peril. It might also be that there was good reason to anticipate an increase in nationalist support as the crisis in the Scottish economy deepened. This after all was what happened in Germany and Italy at the time. According to Archibald Sinclair, Secretary of State in the National government of Ramsay MacDonald, the Great Depression had caused some to seek a solution by setting up a parliament in Edinburgh. That concerns were not confined to the Left in Scottish politics was shown in 1932 when, after a secession from the Cathcart Unionist Association, which blamed Westminster for indifference to the serious difficulties north of the border, the moderate right-wing Scottish Party was established. This eventually joined with the National Party of Scotland to form the Scottish National Party (SNP) in 1934.

However, the Nationalists wholly failed to capitalize on the anxieties of the electorate. In the general election of 1935 the SNP failed to win any of the seven seats it contested. Some may have argued that the blight of the Great Depression proved the bankruptcy of the Union so far as Scotland was concerned. Yet the SNP never developed any coherent or convincing alternative strategy of economic reconstruction to put forward. For its part, the government insisted that it would be suicidal for Scotland to loosen the ties of union at a time of serious recession and increasing international tension in Europe. It also sought to appease national sentiment when the Scottish Secretary, Walter Elliot, moved the Scottish Office from London to Edinburgh in 1937, a development that has been seen as having 'immense symbolic value, making Edinburgh once again a seat of government, truly a capital, rather than just the headquarters of the Kirk and Judiciary'.[10] The SNP soon started to disintegrate into competing factions of Left and Right. Party discipline collapsed and on the eve of the Second World War nationalism had ceased to be a realistic political force in Scotland – at least for the time being.

Elliot, a 'One Nation' Tory, tried to demonstrate unionist sensitivity to Scotland's enormous economic problems. The Scottish Secretary developed new agencies such as the Scottish Economic Committee, the Scottish Development Council and the Special Areas Reconstruction Association to create employment and plan economic diversification. These only managed to scrape the surface of an intractable problem but did help to pave the way for the much more extensive state intervention during and after the Second World War. Elliot, however, remains best known for his successful transfer of the Scottish Office to Edinburgh from London. The objective was to extend administrative devolution while legislative power remained firmly in Westminster. Nevertheless, it was indeed ironic that it was a Scottish unionist who was responsible for this movement of bureaucratic authority north of the border at a time when nationalism had been rendered impotent by electoral humiliation and the cause of home rule was in eclipse at the same time.

8

Britishness, 1939–1960

I

Total war between 1940 and 1945 did much to strengthen British identity among all the nationalities of the United Kingdom. Unlike the Great War, the struggle was also fought to a considerable extent on the home front and so the entire nation became integral to the prosecution of the global conflict. The struggle against the Axis powers became an enormous collective effort. Conscription was imposed from the outset and mass evacuation of children from the cities took place soon after war was declared on Germany by Neville Chamberlain in September 1939. In Scotland nearly 40 per cent of the school population was affected. The people of Britain also confronted a much graver threat to their country than in the last world war: systematic bombing from the air; the even more potent menace of unrestricted submarine warfare in the Atlantic to the safe delivery of vital foods and raw materials to the homeland; and for a time in 1940 and early 1941, the very real possibility of German invasion. The employment of women in the munitions industries, a common feature of 1914–18, expanded on an even greater scale after 1939 as the country geared up for total war and the menfolk joined the forces in large numbers. At the giant Hillington aero-engine factory near Glasgow, for instance, almost 10,000 women formed a massive majority of the labour force, well in excess of a small minority of fully skilled men. In December 1941, Britain became the first combatant nation to conscript women aged between 20 and 30.

English, Welsh, Irish and Scots experienced the conflict together in the ranks of the Royal Navy, the Royal Air Force and, to a greater extent than before, the Army. Between 1939 and 1945, Britain mobilized around 5.8 million men and 640,000 women for military service. The figure for men represented nearly one in four of the country's male population and a significantly higher proportion for those in the age group 20 to 40. Three out of every five men born between 1905 and 1927 served in the armed forces during the Second World War. Around 3.8 million of the male total of 5.8 million spent the years of conflict in the British Army and the vast majority of those had been civilians on the day Britain declared war on Germany. Over 3.5 million men from all parts of the UK were united in the common cause for up to seven years of military service. The grim ordeal of the Great War when 'pals' battalions' and units were recruited from specific localities, trades and professions, and which often resulted in horrendous casualty figures in some communities, was not to be repeated. Instead, there was more mixing of recruits from all corners of the country, made easier by the regulated processes of conscription. Even elite Highland regiments had many Taffies, Cockneys and Geordies among their rank and file. The famous Argyll and Sutherland Highlanders became known for a time as 'the Argyll and Bolton Wanderers' because of the number of English recruits within the regiment.

Scottish soldiers often trained in England, were billeted there in their thousands, and left for overseas service from English ports. For most Scotsmen it was their first experience of life in England. In Scotland, Atlantic convoys assembled and sailed from the Clyde and Loch Ewe in the western Highlands, while commando and other special forces were trained in the wilds of Lochaber. As in the First World War, the Navy maintained two great bases for the Home Fleet at Rosyth on the Firth of Forth and Scapa Flow in the Orkneys. The resulting mixing of servicemen and women could not help but break down levels of basic ignorance and some prejudices among the different nations and regions of Britain. Britishness was also fortified by cinema and radio, which in newsreels, political speeches and propaganda films relentlessly drove home the message of a courageous and unified island race in righteous defence against a monstrous totalitarian tyranny. Winston Churchill became, of course, the voice of the British people with his series of powerful and eloquent radio addresses to the nation during the five years of global conflict.

The powerful impact of the war on British identity did not disappear with victory in Europe and the Far East in 1945. The world conflict thereafter was remembered as a 'good war', justifiably fought against a terrible moral evil. British national pride was boosted by the collective courage shown in 1940 when the nation, both military and civilian, stood alone with the empire against the mighty all-conquering German military machine. It was also significant that casualties were significantly lower than in the enormous bloodletting of the Great War. The industrialized slaughter of 1914–18 was not repeated. Some 722,785 Britons were killed during that epic conflict. The Army's losses from 1939 to 1945 were 146,346, or a fifth of those suffered in the war to end all wars. The national memory of conflict in the 1940s and 1950s was not therefore scarred to the same extent as it had been in the late 1920s and 1930s.

Service for young Scots in the British Army did not end in 1945. National Service, as peacetime conscription became known, was placed on the statute book by an Act of Parliament in 1948. From 1 January 1949, all healthy men aged between 17 and 21 were expected to serve in the armed forces for 18 months and then remain on the reserve list for a further four years. In 1950 during the Korean War the period of service was extended to two years. National Servicemen saw combat in Korea, the Malayan and Cyprus Emergencies, in Kenya against the Mau Mau, and during the Suez crisis of 1956. In November 1960 the last civilian entered conscripted service and in May 1963 the last National Serviceman left the armed forces. All in all, this meant that for almost a quarter of a century from the outbreak of the Second World War, successive cohorts of young Scots experienced the discipline, traditions and *esprit de corps* of an all-British fighting force.

In the immediate post-war years the British contribution to victory, especially after 1942, was probably exaggerated in the public mind. At the time there was little real awareness or recognition of the tremendous sacrifices of the Russian people, who suffered 27 million dead on the Eastern Front and whose armies inflicted 92 per cent of the total casualties suffered by all German forces during the Second World War. In the Far East and in the Pacific, of course, the Americans bore by far the greatest burden of combat against the Japanese empire.

But the British achievement was still remarkable. The experience of service on both the home front and the battlefield moulded the memories of an entire generation of men and women, and also indeed of their children. Memories of the war were celebrated well into the 1960s through books, boys' comics and, above all, such classic 1950s films as *The Dam Busters* (1955), *Cockleshell Heroes* (1955), *The Battle of the River Plate* (1956) and *Ice Cold in Alex* (1958). Major war-crime trials were still going on into the late 1940s. They confirmed the realities of genocide and other unspeakable horrors, and unequivocally confirmed the horrendous evils that might result from extreme ethnic nationalism and fascism. Internationalism, supranationalism and collaboration between nation states became the new aspirations and engendered a spirit that helped to give birth to the United Nations and other global agencies. It was not a good time for nationalist movements anywhere in Europe.

The Second World War crucially influenced Britain in another way. The state established a command economy to mobilize all resources of labour, capital, industry and agriculture in pursuit of final victory. One result was that the Scottish manufacturing economy came into its own again as a producer of ships, shells, fuses, guns and a host of other war materials. Already by the end of 1938 the demand for sandbags had become so huge that it absorbed the entire output of the Dundee jute manufacturers. The Clyde was rejuvenated after the dark years of Depression and unemployment in the early 1930s and by 1943 the shipyards were turning out an average of five vessels a week to replace British losses sustained in the Battle of the Atlantic. In 1945 the ascendancy of the heavy industries in the Scottish economy was therefore not only consolidated but expanded. At the end of the war, coal, steel, iron and engineering employed around a quarter of the labour force compared to around 16 per cent in 1939. The full order books for the traditional industries and the imposition of conscription from the beginning of the war meant that unemployment declined rapidly and virtually ceased to exist by 1943. For most of the war years it remained around 1.6 per cent of the employed labour force, effectively a condition of full employment. The controlled movement of labour and a system of regulated purchase and distribution through the 'bureaucratic Leviathan', the Ministry of Supply, had its primary impact on the population in the rationing of essential foods, such as tea, butter, sugar, jam and meat. Rationing of major foodstuffs lasted until 1954.

Much power was devolved in Scotland to Tom Johnston, the new Secretary of State from February 1941. Herbert Morrison recalled in his *Autobiography* (1960) how Johnston 'would impress on the [Cabinet] committee that there was a strong nationalist movement in Scotland and it could be a potential danger if it grew through lack of attention to Scottish interests'.[1] Johnston exaggerated the nationalist threat but this was one of the reasons why he was given a virtual free hand in Scotland. He fought energetically against the concentration of industrial production in the Midlands and south of England, and managed to attract 700 enterprises and 90,000 new jobs north of the border through the establishment of a Scottish Council of Industry. By doing so, he helped strengthen the Union by demonstrating that political muscle was capable of exploiting the relationship to Scotland's material advantage. Post-war reconstruction was also high on Johnston's agenda, with no fewer than 32 subcommittees set up to tackle a host of problems, ranging from juvenile delinquency to hill sheep-farming. Scotland also became the first part of the United Kingdom to operate tribunals to regulate the level of wartime rents. Even more spectacularly, Johnston created a kind of prototype National Health Service on Clydeside. On the expectation that enemy bombing would cause enormous civilian casualties, several hospitals had been built in the late 1930s to take the many hundreds of thousands who were expected to be killed and maimed by the Luftwaffe. But slaughter on that scale never came to pass and some hospitals, though well staffed, were lying virtually empty. Johnston now used them to treat workers in the munitions factories. As he recalled in his *Memories* (1952): 'The success of the experiment – by April 1945 we had wiped out the waiting lists of 34,000 patients on the books of the voluntary hospitals – was such that our scheme had been extended from the Clyde valley to all Scotland, and blazed a trail for the National Health Scheme of postwar years.' Perhaps, however, Johnston's most enduring achievement was his creation of a comprehensive scheme for the provision of hydroelectric power in the Highlands. The idea had been around for a long time but its implementation had been obstructed by vested interests. Johnston managed to obtain parliamentary support in 1943 for the scheme and a guarantee of £30 million to bring domestic electrical supply to the northern glens. The relevant legislation went through the House of Commons without resistance.

Johnston's administration in wartime Scotland was a strong vindication of the idea that the power of the state could be an effective instrument for the improvement of the lives of all citizens. It raised expectations that the post-war world would bring with it better times and that the misery of the 1930s might finally be consigned to history. If state intervention could help defeat the might of Hitler's armies, then surely it was also capable of tackling the evils of poverty, unemployment and social deprivation. Moreover, those who had argued in the dark days of the Depression that governments were powerless to combat the world economic crisis then, were now proved wrong. The class system and class tensions did not disappear during the war, but the government had worked hard to instil a sense of collective purpose where citizens were expected to make a contribution in the fight against the common foe. Those who had made that sacrifice, however, were not prepared to return to the bad old days before 1939. In essence, a new political contract was being worked out between the British state and its citizens. 'Never again' became the watchwords. It was no surprise that any issues of identity or constitutional politics were driven to the far margins amid these new demands for improved welfare, better housing and state intervention in industry.

Yet that was not entirely the case. Tom Johnston consistently argued that Scotland was neglected by government in London and that the signs of indifference were plain to see in the interwar collapse of the Scottish economy. He was a proponent of British state planning but also endorsed home rule or devolution as complementary to such a strategy. To this end, Johnston resurrected the idea of the Scottish Grand Committee sitting in Edinburgh and claimed that devolution was desirable, not for any reasons of nationalism but because there was not enough time in the Westminster Parliament to deal effectively with Scottish business. It was a view not unlike that of the moderate home rulers of the later nineteenth century. Labour's official commitment to a Scottish assembly did therefore remain throughout the war years despite the scepticism shown on the issue before 1939. Indeed, the aspiration ranked second in the party's 1945 manifesto only after the need to delivery victory against Japan.

This did not mean, however, that the SNP was able to exploit these positive notions about devolution, although it did manage to achieve some minor electoral success. A political truce between the main British parties had been agreed during the war. In the event of a by-election, the sitting party could field a candidate but not the opposition. Since the SNP was not part of this arrangement, it was free to stand whenever and wherever the decision to fight a seat was taken. In one by-election, at Cathcart in April 1942, the SNP candidate polled only 5 per cent of the vote and finished last. This disaster triggered a split in the party. At the SNP's annual conference John MacCormick and his fellow moderates walked out and went on to form the Scottish National Convention in an attempt to work for cross-party support for home rule. Those who remained, led by Arthur Donaldson and Dr Robert McIntyre, decided to promote the cause of Scottish independence, not home rule, at all future elections. This was with hindsight a momentous decision: 'In effect, the SNP as we now know it was born.'[2] The strategy seemed at first to have some traction with the electorate. At the time there was concern about the plight of 13,000 young Scotswomen who had been conscripted to be sent south for work in Midlands factories. This seemed to crystallize the complaint that not enough munition plants were being built in Scotland. Feelings ran high and in the winter of 1943 six members of two nationalist youth organizations bombed and slightly damaged the ICI headquarters in Glasgow in protest.

The SNP then won its first ever parliamentary seat, at Motherwell in April 1945, when Robert McIntyre defeated the Labour candidate, almost certainly because of tactical backing by Tory and Liberal voters in the constituency. The result was, however, very much a false dawn as the seat was lost three months later in the general election of July 1945.

The reasons for the political irrelevance of nationalism in that year of British victory were self-evident. The majority of the population looked forward to reconstruction and improvement after the war and had little doubt that such a huge challenge needed the resources and power of the

British state if it was ever to have any chance of success. Of the nine SNP candidates who stood for election in 1945, therefore, seven forfeited their deposits and the party managed only 1.27 per cent of the poll. The old hybrid identity of Britishness and Scottishness, which had been in place since the early nineteenth century, did not crumble as the concept of nationalism imploded. Four years later in 1949, John Mac-Cormick's Scottish Convention gathered around 2 million signatures for the Scottish Covenant in support of home rule. The petition stated:

> WE, the people of Scotland who subscribe to this Engagement, declare our belief that reform in the constitution of our country is necessary to secure good government in accordance with our Scottish traditions and to promote the spiritual and economic welfare of our nation.
>
> WE affirm that the desire for such reform is both deep and widespread throughout the whole community, transcending all political differences and sectional interests, and we undertake to continue united in purpose for its achievement.
>
> WITH that end in view we solemnly enter into this Covenant whereby we pledge ourselves, in all loyalty to the Crown and within the *framework of the United Kingdom* [my italics], to do everything in our power to secure for Scotland a Parliament with adequate legislative authority in Scottish affairs.[3]

This was not a nationalist document but rather one that aspired to constitutional reform *within* the framework of the United Kingdom. It was therefore a public renewal of the interest in home rule that had surfaced before the Great War. Indeed, the higher public profile of the Covenant helped to draw support away from the SNP, which undoubtedly also suffered from the contemporary public perception of ethnic nationalism as an ideology that had spawned Nazism and devastated Europe in a terrible war. The spirit of the times was much more in favour of international cooperation rather than the promotion of new national divisions that had come to be associated with bitter conflict and racial intolerance. The Scottish Convention was in tune with these ideals. It was non-partisan, consensual, and did not fight elections. The Convention had a gradualist agenda and a moderate approach to constitutional reform, preferring Scottish self-government within the UK to full-blown separatism. Even during the war it had some impact, with branches established across Scotland. In March 1947 a Scottish National Assembly was held in Glasgow with 600 delegates from a number of bodies, including the Church of Scotland, trade unions and Chambers of Commerce. The Assembly produced proposals that became known as the 'Blue Print for Scotland' by advocating a Scottish parliament which would have authority over most areas of government, apart from defence, foreign affairs and the currency. The campaign was then taken further through MacCormick's idea of establishing a new 'national covenant' of the kind that had expressed Scottish religious ideals in the seventeenth century.

When the Covenant was presented to the third National Assembly on 29 October 1949, MacCormick waxed eloquent in his description of the occasion:

> Unknown district councillors rubbed shoulders and joined in pledges with the men whose titles had sounded through all the history of Scotland. Working men from the docks of Glasgow or the pits of Fife spoke with the same voice as portly business-men in pin-striped trousers. It was such a demonstration of national unity as the Scots might never have hoped to see, and when, finally, the scroll upon which the Covenant was inscribed was unrolled for signature every person in the hall joined patiently in the queue to sign it.[4]

Even if the document did contain some forgeries and the names of a few dead celebrities, the Covenant had undoubtedly attracted popular support. However, as a vehicle for delivering home rule it proved ineffective. Self-government could only be achieved through the ballot box by voters backing candidates who were prepared to advocate and support self-government in Parliament. The Covenant was therefore simply ignored by ministers and the movement soon crumbled into political irrelevance, making little impact on the general elections of 1950 and 1951. Nationalist sentiment was now channelled into publicity stunts, as when four young student supporters of MacCormick seized the Stone of Destiny from Westminster Abbey on Christmas Day 1950. The Coronation Stone of the kings of Scotland was a powerful symbol of national sovereignty that had been plundered from the Abbey of Scone near the town of Perth as the spoils of war and moved to London by Edward I, the so-called 'Hammer of the Scots', during the Wars of Independence in order to confirm the suzerainty of the English royal line over the Scots. Each new monarch would be crowned by sitting on the Stone, which was placed in the coronation chair. Eventually it turned up again in Arbroath Cathedral, covered in the Scottish saltire. Sceptics took the view that this tokenism simply confirmed the political impotence of the nationalists since they were forced into colourful gestures in order to attract some public interest to their cause.

Nevertheless, the contention of the Tory opposition in 1950 that socialist nationalization north of the border would result in the transfer of control of Scottish industry to a centralized Whitehall bureaucracy still did hit a nerve in Scottish sentiment. Hector McNeil, the Labour Scottish Secretary, admitted as much in a memorandum to the Cabinet that year. Indeed, the Scottish Unionists thought there was considerable electoral mileage in exploiting Scottish national sentiment and they played the Scottish card to the full during their years in opposition. Winston Churchill told an Edinburgh audience that a London-based Labour autocracy threatened to absorb the Scottish nation in a 'serfdom of socialism' which was in conflict with the Treaty of Union of 1707. Some Scottish sensitivities were also roused by the decision to call the new monarch Elizabeth II, not Elizabeth II and I, although she was first by that name in the history of Scotland. Legal challenges against the decision were mounted and a few post-boxes with the QEII symbol blown up. The Scottish factor also entered the realm of religious dispute in the 1950s with the 'Bishops in the Kirk' controversy. The Anglican and Presbyterian Churches had been having joint discussions on closer relations for some time and these culminated in the publication of a report in 1957 which recommended that the Church of Scotland should adopt a form of episcopacy in the interests of potential unity and each presbytery would have a bishop selected from its membership. The idea might have been good for ecumenism, but it provoked fierce opposition when made public, including widespread and vitriolic condemnation in the press, led by the *Daily Express*. The criticisms were as much inspired by rejection of anglicizing forces as by the need to maintain the ecclesiastical purity of the Scottish Kirk.

The Scottish dimension, therefore, never entirely disappeared from politics between 1945 and the early 1950s despite the irrelevance of the SNP and the collapse of the Covenant movement. But the cause of parliamentary devolution was certainly in the doldrums. Unionists had never supported the aspiration and now Labour too began to falter also in their historic commitment to it. The pledge to establish home rule was still in the party's manifesto in 1945, but five years later the Scottish Trades Union Congress overwhelmingly rejected a motion from the miners to support a Scottish parliament. In the 1950 general election Labour finally dropped its commitment to Scottish self-government. Six years later the party leader, Hugh Gaitskell, confirmed that Labour was opposed to Scottish home rule. Finally, in 1959, the Scottish conference itself withdrew support. For the first time in a long time, even modest forms of devolution were off the political agenda.

II

For most of the 1950s the issues of Scottish home rule and nationalism virtually disappeared from public discourse and electoral history. Even in the early 1960s there was little sign of the national question reappearing. In the general election of 1964 the SNP contested 15 seats; 12 of the candidates lost their deposits. As one observer concluded wryly: 'It was hardly an edifying record.'[5] This period was indeed the high noon of unionism. The Scottish Unionists and their allies secured a majority of the Scottish vote in the 1951, 1955 and 1959 general elections. In 1955 they famously became the only party in Scottish electoral history to that date to win over 50 per cent of the popular vote. This was near the beginning of a 13-year period of Tory rule in the UK, from 1951 to 1964, by a party resolutely opposed to devolution for Scotland. The politics of economics and class were now omnipotent. A poll taken in Glasgow in 1950 showed that the working-class sample in the city who were interviewed believed that they had more in common with their fellow workers in England than with the middle and professional classes in their own country.

The reasons for the triumph of unionism in these years are not hard to find. From the later 1940s the British state had delivered a higher standard of living than ever before, together with almost full employment and a comprehensive system of social welfare. In the heydays of empire and industrial achievement during the Victorian era, most of the material rewards had gone to the affluent classes, with only modest improvements experienced in the lives of the majority of the population. By contrast, in the middle decades of the twentieth century the common man was starting to gain on all fronts. It was indeed a remarkable period of social and economic amelioration.

At first, following the victories over Germany and Japan in 1945 this seemed an unlikely scenario. The nation was exhausted and virtually bankrupt after its enormous wartime effort. The cost of the Second World War was twice as great as the Great War. No less than 28 per cent of Great Britain's wealth was wiped out and a huge balance-of-payments debt of £33 billion had been accumulated. Strict rationing continued in the years of peace and was only finally abandoned in 1954. Post-war woes reached a new low in 1947 when the winter of that year was the coldest of the century, compounding the misery of continuing austerity.

But from that year everything seemed to improve. Marshall Aid from the USA poured into a war-devastated Europe and quickly opened up huge new export markets for British industry on the devastated Continent. At the same time, the government maintained a fiscal squeeze on home consumption in order to allow resources to flow into a drive for the exports that were now deemed vital to national survival. This was all to the benefit of Scottish heavy industry, which had traditionally been strongly committed to overseas markets. In addition, the war eliminated for at least several years the impact of competition from Germany and Japan, two of Scotland's most formidable rivals in the shipbuilding and heavy-engineering industries before 1939. The country also gained from high replacement demand for capital goods and manufactures, which was given even more impetus by the Korean War. Shipbuilding is a case in point. In 1951 it was still very much the biggest industry in Scotland and now forged ahead to a position of rejuvenated pre-eminence. Between 1948 and 1951, Scottish shipbuilders launched no less than 15 per cent of the world's and 33 per cent of British tonnage. Their success was mirrored in the resounding export achievements of the other great staples of steel and engineering. In effect, the post-war boom had entrenched the hegemony of Scotland's traditional industries even more than before. By 1958 the country was more dependent on them for employment than it had been in the 1930s.

The state also began to flex its muscles across British society as between 1945 and 1950 Labour delivered on its election-winning manifesto, *Let Us Face the Future*. The Beveridge Plan of national compulsory insurance to support social security 'from the cradle to the grave' was put into effect, with child allowances, universal state retirement pensions and unemployment benefits. The jewel in this crown of social emancipation was the foundation of the National Health Service in 1948. Scotland's problems of poor health and poverty had long been worse than the average for the UK and the historic reforms were therefore likely to have a disproportionate effect north of the border.

The commanding heights of the economy came under state owner-ship when coal was nationalized in 1947, railways and electricity in 1948, and iron and steel in 1949. The state intervention that had helped to achieve victory in war was now geared up to secure eco-nomic improvement in peace. By 1950, through government-inspired redistribution of industry, Scotland acquired 13 per cent of all new manufacturing units in Britain, a higher proportion than its share of the UK population. American inward investment, already present pre-war, became much more familiar, with the arrival of IBM, Euclid, Honeywell, Goodyear and Caterpillar, which not only provided new jobs but new diversity in Scottish industrial specialisms.

At long last the age-old crisis in Scottish housing was also going to be tackled. Houses were now built at a staggering pace, over 564,000 of them in the 20 years after 1945, an increase of around two-thirds on those constructed between the wars. The striking feature in Scotland became the overwhelming predominance of council houses, with some 86 per cent of those built between 1945 and 1965 in the public sector. In cities such as Glasgow and towns like Airdrie, Coatbridge and Motherwell, the proportion was even higher. This was much greater than anywhere else in the UK and so much so that Scotland by the 1970s had probably the largest share of public housing of any advanced economy outside the communist bloc. The state underpinned new building with a system of subsidies and rent controls, while private building was limited in the immediate post-war years because of the shortage of materials and elaborate licensing procedures. In the final analysis, therefore, the numerous Scottish tenants who benefited from the vast building programmes of the 1940s and 1950s were being shielded from the economic realities and real costs of housing. In the long run the development of Labour control in local authorities reinforced and protected this subsidized system. The council estates or 'housing schemes' soon became veritable fiefdoms of the People's Party. In all, between a million and a million and a half Scots, over a fifth of the population, moved into a new home between the early 1950s and 1960s. For the first time those vast numbers were able to experience the luxuries of fixed baths and inside toilets.

Scotland also had more to spend as average real wages rose by over two-thirds between 1952 and 1964. The earnings of working women now contributed to household incomes on a scale never before seen in the past. In 1957, Prime Minister Harold Macmillan made his famous remark: 'Let's be frank about it, most of our people have never had it so good.' No dissenting voices were heard in response. It was a comment that had special resonance in Scotland, which had had such a hard time between the wars. Unemployment, the curse of the 1930s, now fell to historically low levels. Between 1947 and 1957, Scottish unemployment was remarkably stable and only varied between 2.4 per cent and 3 per cent of a labour force that actually increased significantly by over 690,000 between 1945 and 1960. There were now jobs for virtually everyone who wanted to work. Full employment also helped the trend towards rising material standards. The income of the average working-class household in 1953 was reckoned to be two and a half to three times greater than in 1938. For a time, even the gap in the average wage levels between England and Scotland narrowed. The nation's health improved, not simply because of the new prosperity but also as a result of legislative changes and scientific advances. The National Health Service from 1948 extended free treatment to all, while by the Education (Scotland) Acts of 1945 and 1947 local authorities could insist on the medical inspection of pupils and provide free treatment for them. Antibiotics were introduced for the first time on a large scale in the mid-1940s and soon wiped out tuberculosis, the feared killer disease of children and young adults in the past. By 1960, Scotland's infant mortality rate had come down to the same level as the USA – from 37.1 per 1,000 in 1951 to 28.1 per 1,000 in 1961 – and also moved close to the figures for England and Wales. The range of new labour-saving household appliances – washing machines, vacuum cleaners and electric cookers – were in high demand. Leisure patterns were transformed by television and, for some time after its introduction, cinema audience figures tumbled. The number of TV sets grew from 41,000 in 1952 to well over 1 million 10 years later.

It was only in the late 1950s that some politicians and economists began to detect signs that these good times might not be permanent. One distinguished Scottish historian, looking back from 1969, in fact argued that the nation seemed to be living in 'a fool's paradise' for much of that earlier period.[6] If this was the case, almost the entire country remained oblivious to such unwelcome realities. The 1950s was a decade of considerable material satisfaction for the majority and a time of dominant Britishness that Scots seemed able to comfortably combine with their own sense of national identity.

PART TWO

The Union Challenged

9

Nationalism

It has become known as the most famous by-election in modern Scottish history. In November 1967 a young and articulate Glasgow lawyer, Winifred Ewing, captured the rock-solid Labour seat of Hamilton for the SNP, with 46 per cent of the total vote, in the very heart of Labour's political empire in the west of Scotland. It was the nationalists' most spectacular success since the foundation of the SNP in the 1930s. The Scottish media went into overdrive, seeing the result as an unusually exciting and dramatic event that stood out from the humdrum routine of Scottish politics. The *Scotsman*, at the time pro-devolution in sympathy, came out in early 1968 with a bold statement that Scotland should become 'a sovereign state within a federal UK framework'. Winnie Ewing became an instant media personality. As one comment had it, 'Television cameras and photographers' lenses gobbled her up.'[1] Both the *Express* and *Daily Record* offered her a weekly column. She decided on the *Record* because of the paper's traditional loyalty to Labour. Mrs Ewing's journey to London in November 1967 to take up her seat became a triumphal progress accompanied by enthusiastic SNP supporters. She was driven from the train in a Scottish-built scarlet Hillman Imp, which was especially brought down for the purpose. The victory in Hamilton put the SNP on the British political map for the first time in its history.

Behind the scenes politicians and strategists from other parties hurriedly tried to work out what all this meant. For some, especially at the Tory grassroots, it was judged simply as a freak result, blown out of all proportion by press coverage. But others were not so sure, even in the ranks of the Conservative Party. Their leader, Ted Heath, according to the Labour diarist Richard Crossman, was said to have remarked in the aftermath of the SNP victory in Hamilton that nationalism was 'the biggest single factor in our politics today'.[2] The Conservatives were already becoming anxious about declining popularity north of the border, which might explain why the leadership of the party initially took the nationalist threat more seriously than its rivals. As the official opposition in Parliament, they may also have grasped the opportunity to exploit the constitutional issue in order to put pressure on the Labour government led by Harold Wilson. Whatever the reason, after the Hamilton result the Conservative Party, the most unionist of all the UK political parties, was the first to float publicly for the first time the idea of devolution for Scotland. In a remarkable speech at the Scottish Conservative Party Conference in 1968, Ted Heath committed the party to a devolved Scottish Assembly. To the absolute horror of most of his audience, the Declaration of Perth, as it became known, reversed at a stroke an entire century of unyielding Tory opposition to home rule. The announcement was remarkable at the time, even if, in due course, the commitment was to prove ephemeral.

Undeniably, for those at the time, it was difficult to read the runes of Hamilton. On the face of it, the SNP victory did not simply come out of the blue. At the local elections in May 1967 the party had won over a third of the votes cast, performed well in the Labour fiefdom of Glasgow, and then governed the city in a coalition with the Conservatives. This was a clear warning to Labour, which was increasingly dependent on support from Scotland and Wales to counter the effect of growing Conservative strength in England. In 1966, too, Plaid Cymru in Wales also achieved some success in a by-election and in local contests against Labour. Some asked whether rampant nationalism was about to wipe out Labour's traditional hegemony in the Celtic fringe.

That anxiety soon evaporated. In the general election of 1970, Labour regained Hamilton while the SNP only managed to gain one seat, the Western Isles. Moreover, the nationalist gains in local elections soon evaporated as it became clear that many of the new SNP councillors were not only inexperienced but also ineffective. Unlike Ted Heath, Harold Wilson adopted a policy of wait and see in response to the threat of the SNP. It soon seemed justified. The party's performance in the 1970 general election, though its best to date, resulted in 13 per cent of the total vote, the gain of one seat and the loss of another. Wilson had appointed Lord Crowther in 1969 to head a Royal Commission on the Constitution, which was a sure sign that he did not regard nationalism as an imminent or a potent threat. The Prime Minister had once joked that Royal Commissions were famed for spending years taking minutes.

But for subsequent events, the win at Hamilton could well have been simply remembered as a mere flash in the pan. Even Winnie Ewing recognized that her achievement had less to do with any aspiration for the independence of Scotland and much more with the familiar mid-term unpopularity of a government and the early surfacing of significant economic problems in Labour's heartlands. The Wilson government had also been forced to devalue the pound, which famously led to the Prime Minister's risible comment that, despite the decision, 'the pound in your pocket' remained secure and unchanged in value. Third parties were always likely to perform well for a time in such circumstances. SNP success in Scotland, for instance, was paralleled elsewhere in the UK by a Liberal revival under the charismatic leadership of Jo Grimond. But the conventional wisdom after the 1970 general election was that the SNP bubble had finally burst. Academic articles soon began to be published that provided detailed analysis of the reasons for the collapse of nationalism.

But the Nationalists had not entirely run out of steam. Even during a period of poor results between 1979 and 1987, they never retreated into the invisibility of the innocuous and eccentric political space they had occupied as recently as the 1950s and before. Indeed, though their performance continued to be both erratic and volatile, the SNP remained a permanent fixture of the Scottish political scene from the 1960s. Early indications suggesting that the party was once again on the move came in March 1973, when it polled 30 per cent of the vote in Dundee East, and again in November of that year, when the so-called 'blonde bombshell and darling of the media', Margo MacDonald, won the old Labour seat of Glasgow Govan. Then, in the first general election of 1974, in February, the SNP broke through as a real parliamentary force in Scotland, winning seven seats and 22 per cent of the vote. Within a week the incoming Labour government, again under Harold Wilson, had embraced devolution as a real commitment, despite having fought the election on a platform opposed to home rule. Even diehard Labour opponents, like the formidable Secretary of State for Scotland, Willie Ross, the 'Hammer of the Nats', were forced to eat their words. In the second general election of that year, in October, the SNP did even better by pushing the Tories into third place in Scotland and achieving just over 30 per cent of the national vote. The party won 11 seats, but more alarming from Labour's point of view was that the SNP had come second in no fewer than 42 constituencies. As Michael Foot, Secretary of State for Employment, confided to Winnie Ewing: 'it is not the 11 of you that terrify me so much, Winnie, it is the 42 seconds.'[3] Within three months Labour published a White Paper, *Devolution within the UK – Some Alternatives for Discussion*, which set out five options for change. Even though it is probable that a majority in the Labour Party in Scotland were opposed to such appeasement of the nationalists, the Cabinet was determined to press on with some form of change in order to destroy the threat of separatism. Roy Jenkins, then Home Secretary, later admitted:

> The fundamental trouble was that the Labour Party leadership, I think this was true of Wilson, I think it was true of Callaghan, I think it was to some substantial extent true of Willie Ross, saw the need for some devolution to avoid losing by-elections to the Nationalists, and not to produce a good constitutional settlement for Scotland and the UK.
>
> Any question of separation would be very damaging for the Labour Party because, while it might give Labour a very powerful position in Scotland, if you do not have Scottish members of parliament playing their full part in Westminster then the Labour Party could pretty much say goodbye to any hope of a majority ever in the UK.[4]

Constitutional change for Scotland was therefore firmly back on the political agenda again within seven years of the SNP's victory at Hamilton because of the surge in support for the party in 1973 and 1974.

The SNP remained a political force but its history between 1967 and the first referendum on devolution in 1979 was one of stop and start, temporary success followed by a time in the electoral doldrums. There was no sign that the party would emerge as the formidable political machine that it had become by the early twenty-first century. Both its ideological and organizational coherence were found wanting. Even on the party's core policy of Scottish independence there was disagreement between those who were essentially home rulers and those who were fundamentalists for whom the rapid liberation of Scotland from the Union was their holy grail. Another consistent problem was that opinion polls showed at most no more than 20 per cent of Scots willing to support the central aspiration of independence for the country. The broad electorate from time to time was prepared to go some way with the SNP but not the whole hog. Surveys from the late 1970s confirmed, disappointingly, that two-thirds even of SNP voters were not prepared to support the independence agenda. It was a problem too that in Westminster the SNP leadership showed little dynamism or charisma. In addition, much of the party's support came from younger voters, traditionally the most volatile section of the electorate, which might help to account for the fluctuating nature of SNP support. There was a sense that if the SNP came closer to a breakthrough, then the protest voters who allied with it but who were not convinced by the independence option would rapidly switch sides in significant numbers.

In the late 1960s the credibility of Labour, increasingly the main rival to the SNP by that time, had been undermined at the UK level when the government abysmally failed to generate improvement in economic and social conditions. Labour's weakened position in 1967 due to the by-election loss of Hamilton to the SNP and Plaid Cymru's successes in Wales had a particularly serious impact on the party's position in Scotland. Some of its followers, though a minority, were now prepared to look elsewhere, at least for a time. The party's organization was regarded as both weak and ossified. So much was this the case in Glasgow that the London headquarters ordered the dissolution of the main branch of the party in a city famed for its strong socialist traditions. It was noted by Labour itself that there was precious little evidence of any energetic grass-roots activism. Labour's loss of Govan in the 1973 by-election was put down much more to inadequate organization and membership torpor than the allure of the SNP.

But Labour recovered and the SNP bandwagon stalled. Ironically, the first signs of resurgence came with the increasing influence of a new generation of Labour politicians who had started to become interested in devolution as an effective means of dealing with Scotland's special needs. They saw this as extending democratic accountability rather than simply as a defensive response to nationalism. They included such rising stars as Gordon Brown, Donald Dewar, Jim Sillars, Harry Ewing and John Smith. Some of the SNP's constitutional clothes were being stolen. Labour soon developed a scheme of devolution, made easier politically as the party's strategists had noted that the Nationalists' central policy of independence in practice attracted only limited support. Devolution, a moderate halfway house between the status quo and separation, was likely to have more appeal. The SNP could therefore be easily outflanked in the process and Labour hegemony in Scotland further embedded.

The Labour Party therefore went to the country in October 1974 as a supporter of devolution. The first attempt at honouring its election pledges came in 1975 when *Our Changing Democracy* was published, proposing a Scottish Assembly of 142 members, funded by a block grant and with control over most Scottish Office functions but with no revenue-raining powers. Jim Sillars, probably the party's best orator, and by now a convinced and enthusiastic devolutionist, thought the blueprint lacked economic teeth. He and one other MP, John Robertson, defected to form the Scottish Labour Party in early 1976, an ephemeral grouping prone to Marxist infiltration that lasted for a mere three years. The bigger challenge was that devolution did not yet have much appeal across Labour as a whole. Some in the party still believed in the view that had prevailed across so much of the period: that strong British centralist powers were needed to solve Scotland's economic problems. Others thought that identity politics were a barrier and a diversion to the final success of the class struggle. The more pragmatic took the view that devolution was essential to stop the SNP bandwagon but were strongly opposed by others who were convinced that conceding anything to the nationalists would be the slippery path to the final break-up of the United Kingdom. Tam Dalyell, MP for West Lothian and arch-enemy of home rule in all its forms, was able to mount a sustained and effective campaign against what he contemptuously dismissed as illogical proposals designed merely to placate nationalism but which would lead inevitably to the separation of England and Scotland. Given these divisions, it was unlikely that Labour would be able to generate much effective enthusiasm either within or outside the party to deliver home rule for Scotland.

By 1977 the Labour government was weak in the extreme. It had only a small majority and from March of that year depended on Liberal support for its very existence. The Cabinet also faced a multitude of intractable economic problems. Throughout the UK over 1.25 million were unemployed, the balance of payments deficit approached £1 billion and annual inflation stood at 16 per cent. The Chancellor, Denis Healey, had been forced to go cap in hand to the International Monetary Fund for a substantial loan during the sterling crisis of September 1976. This rescue package was to be agreed only if draconian cuts in UK government expenditure were implemented. The government had by now become widely unpopular. It neither possessed the moral authority nor the political will in Parliament to deliver Scottish devolution, the most important constitutional change in the United Kingdom since the foundation of the Irish Free State in 1922.

Difficulties soon emerged when the Scotland and Wales Bill was presented in the House of Commons. In order to avoid intensifying the damaging splits on devolution, the government was forced to concede a referendum. Michael Foot, who was responsible for taking the bill through Parliament, admitted that the decision was forced on the Cabinet by threatened backbench disaffection. At least 140 MPs signed a motion urging a referendum and stating they would not vote for the bill unless it was granted. A government with a tiny majority had no choice but to concede in the face of this potential revolt.

The referendum was intended by its supporters to be at best a delaying tactic and at worst a wrecking device. Cheered by this victory, the anti-devolutionists pressed on to other triumphs. The attempt to impose a guillotine on further parliamentary discussion of the bill after its second and third readings failed, giving opponents of the legislation the opportunity to table amendments that could water down the original proposals even further. The most crucial of these was the motion proposed by the Labour MP for London Islington, the expatriate Scot, George Cunningham, that if fewer than 40 per cent of those who could vote in the referendum voted 'Yes', then an order should be laid before Parliament for the repeal of the Scotland Act. This amendment was passed on Burns Night, 25 January 1978. For those bent on destroying devolution it proved a potent weapon. Cunningham's coup has been described by some political scientists as the most significant backbench intervention in any parliament since 1945. The Scotland Act was finally agreed by the Commons in February 1978. Now the verdict of the Scottish people on the legislation was awaited.

When the nation gave its answer on 1 March 1979 it was inconclusive, ambivalent and unclear. The majority of those who voted did record a 'Yes' vote, by 51.6 per cent or 1.23 million Scots, as against 48.4 per cent on the 'No' side. But on such a major constitutional issue the margin of victory was very slim indeed. Since the 'Yes' vote represented less than a third of the electorate, it was well below the 40 per cent required by the Cunningham amendment. It was hardly a ringing endorsement of home rule. Moreover, just 63.8 per cent of those entitled to vote did so, which does not suggest that the prospect of devolution had engendered a great deal of mass popular enthusiasm. Much of the rural north and south of Scotland voted against devolution. The Borders, Dumfries and Galloway, Tayside, Grampian and the Orkney and Shetland Islands all recorded No' majorities, suggesting they were more in fear of domination from the Labour-controlled cities of the Lowlands than London rule.

The SNP launched a 'Scotland Said Yes' campaign to urge the government to press on with devolution. But the cause was lost. The truth was that less than a third of the electorate had actually voted for the most important constitutional change in Scotland's history since the Union of 1707. The results of the referendum demonstrated conclusively that the Scottish people were hopelessly divided on the issue. Since the Labour government of Jim Callaghan failed to deliver devolution and had proved incapable of controlling its backbenchers during the passage of the bill through Parliament, the SNP tabled a motion of no confidence in an increasingly discredited administration. This succeeded by one vote. In the general election that followed in 1979 the Conservatives under Margaret Thatcher swept to power with a radical agenda for curing Britain's ills in which constitutional change had no part.

For the SNP, the election was a disaster: 9 of its 11 seats were lost. In effect it had committed political suicide, thus confirming James Callaghan's gibe that the censure of the nationalist MPs on his government was the first recorded instance in history of turkeys voting for an early Christmas. The campaign for home rule that had dominated much of Scottish politics in the 1970s now collapsed in acrimony, bitterness and disillusion. Jimmy Turnbull's cartoon in the *Glasgow Herald*, depicting the Scottish lion cowering in the corner of an open cage and murmuring 'I'm feart', captured the mood of utter despondency in the pro-devolution camp.

A number of factors combined to cause the failure of 1979. The nationalist tide had been rising in 1977 and the SNP did well in the district elections of that year. But by 1978 the party was much less popular and lost two important by-elections to Labour. Significantly, a *Scotsman* opinion poll, published a fortnight before Referendum Day, showed the SNP as a poor third in national popularity, winning only half the support of the Conservatives and Labour. Not surprisingly given the times, the electorate were mainly concerned with strikes, industrial relations and unemployment. A mere 5 per cent of those interviewed gave any priority to devolution as an issue of major concern. Equally significantly, the Tories did well in these surveys and, alone among the major parties, were committed to opposing devolution. At a time when the country seemed to lurch from crisis to crisis, people were naturally more anxious about jobs and living standards than constitutional reform. The year 1978–9 saw the notorious 'Winter of Discontent', when Britain was rocked by a series of industrial disputes as the big unions smashed through the government's attempt to keep public-sector pay increases below 5 per cent. Television images of uncollected rubbish piled high on the streets and hospital workers out on strike conveyed a sense of public anarchy. At one point even the dead went unburied. A government that had demonstrated such incompetence was hardly in a position to convince the Scots of the merits of the Scotland Act.

The 'Yes' camp was also fundamentally split. Indeed, the divisions within it were almost as deep as those between them and the opponents of devolution. The SNP and Labour 'Yes' campaigns would not cooperate, in part because they had different aspirations, the former seeing the Act as a stepping stone to full independence, the latter arguing that devolution would help to strengthen the union. Three high-profile Labour MPs, Robin Cook, Brian Wilson and Tam Dalyell, ran a 'Labour Says No' campaign that managed to attract considerable media attention. It did not help that the Scottish Assembly, its powers mangled and diluted by Parliament and the Civil Service, was 'an emaciated figure' by the time the Scotland Act reached its final stages, and not a national body likely to inspire either confidence or enthusiasm.[5]

On the other hand, the 'No' campaign was much better organized and well financed from the massed ranks of the Scottish business community, which denounced the proposed legislation as likely to raise taxes, endanger industry, produce yet more bureaucracy, and increase the danger of conflict with London at a time of mounting economic difficulty in Britain as a whole.

The 'Yes' camp had little effective answer to this heady mix of reasoned argument and hysterical scaremongering. The 'No' campaign was boosted further in the final weeks before the referendum with the late intervention of the former Scottish Tory Prime Minister Lord Home, who had been chairman of Ted Heath's constitutional committee a decade before. Lord Home had acquired a reputation in some quarters since then as a devolutionist. He used his authority to condemn the Scotland Act root and branch as inadequate and dangerous. Only through the rejection of this patently flawed legislation could a better set of proposals be put together by a future Conservative government. Whatever its impact on Scottish opinion as a whole (which must be doubted), Home's intervention, in the words of one Glasgow Conservative activist, had a 'powerful, indeed devastating effect on Scottish Tory voters', although it is likely they would have voted 'No' anyway.[6]

So ended the first attempt to devolve power to Scotland. It would be 18 years before another proposal for home rule was laid before the UK Parliament. The incoming administration of Margaret Thatcher repealed the Scotland Act and thereafter was a resolute opponent of any form of devolution. Mrs Thatcher and her ministers took the view that the Scots had been offered more say in their affairs but had rejected home rule. There was no need to raise the issue again. It had been dealt with. That conclusion was not entirely accurate. But for the Cunningham amendment, the devolution referendum would have decided in favour of a Scottish Assembly, even if support for it was less than whole-hearted. Nevertheless, for successive Conservative governments devolution was now dead in the water and no attempt should be made to resuscitate it. In the long run, that was to prove a very costly mistake for the fortunes of the Tory Party in Scotland.

10

Seeds of Discontent

The question of the constitutional future of Scotland within or outside the United Kingdom has rarely been off the British political agenda in recent years. Over that period there have been two dramatic moments relating to the question, the opening of a devolved Scottish Parliament in 1999 and the referendum on Scottish independence in 2014. Scottish home rule had been an issue, but not a pressing one, from the later nineteenth century to the Great War. It then sank into obscurity, only to be revived in any significant fashion from the 1960s. Moreover, before 1914 the movement was reactive, in large part a Scottish response to the much bigger political challenge of Irish nationalism and the concern with the possibility of unfair treatment within the Union. In the 1950s few could have guessed that that decade of unionist ascendancy would soon be followed a few years later by SNP electoral successes and the renewal of public interest and a national debate on the Scottish question. Nor would it have been credible to imagine that in subsequent decades the constitutional future of Scotland would assume a place in British politics not entirely dissimilar to that occupied by the Irish question before 1922 but without the element of real or potential physical force.

Why this happened is an intriguing puzzle and one that has drawn the attention of a number of historians and social scientists in recent years. The answers to the puzzle have varied from the decline of empire to the discovery of North Sea oil, from the increasingly centralized policies of the British state to the economic crisis in the UK in the 1970s. No final consensus has yet emerged. It is clear, however, that there is no single explanation but rather there were a series of influences that came together to place the Scottish question firmly on the political agenda.

I

Since Tom Nairn's controversial treatise, *The Break-Up of Britain* (1969), it has been common to argue for a causal relationship between the decline and fall of the British empire and the rise of Scottish nationalism. As one writer concluded recently: 'The sudden rise of the SNP can be mapped almost exactly on to the acceleration of the decolonisation process abroad . . .'[1] At first glance, the case seems plausible. The British empire took centuries to develop and only reached its apogee after the First World War when further significant territorial gains were won by the annexation of German colonies in Africa and great swathes of the former Ottoman empire in the Middle East. As late as 1945 the empire on which the sun never set remained virtually intact. British rule extended across the oceans of the world with a subject population of over 700 million people. Thereafter, however, decolonization took place at breakneck speed. India became independent in 1947 and Burma in 1948. Between 1960 and 1967 nearly 25 colonies in Africa, Asia, the Caribbean and the Mediterranean achieved their freedom. By 1970 the once mighty empire had a mere 5 million subjects, of which 3 million lived in Hong Kong. That last major Crown colony then became part of the Chinese People's Republic in 1997. As previous chapters have shown, imperial opportunities in careers, markets and commerce had helped to bind Scotland tightly to the Union. It surely seemed inevitable that the complete disintegration of empire would hasten an end to that historic relationship.

Perhaps that might be the case in theory, but historical analysis depends in the final analysis on hard evidence. To begin with there is a problem of logic. Because two developments occur one after the other it does not necessarily follow that the two are causally linked. Because one event takes place after another, it cannot be assumed that the latter was necessarily caused by the former.

In fact as the pace of decolonization accelerated, the Scots seem to have been surprisingly unconcerned. In Scottish press files there is little evidence that the end of empire was seen as a serious threat to Scottish interests. Perhaps not surprisingly, some Scots-born imperial civil servants and other officials in the bureaucracies of the African empire were, on the whole, opposed to decolonization, not simply as a result of vested career interests, but because many thought that the African colonies were not yet ready for full independence. Those responses apart, it is difficult to find outside the columns of the empire-leaning Beaverbrook Press's *Scottish Daily Express* any particular opposition to or anxiety about the retreat from empire in the public prints. The files of the *Glasgow Herald* and *Scotsman* for 1947, the year when India and Pakistan both became independent, do not even mention the possibility of any likely adverse effect on Scotland. Instead, the tone in both news and commentaries was one of acceptance, some praise for the contribution of the Raj to Indian development and warm good wishes for the future of both India and Pakistan as independent states. The Scottish role in the Indian empire was not discussed or even hinted at in the sympathetic valedictory opinion columns. If there was any concern it was about the menace of possible racial tension and conflict between Hindu and Muslim in the subcontinent after the British had gone. Even the *Dundee Courier*, the newspaper of the city with the deepest Scottish connection to India in the past through jute manufacture, did not voice regret and remarkably did not even allude to the long historical relationship between Dundee and the new states.

One fact also to be borne in mind is that in the campaign against the Imperial Japanese Army in the Far East between 1942 and 1945, most Scottish soldiers had encountered for the first time the realities of life in the 'jewel of the imperial crown'. They of course knew something of India through tales of the Black Hole of Calcutta and the heroic relief of Lucknow, which they had heard about in school. In books for boys, India was presented as an exotic place of derring do, elephants and tigers, friendly and deferential natives, and picturesque scenery. However, troops stationed there in order to be acclimatized before heading for the front line in Burma in many cases formed a radically different impression of the Raj. Not for them was there an abundance of servants, easy living and polo matches at the officers' clubs, nor the soothing coolness of the hill stations during the torrid summers. The ordinary Tommies experienced a different India in overcrowded and stifling barracks. They hated the terrible squalor, the unbearable heat, and the constant threat of being struck down by tropical disease. George MacDonald Fraser, later to achieve literary fame as the author of the *Flashman* novels, served in the Border Regiment. He loathed Calcutta as 'a vast proliferating Augean stable'. Others were franker: India was 'the arse of the world', wrote another soldier. It did not help that the subcontinent was already seething with nationalist discontent and opposition to British rule.

Burma was even worse, 'a stinking hell on earth', where malaria and dysentery were a much more potent threat to life than the Japanese Army. On their return home, the many thousands of British veterans who had fought in India and Burma were hardly likely to suggest from their experience that colonial rule had to be maintained over these lands at all costs to prevent the crumbling of empire. As one private soldier wrote to his mother, 'it says in this book I'm reading that India is the Crown Jewel of the British Empire. If so, take it from me, they ought to pawn the bloody thing.' One historian summed up the feelings of the British Army in south-east Asia at the end of the war:

> As for the Empire: its poverty and chaos looked too permanently entrenched to ever possibly change. Those ungrateful natives had not shown much enthusiasm for the presence of the long-suffering British anyway. So why not let them stew in their own juice? To hell with the Empire. *That* was the lesson that many soldiers took home from the war. Britain – 'alone, self-contained, redoubtable' – had confronted the evils of Continental fascism and Asiatic fanaticism by relying on its own values and virtues ... decades of national psychic isolation would follow V-E Day and V-J Day.[2]

Of course, not all veterans necessarily felt this way. Some who had belonged to an army that garrisoned a quarter of the globe might well have felt dismay at the dramatic retreat from Britain's status as an imperial great power. It would have been hard not to wonder whether their sacrifice and that of the many thousands of dead comrades had been for nothing.

When considered over time, the British empire was not as crucial to the economy of Scotland in the 1950s as it had been in the Victorian era. Trade data confirm that the USA, Europe and other non-empire countries had already become much more important for trade and markets by 1914. Scotland was by then a global and not simply an imperial player. The empire had not saved Scotland from the great crisis of the interwar period and, indeed, the nation's external markets among the world's primary producers of foods and raw materials were especially badly hit, with Canada, Australia, New Zealand and India being among the most significant of these. The most arresting illustration of the new economic context of empire was the experience between the wars of the Dundee jute industry. As early as the 1890s, Bengal had overtaken its Scottish parent to become the world's dominant centre for the jute sacks and hessian cloth that carried many of the world's foodstuffs. Not surprisingly, in the depressed market conditions of the 1930s, Dundee jute interests pleaded on numerous occasions for tariffs to be imposed on the cheap imports from Calcutta. But their pleas were in vain. Now it was Dundee that looked more like the colony, and Bengal the metropole: '. . . jute presents an unusual example of a powerful industry emerging in a colonial setting which almost destroyed the rival industry back in Britain while the empire was still flourishing'.[3]

Moreover, experience of the hard times of the 1930s and total war from 1939 had begun to convince most Scots as never before of the far higher priorities posed by the social issues of employment, welfare and personal security. This new mood was crystallized after the publication of the famous Beveridge Report in December 1942. Immediately, the Report and the Summary became best-sellers; large queues formed outside the shops of His Majesty's Stationery Office to buy them and a Gallup Poll discovered that 19 out of 20 people had heard of the proposals a mere fortnight after their publication. Beveridge provided a blueprint for the post-war society that would commit government to conquest of the historic enemies for ordinary people of want, disease, ignorance, squalor and idleness. Family allowances should be provided for all children, mass unemployment could be avoided by state planning and intervention in the economy, and a National Health Service would be established. Citizens would be covered for all their needs from cradle to grave through a single weekly contribution. At the heart of the proposals was the idea of the 'national minimum', a basic level of income below which no one should be allowed to fall. All these helped to form the basis of the policy of the Labour Party after its landslide victory under Clement Attlee in the 1945 general election. When the anticipated independence of India became a settled fact in 1947, the concerns of most Scots were more focused on the new welfare reforms in health, social security and pensions, and the employment prospects in an economy now emerging from post-war austerity. The Welfare State and the commitment of the Labour government to the pursuit of policies of full employment rather than nostalgic dreams of empire were now becoming the new anchors of the Union state.

Two other factors also deserve consideration. First, Scottish emotional links of family and kindred were not to any great extent with India and the former African colonies but rather with the Dominions of Canada, Australia, New Zealand and South Africa, the countries that had experienced mass Scottish settlement over many generations. Their autonomy as members of the British Commonwealth of Nations had been confirmed not in the 1950s but much earlier by the Statute of Westminster of 1931. But such 'independence' in no way destroyed the links of kith and kin with Scotland. On the contrary, the enthusiastic commitment of the Dominion forces to the war against Nazi Germany and their courageous contributions to victory confirmed that the bonds with the mother country still held very fast. The renewal of Scottish emigration after 1945 continued to refresh these links where it really counted, at the human, personal and familial level. Over 300,000 Scots left their homeland between 1950 and 1970, many for these destinations, both to join friends and family already in the Dominions and also because during these decades the Dominions were more broadly giving very strong encouragement to immigration from Britain.

Second, by the 1950s two influential institutions in Scotland were becoming concerned about the morality of continued imperial rule. This was particularly the case in relation to some of the African colonies that had long had close associations with Scotland through Victorian missionary networks and where nationalist movements, notably in Kenya during the Mau Mau 'emergency', were causing terrible atrocities committed by both ruled and rulers. In the 1950s the General Assembly of the Church of Scotland enthusiastically advocated the cause of black nationalism and, especially in Nyasaland (modern Malawi), vehemently opposed the pressing menace of white racist minority rule. This was at a time when Scotland's so-called 'surrogate parliament' was listened to, its deliberations reported at length in the national press, and when membership of the Church of Scotland stood at an all-time high, especially among the Protestant business and professional classes and skilled workers. In similar vein, the Scottish Trades Union Congress received regular reports on the colonies and again strongly supported 'the native peoples [who] were entitled to the same freedom, liberty and opportunities as were the people of Britain'.[4] British policy in Kenya came in for special criticism when it was denounced by the STUC as 'a war of extermination' and much else. Some delegates extended specific comment from that case to a general condemnation of British imperialism writ large. If the position of the Church of Scotland and the STUC reflected a wider constituency (and that has yet to be determined by future research), some Scots were ending the imperial connection not only with relief but with some distaste for the colonial past.

Perhaps this may account for the post-imperial silence on Scotland's central historic role within the British empire. Between 1937 and 2001 not one book was published on a subject that many scholars now regard as being as important in Scottish history as the Reformation, the Enlightenment and the Industrial Revolution. Ironically, the 1960s and 1970s were decades of lively advances made in Scottish historiography, but empire as a subject was hardly studied. Indeed, some sociologists in the 1960s began to suggest that Scotland was more of a country colonized by England than an enthusiastic colonizing nation in its own right. Theories of 'internal colonialism' and 'under-development', which purported to demonstrate England's exploitation of Scotland, threatened to unceremoniously bury all memory of the country's imperial past. As the nation moved increasingly to the left in political allegiance from the 1960s, a kind of collective amnesia set in. There was no kind of intellectual conspiracy at this time that sought to conceal Scotland's engagement with empire;

rather, the subject was simply ignored or, when mentioned, thought worthy neither of celebration nor of pride but rather a matter for apology and embarrassment.

As far as Britain was concerned, the pinnacle of its glorious history was the Second World War when England and Scotland shared both in sacrifice and victory. But since the 1950s there has been a marked decline in Britain's significance as a great power. The end of empire was part of this process but it was not the only influence. Britain was seen to be a nation of declining influence on the world stage. Having won the war, the country seemed to be losing the peace. Successive British governments continued to have great-power pretensions but that facade could not disguise the real erosion of Britain's standing. The Suez Crisis in 1956 conclusively demonstrated the international dominance of the USA, with Britain tagging along as a junior and dependent partner in the 'special relationship'. From the late 1960s, also, Britain became the so-called 'sick man of Europe' as the economy lurched from crisis to crisis under the pressures of high inflation, balance of payments emergencies and trade union recalcitrance. In 1963 the British government of Harold Macmillan was humiliated when its application for membership of the Common Market was summarily rejected at the insistence of the French President, Charles de Gaulle, who dismissed the idea by claiming that the United Kingdom was unfit for full membership. Not until 1973 did the UK finally join Europe. A year later the academic and politician, John Mackintosh, argued in the *New Statesman* that whatever the other political parties offered to stem the SNP advance would not be enough 'so long as there is no proper pride in being British'.

II

By the early 1960s it had become evident that the post-war economic boom was dependent on the temporary conditions of replacement demand after 1945 and the virtual absence of international competition while the ravaged economies of Europe and the Far East recovered from the devastation of world conflict. There had still been precious little industrial diversification in Scotland. In the west, heartland of the traditional industries, the rate of entry of new companies in the 1950s was about half that of the 1940s. The most serious concerns were voiced about the condition of the industrial staples. Coal in particular faced a bleak future. The once rich Lanarkshire field was virtually worked out, while many consumers were moving to electricity, oil and gas. The conversion of locomotives from coal-burning to diesel engines and steel furnaces to oil-burning cut deeply into much of the traditional market for coal. Steel was better placed. In 1957 Scotland's first integrated iron and steel works, built at a cost of £22.5 million, was brought into production at Ravenscraig near Motherwell. But by the later 1950s Europe had recovered from the war, much more steel was being produced, and, with a world surplus building up, price-cutting became a common strategy. Despite the Ravenscraig works investment in Lanarkshire, the Scottish steel industry remained vulnerable because of its inland location and consequent high costs for ore and delivery of finished products.

Also, before 1960 shipbuilding was losing much of its world ascendancy. Although global demand for ships was still very buoyant, the Clyde's share of output was already in steady decline. In 1947, Clyde yards had launched 18 per cent of world tonnage, but its share slumped to 4.5 per cent in 1958. Scottish shipbuilding, once a world-class industry, was in a sorry state and it seemed that the many structural problems had simply been temporarily concealed by the post-war replacement boom. Certainly German, Dutch, Swedish and Japanese yards had the benefit of more lavish state support, but it was still the case that many of the wounds of Scottish shipbuilders were self-inflicted. While their rivals adopted streamlined assembly-line techniques, invested extensively in mechanization and designed well-planned yards, the Scots stood still, apart from the replacement of riveting by welding and improvements in prefabrication. They were now losing their competitive edge. In the later 1950s German yards could frequently deliver ships in half the time quoted by Clyde builders. Indecisive management and workers caught up in numerous demarcation disputes bore a collective responsibility for this state of affairs, which was by no means inevitable but before too long would bring a once mighty global industry to the brink of total collapse.

In truth, Scotland was no longer the economic superpower that it had been in the past. The old commercial empire was in its death throes. The nation's impact on the world economy receded with the continued malaise of the heavy industries, several of which were now only kept afloat by the nationalization of steel and coal in the 1940s, lavish government subsidy intervention in the 1960s, and the overriding post-war policy by the state of commitment to full employment. It was not, therefore, surprising that when the Thatcher governments withdrew life support in the 1980s and prioritized the control of inflation over the guaranteeing of employment, the traditional pillars of Scottish industry disintegrated with frightening speed. The takeover of Scottish companies by outside interests also speeded up so that by 1960 over 60 per cent of all manufacturing firms employing more than 250 people were owned by non-Scottish interests, primarily with headquarters in England and the USA.

Some concluded gloomily that Scotland was now only 'a branch-plant economy'. The tables had well and truly turned. Whereas Scottish overseas investment had helped to transform the New World in the nineteenth century, companies headquartered abroad or elsewhere in the UK were now becoming dominant in Scotland itself. By 1964 direct investment from the USA alone supported 52,000 jobs. A decade later, 40 per cent of manufacturing labourers in Scotland were employed by English-owned firms. This was also the time that saw the final demise of most of the great Scottish trading companies in the Far East. Acquisitions, mergers and nationalization by post-colonial governments brought to an end the long and independent histories in south-east Asia of such illustrious firms as Gray Mackenzie (1960), the Borneo Company (1967), Wallace Brothers (1977) and Guthries (1981).

Both Labour and Conservative governments in the 1960s and early 1970s recognized the problems that were emerging north of the border. Willie Ross, the Secretary of State in Harold Wilson's administration from 1964 to 1970, was a past master at fighting Scotland's corner in Cabinet. Public expenditure rose spectacularly by 900 per cent to over £192 million during his watch. Identifiable public expenditure moved to one-fifth above the British average. The whole of Scotland except Edinburgh was designated as one large development zone to which over £600 million of aid was dispensed through a new Scottish Office department. No area of the country was left untouched. The Highlands and Islands Development Board was set up in 1965 with executive authority over transport, industry and tourism. The north also gained when the Dounreay fast breeder reactor started in 1966, followed by the Invergordon smelter in 1968. A huge new pit at Longannet was opened, bringing with it the promise of 10,000 new jobs. The Forth Road Bridge was completed in 1964 and the Tay Road Bridge two years later. The largesse was not confined to infrastructure and industry. Following the publication of the Robbins Report in 1963, the number of Scottish universities doubled to eight with the foundation of Strathclyde (1964), Heriot-Watt (1966), Dundee (1967) and the only entirely new institution, Stirling (1967). There was a significant growth in the teaching profession of over 20 per cent between 1963 and 1973, which led to the opening of three colleges of education, at Ayr, Hamilton and Falkirk in 1964–5.

The social and economic impact of all this activity can hardly be doubted. Scotland was directly gaining from the Union as public revenues were channelled north in the form of massive regional assistance and other benefits. Ross had demonstrated that, like Tom Johnston before him, the Union relationship could be maximized to Scottish advantage. Labour was soon rewarded with a general election victory for Wilson's government in 1966 in which the Conservatives lost three of their 24 seats in Scotland. This, however, was the lull before the storm. Planning and lavish state expenditure had created expectations that could not always be fulfilled. The vast spending by Labour on the National Plan made it increasingly difficult to balance the UK budget. This problem soon led to wage restrictions and increases in duties on foreign imports. A dockers' strike in 1966 compounded the difficulties and sterling fell until the government was eventually forced into a devaluation. The number of disenchanted voters started to rise. In Scotland some of the protest was channelled into support for the SNP.

It now became obvious that regional policy, no matter how generous, was but a short-term fix. Scottish economic problems remained endemic. Unemployment was higher than the British average and would have been even more but for the many thousands who migrated, either to England or overseas. A response to a question in Parliament from Winnie Ewing for the SNP revealed that 45,000 had left Scotland in the year to July 1967. Industrial relations went from bad to worse in both traditional and new sectors of the economy, especially under Ted Heath's Conservative administration of 1970–74. The dispute at Upper Clyde Shipbuilders in 1971–2 and the associated 'work in' became a cause célèbre. For some, all this demonstrated that centralized British planning was now intellectually bankrupt and no longer capable of providing a long-term solution to national ills.

The malaise is a necessary context for understanding the rise of nationalism. There had, of course, been many worse periods before, notably between the wars, and they had not triggered a nationalist response. But these were different times that enabled the SNP to exploit economic grievances to the extent that it did. One factor was that by the later 1960s the party was in much better shape to deliver electoral impact. Ian Macdonald, a nationalist farmer from Ayrshire, became the SNP's first full-time organizer, funding his employment from the income released by the sale of his farm. He played a key role in the successful establishment of a branch structure throughout Scotland. This soon attracted enthusiastic activists, a trend that contrasted with the Labour and Conservative parties, which were almost moribund at the grass-roots level during this period.

The Scottish electorate was also changing. A nation that had experienced the good times of the 1950s and early 1960s had much higher material expectations than those of previous generations. State intervention since 1945 was supposed to generate better standards of living and so politicians were now judged on how far they were able to deliver these outcomes. The blame for bad times was no longer visited on the captains of industry or the employers to the same extent as it had been in the past. It is easy to see how a culture of political grievance could develop if aspirations were frustrated and expectations disappointed. The electorate was also now much more prepared to shop around if traditional party loyalties did not produce satisfactory results. The Liberal Party in this period mainly failed to break out of its rural fastnesses in Scotland but it also showed a modest revival by gaining five Scottish seats in 1966.

In part this new political fluidity reflected the patterns of the time in Scottish society. As the old industries declined, people moved increasingly into new jobs. Women had become a major part of the labour force. The new towns of Cumbernauld, East Kilbride and Livingston attracted the aspirational and upwardly mobile skilled working classes. Scotland's youth savoured some of the delights of the Swinging Sixties and were often no longer prepared to follow the traditions of their parents in either politics or religion. The Presbyterian Church, which had moulded the moral values and social conformity of the country for centuries, was in rapid decline. The number of Scots with some form of church connection fell from over 40 per cent of the population in 1960 to just over 30 per cent in the mid-1970s. The losses were especially significant in the Church of Scotland and particularly among its younger adherents. Scottish society in the 1960s was becoming fertile territory for fresh ideas. New political causes such as nationalism and the Campaign for Nuclear Disarmament (CND) were among the most influential.

The changing electoral landscape gave the SNP an opportunity for another reason. The Scottish Unionist Party dropped the 'Unionist' label in 1964 in favour of 'Conservative'. For several decades it had been a doughty champion of the Scottish interest, either when the Tories were in government in Westminster or against the centralizing Labour administration after 1945 when they were in opposition. That commitment to Scotland as well as loyalty to the Union helped to explain the remarkable history of electoral success of the Conservative Party in Scotland between the wars and again in the 1950s. By the early 1960s, however, all was not well with the Tories in Scotland. The party's grandees were already becoming concerned about low levels of membership among the young and a sharp decline in the number of activists. That organizational decay increasingly gave the SNP its chance, especially in rural areas and small-town Scotland, where Labour had never developed deep roots. The revival of Liberalism also clearly offered a choice but the Liberals were never as successful in Scotland in this period as they were south of the border. In the two general elections in 1974 they took over a fifth of the vote in England compared to only around 8 per cent in Scotland.

The decline in Unionist/Conservative popularity was as swift as it was unexpected. As recently as 1955 the Unionists with their allies had attracted just over 50 per cent of all Scottish votes, the only party grouping ever to have managed that electoral achievement. But, in retrospect, this was to prove a watershed in their fortunes. In 1959 the number of Unionist MPs fell from 36 to 31, then to 24 in 1964, and dropped again to 20 in the 1966 general election. It was still not a disaster on the scale to come in the elections of 1987 and 1997, but nevertheless it was an enormous humiliation for a party that had been the most successful in Scotland since the end of Liberal hegemony after 1918.

Increasingly the Scottish Conservatives presented the image of a remote or anglicized elite that seemed out of touch with current Scottish problems. In part this was due to a combination of the difficulties of the older industries and the inexorable decline of indigenous control of manufacturing and enterprise due to nationalization, numerous mergers, and the penetration of American and English capital. The great Scottish captains of industry and leaders of the Clydeside dynasties who had formerly ruled the party were fast disappearing, and their place was once again being taken by lairds and aristocrats who had received an entirely anglicized education. The huge changes in urban housing after the Second World War also affected the party's fortunes. The massive working-class peripheral housing estates around Glasgow, Edinburgh and Dundee established new Labour fiefdoms in former rural areas, while the flight of the middle classes to the suburbs eroded the Conservative vote in the heart of the cities. It may seem remarkable today, but in 1951 the Conservatives held as many as seven seats in Glasgow, only one fewer than Labour. By 1964, however, they were left with only two, one of which was already very vulnerable.

The success of Scottish Conservatives for much of the twentieth century was partly base due to their ability to reach out well beyond their traditional support base among the middle classes to many of the respectable, skilled and semi-skilled Protestant working classes in Scotland. To them the party stood for Protestantism, unionism and imperial identity. As late as 1986, 45 per cent of the members of the Church of Scotland claimed to vote Tory. In Dundee in 1968 nearly 40 per cent of Protestant manual workers voted Conservative, compared to 6 per cent of Roman Catholics from the same class. These figures date from the period when the pattern of voting along religious lines – at least for Protestants – was already in decline. It is very likely that in the 1950s and early 1960s the political and religious cleavages in Scotland went even deeper. Nevertheless, the bedrock Protestant working-class support for Conservatism was crumbling in the 1960s and 1970s. Many young people were losing contact with religion altogether: the numbers attending Sunday School plummeted; the Boys' Brigade, closely attached to the Kirk, was no longer as popular; and the proportion of marriages being religiously solemnized fell, especially from 1965. That Scotland was becoming a more secular society was also illustrated by the partial erosion of sectarian employment practices, driven by a variety of factors: the impact of new foreign-owned industry; the nationalization and/or decay of the older staple manufactures (where discrimination in the skilled sector against Catholics had flourished); the growth of employment in public services; and the effect of full employment in the 1950s and early 1960s on the labour market. As a result, the old Protestant monopoly of many skilled jobs was breaking up.

The Conservatives suffered most as a result of the growing secularization of Scottish politics, while the now traditional Catholic vote for Labour remained rock-solid. As early as 1964, when they suffered an important defeat in the Pollok constituency in Glasgow, Conservative Party managers had first become aware that they were losing the working-class religious vote. On the other hand, the Catholic block vote for Labour remained loyal for at least another generation. Catholics on the whole distrusted the SNP as a 'Protestant party'. The Tories were therefore squeezed by two forces: the desertion of many of their working-class supporters to new allegiances and the still unquestioning loyalty to Labour of the Catholic population in numerous constituencies in the west of Scotland. Tory problems were brought into stark relief in a survey carried out for Conservative Central Office on the motivations behind Scottish nationalism. It concluded with a very downbeat assessment after analysing the views of electors:

> The Scottish Conservative Party has got an exceedingly bad image. It is thought to be out of touch, a bastion of 'Foreign' privilege, Westminster orientated, associated with recalcitrant landowners ... the only party

which on mention often elicited mirthful or mirthless laughter. It was variously described as 'run by lairds, landowners and the business community'. Among the insults heaped upon it were that 'Conservatives are the dregs from England' and that Conservatives [sic] MPs with Scots names 'are no true Scotsmen'. The Scottish Conservative Party was described as being comprised of 'misguided Scots'.[5]

The death of Toryism in much of Scotland is often ascribed to the impact of the policies of the Thatcher governments in the 1980s. Clearly, however, the roots of the party's decline are to be found much further back in earlier decades.

III

In October 1970, BP struck oil over 100 miles off Aberdeen in what was to become the giant Forties field. The subsequent massive hike in oil prices after the Yom Kippur War in the Middle East in 1973 meant that even marginal discoveries could now have huge potential value. The 'black gold' came as a godsend for the British government and an asset it simply could not afford to lose. In 1975 the UK was edging close to bankruptcy. Lord Balogh, Harold Wilson's economic adviser, stated that the country faced 'possible wholesale domestic liquidation'.[6] But at the same time it was also recognized within government that the discovery of oil would have a significant impact on the debate over the national question in Scotland.

A confidential, unsigned and undated memorandum on the subject, written in the early 1970s, has only come to light recently as the result of a Freedom of Information request in 2005.[7] The mysterious author was almost certainly a senior civil servant in the Scottish Office. The content of the report was potential political dynamite. It argued that the discovery of oil had now transformed the economic case for independence. Scotland could become the 'Kuwait of the North'. The economy of the independent country would be massively in surplus and living standards were bound to rise spectacularly. The nation's currency would be the strongest in Europe, with the possible exception of the Norwegian krone. Scotland could become another Switzerland: 'as deposed monarchs and African leaders have used the Swiss franc as a haven for security so now would the Scottish pound be seen as a good hedge against inflation and devaluation'. Scottish banks in the event of independence could be expected to receive a massive inundation of foreign funds. Most remarkably, the paper also added that 'for the first time since the Act of Union was passed, it can now be credibly argued that Scotland's economic advantage lies in its repeal'.

An associated memorandum entitled 'The Economics of Nationalism Re-Examined', compiled by Dr Gavin McCrone, then Chief Economic Adviser to the Secretary of State for Scotland, went further by stressing the additional advantages that had emerged for Scotland as a result of Britain joining the European Economic Community (EEC) in 1973. It asserted that the EEC now offered even bigger markets to Scotland than the Union of 1707 had done in the past. While these confidential documents went no further than the eyes of ministers, it is clear from the trend of future policies that there was widespread recognition in government of the acute danger faced by the UK state if there were any attempted redistribution of oil revenues contemplated in order to appease the Scots. The Cabinet Secretary, Sir John Hunt, was adamant that in the event of any future devolved arrangements for Scotland, all effective control of North Sea oil resources had to remain within the complete control of Westminster.

In the event, the oil and gas discoveries had four effects on the Scottish question. First, they help to explain the SNP comeback in Labour's general election victory of October 1974 under Harold Wilson, when the SNP won just over 30 per cent of the vote, achieved the election of 11 MPs, and came second in 36 of Labour's 41 seats. Senior government officials at the time had little doubt that the (temporary) SNP advance was due to the oil factor. The party for a time brilliantly exploited the stark contrast between the fabulous wealth in Scottish waters and the relatively high unemployment levels in Scotland compared to most countries in Western Europe.

Second, both unionists and nationalists agreed that oil had massively weakened, and in the view of many, destroyed the old argument that Scotland could not go it alone as an independent state. As Billy Wolfe, the then leader of the SNP, asserted in 1973: 'The wealth of the oil destroys the myth that Scotland is too poor for self-government. It gives the Scots confidence to run their own affairs.'[8]

Third, the windfall from the North Sea led to the campaign 'It's Scotland's oil – with self-government'. The posters that appeared all over the country displayed the 'black stuff' pouring from the large capital letter 'o' in the word 'oil'. The campaign restored the SNP's credibility for a time but it did not lead to the hoped-for electoral breakthrough. Eventually, some senior members of the SNP became embarrassed by it and were sensitive to accusations that total Scottish control of the new wealth might be viewed as unadulterated selfishness by the electorate.

Fourth, the possibility of apparently limitless energy resources off the Scottish coast concentrated the minds of UK government ministers. A Department of Energy paper in 1974 came to the conclusion that the discoveries off Aberdeen were 'probably one of the most important events in the UK since the industrial revolution' and hence were fundamental to both the economic and strategic vital interests of Great Britain as a whole. In consequence, it was decided not to publish formal government estimates of the likely future supplies of oil. Instead, the message went out to the public that North Sea oil would not last for very long and the estimates made by the SNP about potential reserves were grossly exaggerated. The SNP campaign soon fizzled out and died.

I I

Scotland Transformed

The Labour defeat of 1979 was the prelude to 18 years of Conservative rule in the UK, first under governments led by Margaret Thatcher, who won three consecutive general elections in 1979, 1983 and 1987, and then by her successor, John Major, from 1990 to 1997. During the Thatcher years in particular the economy of Scotland was transformed, social change accelerated, opposition to the government's policies became entrenched, and policies were introduced by the UK state that did much to weaken the stability and integrity of the Union. Indeed, some later viewed Mrs Thatcher as 'the midwife of the Scottish Parliament' since during her administrations a new and stronger commitment eventually emerged in the movement for home rule, in large part as a reaction to her policies.

Yet in 1979 the outlook for devolution seemed bleak indeed. The new Tory government was firmly opposed to the Scotland Act and one of its first decisions was to secure its repeal in Parliament. As a token gesture to home rule sentiment the Scottish Grand Committee began to meet in Edinburgh, though it failed to elicit much public interest or response. The two pro-devolution parties, Labour and the SNP, were in disarray and soon became mired in serious internal difficulties for some years. Labour became virtually unelectable at the national level for a period while the SNP imploded into fratricidal dispute. With the opposition practically emasculated, life at first was relatively easy for the Thatcher government. The SNP was demoralized and internal tensions that had been festering for some time now came to the boil. The party had suffered an electoral humiliation in 1979 as the number of MPs fell to only two. The post-mortem on this debacle and the debate on the best way forward triggered a state of open warfare among different factions. The '79 Group, which included Margo MacDonald, Jim Sillars and a young Alex Salmond, tried to move the party to the left in order to give it a distinctive ideological identity that would be recognized by the electorate. The newsletter of the Group carried the masthead 'For a Scottish Socialist Republic', and the members gave vocal public support to workers whose factories were threatened with closure, such as the Invergordon Aluminium Smelter and the British Leyland Bathgate truck plant. The right to civil disobedience was also asserted.

The most notorious example of this commitment came in October 1981 when Sillars and some companions broke into the Royal High School building in Edinburgh, which had been refurbished in preparation for housing the anticipated new Scottish Assembly. The aim was to hold a symbolic debate on Scottish unemployment in the empty chamber. Sillars was arrested and fined £100 for vandalism. Another group to emerge at the same time was Siol nan Gaidheal, ('Seed of the Gael'), comprising young men from the traditionalist wing of the party who liked to parade in Highland dress with bagpipes, drums and dirks. They posed as a kind of nationalist militia and were fond of the ritualistic public burning of Union Jacks. While their militaristic image pleased some supporters who were in despair at the collapse of the SNP's electoral fortunes, the '79 Group and their allies regarded the antics of Siol as tantamount to embracing fascism. The SNP leader, Gordon Wilson, concluded that his party would inevitably disintegrate into hostile factions if drastic action were not taken. At the annual conference in Ayr in 1982 it was therefore agreed that all groups should be disbanded forthwith. Eventually, six members of the '79 Group, including Alex Salmond, were expelled from the party, though most returned after eventually accepting the conference decision. The events of 1982 left a legacy of great bitterness and personal animosities within the SNP that took time to disappear. The party's political effectiveness was therefore very limited for several years. At the 1983 general election the SNP held on to its two seats but attracted only 12 per cent of the vote. Not until Jim Sillars's victory at the Govan by-election in 1988 did the Nationalists achieve another significant public success. However, in the meantime, one longer-term effect of the bloodletting of the early 1980s was that the SNP did begin to define itself more distinctively as a left-of-centre party. In due course this was to bring electoral dividends.

The Labour Party in the UK was in even more serious trouble than the Nationalists after 1979. Its response was to swing far to the left, a process accompanied by the infiltration of the Trotskyist Militant Tendency into many local constituency organizations in England. At the 1980 annual conference, the Left coasted to a sweeping victory as the party adopted a policy of withdrawal from the EEC, unilateral nuclear disarmament, and removal of the power of MPs to select the leader. While ideologically pure, this programme ensured that Labour would be consigned to the electoral wilderness for some time to come. The following year, the 'Gang of Four', David Owen, Roy Jenkins, Shirley Williams and Bill Rodgers, split from Labour and founded the Social Democratic Party (SDP). The official parliamentary opposition was now reduced to division and impotence, and was unable to exploit the undeniable national unpopularity of the Thatcher government in the early 1980s. Labour's left-wing manifesto for the general election in the summer of 1983 was famously dubbed by one of its MPs, Gerald Kaufmann, 'the longest suicide note in history'. The combination of this programme, a divided opposition and, crucially, the impact of the successful British campaign in the Falklands War of 1982, resulted in a crushing Conservative victory in 1983. Labour's performance was disastrous, its national vote collapsing to a level never seen since the 1930s. Conservative rule was to last without interruption for a further 14 years.

However, Labour maintained its dominance north of the border in 1983 by returning 41 MPs, nearly twice as many as the Tories. Because of this, the first mutterings were heard that the Thatcher government did not have a mandate in Scotland. The Scottish Labour Party also remained more moderate than its counterpart in the south. Significantly, in March 1982, under the new rules for the selection of MPs, not a single sitting member was deselected in Scotland. Nor was there much leakage to the alliance formed by the SDP and the Liberals in June 1981. Charles Kennedy, an SDP MP from 1983, thought that this was because Labour in Scotland was regarded as more sane and responsible than the party in parts of England. John Smith, a future leader of the party, argued that Labour owed a great debt to the Scots because they kept the faith and held the middle ground during the years when the Labour Party in England tried to resolve its multiple problems. It was in the 1980s that talented Scots, such as Smith himself, Gordon Brown, Robin Cook, Donald Dewar, George Robertson and others, came to the fore in the Labour Party, and after the 1997 election they went on to form the largest group of Scottish MPs ever to sit in a British Cabinet. With the SNP irrelevant, Labour was still overwhelmingly the electoral focus for anti-Conservative opposition in Scotland. The problem was, however, that though Labour could win with ease north of the border, the Conservatives were impregnable in the Midlands, London and the south-east, where British general elections were usually decided.

I

The great manufacturing complex of Scotland had grown to maturity in the nineteenth century and especially from the 1830s to around 1900. It now disintegrated in little more than a decade. De-industrialization was of course a common experience of advanced western economies in this period, including those of the north of England. But the industries that dated back to Victorian times had long been central to Scotland's sense of itself as a nation which made things and on whose foundations the public and service sectors ultimately depended. The country's manufacturing base was in serious difficulty for decades before the 1980s despite many millions spent by government in support. Yet, when the end came in that decade, it was frightening in its speed and for a time brought in its train devastating social consequences for the mining and industrial regions of Scotland. Equally concerning was that several of the new industrial plants born from inward investment in the 1970s proved not to be immune from the gathering economic storm. Some of them followed the so-called 'dinosaur industries'.

The worst economic recession since the 1930s was global in scale and in origin. In the late 1970s the impact of the steep increase in oil prices on world demand for manufactured goods was especially lethal in its consequences. But in Britain there was an additional factor, the election of a Conservative government with a radical economic agenda that was hostile to the post-war consensus on full employment and welfare provision and in possession of an electoral mandate to cure the ills of 'the sick man of Europe', once and for all. The last Labour administration had already been forced into cuts on government expenditure as a result of the UK's economic troubles and the spiralling overspend in the public finances. But the incoming Thatcher government possessed an ideological commitment to the control of public expenditure combined with a crusade against the evils of inflation and firm opposition to the provision of state help for so-called industrial 'lame ducks'. These policies were soon imposed on a weakened economy already mired in depression. Inflation was to be squeezed out by a sharp rise in interest rates to halt the growth in the money supply. The old priority of the need to secure full employment, an unchallenged nostrum since the 1940s, was abandoned in this new context of financial rigour. By the end of the first year of the new administration, the Bank of England base rate had soared to 17 per cent. As financial prudence became the new orthodoxy, whole sectors of Scottish industry became vulnerable to the combination of the squeeze on credit and falling markets overseas. This time the state would not attempt to shelter ailing and uncompetitive businesses from the harsh winds blowing through the market economy. Also, the ignominious surrender of Ted Heath's government to trade union power in the early 1970s was not to be repeated, whatever the social costs of the new economic strategy. As Mrs Thatcher famously declared at the Conservative Party Conference in 1980: 'You turn if you want to; the lady's not for turning.'

As will be discussed later, Thatcher and the Tories eventually paid a heavy political price for the collapse of Scottish industry in the 1980s. But at worst, the government of that decade of recession merely hastened this process of dissolution. The complex origins of the death of Scottish industry can be traced as far back as the 1920s or even earlier. The symptoms of the maladies were, however, concealed for many years because of the stimulus of the Second World War, its aftermath, and the post-war support of the state. The Conservatives took the blame but the real villains were successive governments of both political hues, the endemic failings of Scottish entrepreneurs, recalcitrant trade unions, and the misguided ideas of planners dating back half a century and more. Yet this conclusion did not mean that the pain when it came was any easier to bear. With the riches from North Sea oil swelling the coffers of government, much more could have been done to ease the radical restructuring from the old to the new economy that emerged from the later 1980s and beyond. Such an approach was made impossible in reality because of the new market-based ideologies of the Tories. As one historian has put it:

> The Thatcherite response was to take it on the chin. Those firms with competitive ability would survive by becoming hardened to the market's knocks. The industries that collapsed under international competitive blows would be left on the canvas, as there was no point in government picking them up only for them to get knocked down again. Unfortunately, Scotland's economic jawline was brittle . . . It was nasty and brutal medicine.[1]

Between 1979 and 1981, Scottish industry lost around a fifth of all its jobs. Manufacturing capacity fell all over the UK, but the decline in Scotland at 30.8 per cent between 1976 and 1987 was greatest of all. Worst hit was the traditional heavy industrial region of the west of Scotland, which experienced a fall of 36.9 per cent and the textiles area of the Borders, which lost 64 per cent of industrial capacity. The great staples of the Victorian economy all crumbled with astonishing speed. Scottish mining had long suffered from poor productivity levels but had been kept alive because the state-owned electricity industry was required to purchase coal from 1977. In the 1980s, however, the number of active pits fell from 15 to just two. By 1997, with the failure of the miners' buyout at Monktonhall, this once mighty industry was reduced to the single Longannet complex on the Firth of Forth. The fate of shipbuilding was little better. In 1979–80, Scottish yards accounted for half of all the losses incurred by the nationalized British shipbuilders, and a rundown of the labour force was therefore inevitable. Only a handful of yards remained in the 1990s on what was now the almost silent River Clyde: Yarrows specializing in warships, Kvaerner at Govan (whose future was uncertain in 1999), and the small Ferguson company at Port Glasgow. In 1987, when the QE2 was re-engined with diesels, the work could not be carried out on the river that had built her but had to be done in a German yard. It was a potent symbol of de-industrialization and the enormous loss of time-honoured skills that went with it. Textiles were not spared either. The last cargo of jute to Dundee from Bangladesh was landed in October 1998 as the industry fell victim to substitutes such as cardboard and plastic bags, bulk handling and containerization. Indeed, little remained in the 1990s of the Scottish textile industry except high-quality production of knitwear in the Borders.

By the 1970s it was also clear that the steel industry was in acute difficulty. Demand for steel was falling generally in the UK in the later part of that decade and the Scottish plants were exposed in cost terms. Losses per ton were higher north of the border than in any of the other divisions of the British Steel Corporation because of the smaller scale of production and higher fuel and transport costs. But 'rationalization' with limited regard for political and social consequences was much harder to achieve in steel, even if the slimming down of the industry might be justified in the eyes of government by narrow economic and accountancy criteria. The Lanarkshire plants were the biggest electricity customers in the land and provided half of all the freight traffic in Scotland. They were also important suppliers to the North Sea construction yards at Clydebank, Nigg and Ardersier. The closure of the Linwood car plant in 1981, which had been a key market for strip steel, was therefore a serious blow but not a mortal one, because business leaders and politicians of all parties were agreed that a Scottish steel-making presence of some kind was essential in order to attract other industry to Scotland.

The survival of the great Ravenscraig works at Motherwell, the 'Steel Town' in Lanarkshire, began to assume totemic significance as the symbol of Scotland's historic status as a great industrial nation. Its closure was therefore politically unthinkable. Even the Tory Scottish Secretary of State, George Younger, admitted that the closure of 'the Craig' would be for him a resignation issue. But the plant did die, though it was death by a thousand cuts. During the 1980s, Ravenscraig was starved of investment, steadily reduced in capacity (including the closure of the nearby Gartcosh rolling mill), and threatened with a complete shut-down on two occasions. Despite this, a package of productivity reforms meant that the plant soon consistently outperformed the rival works at Llanwern in Wales. Nevertheless, when the privatization of the British Steel Corporation eventually took place, Ravenscraig's days were numbered. In January 1992, British Steel announced that the plant would close in the following year. When production finally ceased in June 1993, the end was accepted with muted resignation rather than angry protest.

Yet it was not simply the old, traditional pillars of Scottish industry that vanished during the Thatcher years. Even many of the regional policy successes of the post-war years succumbed in significant numbers: 'A list of closures included Singers in Clydebank, Goodyear nearby in Glasgow, Monsanto in Ayrshire, Massey Ferguson in Kilmarnock, BSR in East Kilbride, Wiggins Teape pulp mill in Fort William, Talbot's Linwood car plant, the Invergordon aluminium smelter, Caterpillar in Uddingston, Burroughs in Cumbernauld, Plessey in Bathgate, Rowntree Mackintosh in Edinburgh.'[2] Other multinationals, like Timex, Hoover and SKF, shed tens of thousands of jobs between 1976 and 1988, while commentators talked freely of the total de-industrialization of Scotland as unemployment soared. Jim Sillars voiced the worst fears of many when he wrote in late 1985 that even Scottish Conservatives were alarmed at the serious threat to 'Scotland's place as an industrial nation'. The seemingly endless lists of closures were 'hammer blows at main pillars of Scottish economic life' and the optimism of the 1970s was now replaced by a mood of deep pessimism: 'Today, ours is a fearful, anxious, nail-biting nation ruminating on Burns's salutation to human despair, "An' forward tho' I canna see, I guess and fear."'[3] At the end of the 1980s the Scottish novelist James Kelman thought that 'For hundreds of thousands of people throughout Great Britain the last decade or more has been a form of nightmare.'[4]

But it was not entirely a long day's journey into night. What in fact was taking place, though very difficult to see at the time, was not terminal decline but a painful and compressed process of economic transformation. Scotland was going through a revolution that had no precedent since the first industrialization of the country two centuries before. The number of workers in manufacturing, mining and agriculture fell by nearly one-half in less than five years between 1979 and

1984. The 'service' sector, which included everything from menial labour to high-status jobs in finance and higher education, grew exponentially. The jewel in the crown, at least in that period, was finance, where Scotland was reckoned to have become fourth in Europe in terms of the provision of services, after London, Frankfurt and Paris. But many service jobs were part-time and low-paid, and were often taken by women on very modest earnings trying to make ends meet in the family budget. Higher education, the health service and public-sector employment generally began to expand again at the end of the decade. Tourism by the 1990s employed over 220,000 people, more than agriculture, fishing and mining combined. Ironically, some of the new visitor attractions included a plethora of heritage museums and theme parks designed to show the glories of Scotland's industrial past. Making things, however, was not entirely dead. North Sea oil provided spin-offs in well construction, though these companies were not always able to weather the global volatility in oil prices. Electronics manufacture, once thought of as the economic saviour of Scotland, made a recovery, and 'Silicon Glen' soon produced 42 per cent of the country's manufactured exports by 1990. But the new and established plants remained the result of American, Asian and Japanese inward investment, and Scotland therefore remained exposed to the vulnerable 'branch factory' syndrome. International investors were attracted by government support, custom-built factories, a favourable geographical location that enabled speedy and low-cost access to European markets, and, perhaps above all, wages of around half the going rate in such technological hotspots as California in the late 1980s.

By the later 1990s, Scotland had a new economy. It was more varied, stable, and above all tuned to modern international markets. Indeed, during the early 1990s recession, Scotland fared better than many parts of England and had lower unemployment rates than the other de-industrializing regions of the UK in the north-east and Wales. The new structure ended the old risky dependence on a few great but declining industrial giants. Instead it came to resemble the UK as a whole and other advanced economies in the West that had also experienced a massive rise in service employment at this time. One senior economic historian concluded in 1992 that 'industry in Scotland is more healthy than it has been for many generations'.[5] The scale of the revolution is identified in the numbers in Table 3.

Table 3. Employees in Employment in Scotland by Major Industry or Service Sector

Source	Number in Employment (thousands)		
	1979	1989	1994
Agriculture, Forestry, Fishing –	48	29	26
Energy and Water Supply –	72	57	49
Manufacturing –	604	402	354
Construction –	155	130	101
Distribution, Hotels and Catering, Repairs +	392	400	416
Transport and Communication –	135	113	107
Banking, Finance, Insurance and Business Services +	123	176	204
Education, Health and Other Services +	573	651	704
All Industries and Services –	**2,102**	**1,958**	**1,961**

Source: Alice Brown, David McCrone and Lindsay Paterson, *Politics and Society in Scotland* (Basingstoke, 1996), p. 75. Note: – equals fall; + equals increase, 1979–94

II

Some of the generation of working-class Scots who lived through the difficult times of the early 1980s had already experienced the even greater miseries of the 1930s, half a century before. It was a bitter pill for them to swallow to see their children and grandchildren confronted once again with the harsh realities of mass unemployment. The older generation had assumed that the evil of long-term loss of jobs had been banished in Britain after 1945 by the political consensus on full employment shared by both major parties. Probably even more shocked, however, were younger people who since the 1950s had grown to adulthood in a world of relative material plenty and job security. Of course, as the UK balance of payments position deteriorated, inflation spiralled out of control and industrial relations went from crisis to crisis, few could have been unaware that the good times would soon come to an end and that 'something had to be done'. Yet, when the Scottish economy was hit by deep crisis in the early 1980s, the experience for them was without precedent.

Some perspective and balance are needed in assessing the impact on the population. The historical image of the 1980s in Scotland is dark and bleak – the death knell of the familiar old industries, a growing army of unemployed, especially among the young, derelict factories and redundant pits. It is, however, important to remember that most Scots were still in work, even in the worst times, and that much of the country, especially in the east, was not as badly hit as Glasgow and its hinterland, the epicentre of traditional industry. But the constant factor across the country was often fear and insecurity. Manual and semi-skilled workers bore the brunt of the job losses, but the uncertainties were not confined to them. Running in parallel with the recession came a new managerial drive to boost efficiency and the productivity of labour. The words 'downsizing' and 'shake out' entered the common vocabulary. It was a trend that led to even more redundancies. The determination of government to impose more rigorous discipline on the so-called 'feather-bedded' public sector of health services, education and the universities also bred insecurity and anxiety. People may have been in work but there was no certainty that they would always manage to escape the dole queue.

Evidence emerged of acute social problems in some regions. In parts of Glasgow, even after recovery from 1991, unemployment rates were over 38 per cent in the city centre and almost 33 per cent in some of the huge peripheral housing schemes built with such optimism in the post-war years. Despair, alcoholism and drugs took root in many of these communities. Earlier in 1983, unemployment in Scotland as a whole had passed the 300,000 mark, though the figure was probably an underestimate as it did not take account of those on youth work schemes or the numbers who were transferred from unemployment to invalidity benefit. In the same year it was reckoned that over 1 million people were living on or below the poverty line, as defined by contemporary standards. A key social change was the movement of women en masse into the labour force. By this period they formed over 40 per cent of those in work. However, as one analyst claimed at the time, jobs for women were 'low paid, low grade, semi-skilled at best and frequently part-time'.[6] The expanding service sector was not always liberating. Some in science, technology, finance and education provided high-status and satisfying employment, but many in the service sector were also working in fast-food outlets, and cleaning and assembling computers rather than developing them: 'The "service economy" is just as much about these shadowy jobs as about the glitter of the stock market or the pioneering excitement of the laboratory.'[7]

Then there was the issue of health where research began to discover a 'Scottish effect' in illnesses and mortality. Life expectancy for Scottish women in 2003 was the lowest in the EU; for men it was the second lowest. Social scientists showed that compared with England and Wales the Scottish experience could be explained by higher levels of deprivation. Importantly, the data suggested that only from the mid-twentieth-century period of de-industrialization had Scotland declined in indicators of health. Other countries were improving, but Scotland was not doing so to the same extent, as the country began to slide down the league table of life expectancy.

But there were more positive aspects to this highly complex period of social and economic transformation. By the 1990s nearly half of students were completing courses in higher education compared to less than 10 per cent as recently as the early 1960s. As a result, Scotland was beginning to see the emergence of a more critical citizenry whose sense of deference was ebbing away and who were likely to be more willing to challenge authority in all spheres, whether in politics, religion or civil institutions. Career opportunities were increasingly founded on educational credentials, certificates and measurable merit. Meritocracy, however, can marginalize those who, for whatever reason, cannot easily compete in the business of achieving good school results or university honours. The knowledge economy created problems for those without knowledge. The patterns fitted well with an economy that was shedding the need for as much manual labour as before and where brain-intensive, value-added manufacturing was becoming the aspiration of government not only in the UK but across Western Europe and North America. A subset of this need for credentials to get ahead in society was the decline in nepotism, patronage and sectarian employment discrimination. By the early 1990s, Scottish Catholics, mainly from Irish immigrant stock and forming around one-sixth of the nation's population, were no longer under-represented among the class of managers, senior officials or professionals, and by 2001 they had achieved occupational parity with their fellow Scots. This was a historic transition.

Scotland was also becoming a more 'professional society' in the literal sense that those claiming professional status in the 2001 census made up over one-third of the population. A team of Edinburgh University sociologists also showed in a major study that whereas many suffered low wages and unemployment in the 1980s, others had experienced significant upward social mobility:

> Indeed, in all but the youngest cohort of men, a majority [for each sex] had been upwardly mobile. For example, among people born between 1957 and 1966, 55 per cent of men had been upwardly mobile, and 63 per cent of women ... this upward mobility was largely because the professional classes were expanding their share, rather than because of any changes in the relative chances of mobility from a given starting point.[8]

Others, such as Sir Malcolm Rifkind, MP, Secretary of State for Scotland from 1986 to 1990 and a member of Margaret Thatcher's Cabinet in the last years of her term as Prime Minister, also stressed the complicated nature of the 1980s in Scotland. While admitting the errors of the Tory government during those years, he pointed out that when Mrs Thatcher left office in 1990, Scotland's economy had not only been transformed but was outperforming most regions in England. He added that:

> Scotland was a Mecca for overseas investment and thanks to the Right to Buy legislation, home-ownership had gone from one of the lowest levels in Europe to one of the highest. Far from council tenants rebuffing Thatcherism they embraced it with great enthusiasm, buying their homes against the advice of both the Labour Party and the SNP.[9]

The response to the Conservative policy of privatization was similar. Shares in companies that were privatized, like the South of Scotland Electricity Board, the North of Scotland Hydro Board, the Scottish Bus Group and Kvaerner Govan Shipbuilders, were bought up by Scots in the same way as their fellow citizens elsewhere in the UK. No hard data yet exist to prove the point conclusively, but almost certainly the shareholders, homebuyers and the upwardly mobile gained during this period.

Yet despite apparent material progress for some at least, Margaret Thatcher and the Tory Party were condemned by most Scots by the end of the 1980s. Conservatives continued to lose seats, Scots voted against the party's candidates in large majorities, often by tactical voting, and Mrs Thatcher became a hate figure throughout the land. So why, given some undoubted successes in Scotland, did this happen, and how did the Thatcher years become the foundation of the movement to establish a Parliament in Edinburgh?

12

'The greatest of all Scottish Nationalists'*

A few months before his premature death in October 2000, Donald Dewar, Scotland's first First Minister after the establishment of the Scottish Parliament in 1999, gave a fine lecture at Trinity College, Dublin, to a distinguished audience of Irish academics and politicians. This author hosted the dinner in his honour afterwards and in introductory remarks referred to the then cliché that Mr Dewar was the 'Father of the Scottish Parliament'. Donald Dewar cringed, then declared there was no 'Father' – but there was a 'Mother' and her name was Margaret Thatcher. Later, in conversation, he argued that if the 1980s could be counterfactually removed from the history of Scotland, he doubted whether there would have been a Parliament in Edinburgh in the year 2000.

I

No British politician has been more reviled in Scotland than Mrs Thatcher since universal suffrage was established after the Great War. The current First Minister of Scotland (2015), Nicola Sturgeon, admitted recently: 'Thatcher was the motivation for my entire political career. I hated everything she stood for.'[1] Sir Malcolm Rifkind, once a member of Mrs Thatcher's Cabinet, remarked that many 'loathed her during her tenure of power and her name has been used since to terrify the gullible in a manner that used to be reserved for witches and warlocks'.[2] The Scottish novelist Willie McIlvanney, who

* A reference to Margaret Thatcher attributed to Charles Kennedy, MP.

was prominent in the political activities of the 1980s, stated in a lecture 'Stands Scotland where it did?' to huge acclaim at the SNP Conference in 1987: 'Margaret Thatcher is not just a perpetrator of bad policies. She is a cultural vandal. She takes the axe of her own simplicity to the complexities of Scottish life ... if we allow her to continue she will remove from the word "Scottish" any meaning other than the geographical'.[3] A very long compendium of similar condemnations from political and civic Scotland could easily be compiled that are much more abusive than those words. The sociologist Tony Dickson tried to summarize the roots of this Scottish loathing for Mrs Thatcher in an essay published in 1988:

> The public persona of Mrs Thatcher appears to many Scots to capture all the worst elements of their caricature of the detested English – uncaring, arrogant, always convinced of their own rightness ('there is no alternative'), possessed of an accent that grates on Scottish ears, and affluent enough to afford a retirement home costing around £500,000. She is also associated with the conspicuously 'yuppie'/affluent South-East and the City. These are bitter images for Scots well aware of such stark contrasts offered in Scotland by high unemployment, pockets of appalling social deprivation in the major urban areas, and reared in a culture where Scottish Protestantism, while not denigrating the accumulation of wealth, has always emphasised distaste for the flouting of its manifestations.[4]

Sir Malcolm Rifkind talked about Mrs Thatcher as a woman who fell victim to the strongly masculine, if not misogynist, culture of Scottish politics at the time: 'She was a woman; she was an English woman; she was a bossy English woman ... Combined with the cut-glass voice and an apparently patronising manner, they were lethal [together].'[5] George Younger in 1993, another Cabinet colleague, agreed that 'Scots, even socialists, expect women to keep their place. Everyone who ever canvassed during her time experienced the coarse and uncivilised abuse about "that bloody woman".'[6]

Few aspects of the Thatcher years in the modern history of Scotland are immune from the scholarly vices of myth, partiality, bias and stereotype. But there is a more authentic record behind the posturings and exaggeration that can be assembled from her memoirs, correspondence, policies and recollections of colleagues.

When Mrs Thatcher assumed power in 1979 there was much in Britain that she passionately disliked and was determined to 'reform' or even destroy. Socialism was the visceral enemy, the political creed that in her view had brought Britain to its knees by its excesses in the 1960s and 1970s. She was also determined to exact revenge on the National Union of Mineworkers, not perhaps immediately but when a suitable opportunity presented itself. They and their trade union allies were 'the enemy within' who had humiliated the Heath government in which she had served as a minister. Margaret Thatcher also regarded local councils with ill-concealed contempt. The country's economy could only be radically reformed by liberation from state control and from feather-bedding subsidies that would release energies to stimulate individualism, ambition and self-help. Britain's vast social security budget she regarded as a mechanism for transferring the hard-won earnings of taxpayers to the undeserving and indolent. In addition, as was confirmed by Mrs Thatcher's leadership during the Falklands War of 1982 and her diplomatic role in Europe, she was a doughty fighter in the British interest. But that commitment usually failed to acknowledge any real awareness of distinction or difference between the nations of the UK, except, of course, for one of them. At a later date, the former Scottish Tory Chairman, Michael Ancram, was reminded by the Prime Minister, 'Michael, I am an English nationalist and never you forget it.'[7]

As an arch-unionist, she took the view that the issue of Scottish devolution had been finally settled by the failure of the legislation of 1979. There was now no need for any further discussion. On that point she was absolutely resolute, even when later in her premiership the Scottish question did surface again. Nine years after her first election triumph she had not budged an inch on the devolution issue. When the 1988 Scottish Conservative Party Conference in Perth dismissed reconsideration of devolution by 300 votes to 11 (a delegate produced stickers advocating the immediate expulsion of the 11), the Prime Minister rose to the occasion: 'As long as I am Leader of this Party,' she declared to rapturous applause, 'we shall defend the Union and reject a devolved legislature unequivocally.'[8] The economic policies of her successive governments were intended to be implemented across all parts of the UK without fear or favour. The strategy was to be pan-British; all nationalities and regions were required to take the same medicine because, for Mrs Thatcher, the UK was a unitary state. She also faced other challenges in Scotland since her natural support base in the middle classes was numerically weaker than in the south of England, and the skilled and semi-skilled Scottish working classes, who were even more crucial to her electoral successes there, were more inclined to vote Labour north of the border than Tory.

Almost everything in the new Prime Minister's personal and political agenda represented a comprehensive challenge to Scottish society. Scotland was a nation with a long and proud history that had entered into joint union with England in 1707. Its people were not likely to take kindly to being treated like any other region of Britain, especially during a time of serious recession, and with a population accustomed to a post-war consensus favouring full employment guaranteed by the intervention of a benevolent state. The enduring stability of the Union was based historically in large part on Westminster's traditional recognition of Scottish nationhood and identity, and a balanced partnership between Scotland and England within the Union state. The welfare reforms of the Labour government of the 1940s had also been welcomed with great enthusiasm by Scots after the miserable experiences of the 1930s. The experience of administrative devolution from the Scottish Office was seen as very beneficial, not least interventions in the industrial sphere where nationalization and state subsidy had kept the great staples of the economy afloat as they became increasingly battered by the harsh winds of international competition. Moreover, the long hegemony of Labour Party influence in Scotland at both national and local levels had been in place since the 1960s. Socialism north of the border thereafter had been advancing and not in any way contracting. The trade unions were also well entrenched in Scottish mining and manufacturing, a sector that itself formed a larger part of the economy in 1979 than elsewhere in the UK.

The public sector was also very significant as an employer north of the border. By 1980, one in three Scots worked in central or local government. The Barnett formula for the distribution of government spending to the nations and regions of Britain allocated around 20 per cent more to Scotland on an annual basis than the UK average. Only Ulster, with its special political circumstances, did better. This largesse partly reflected the success of the relentless campaigns in Cabinet conducted by the former Labour Secretary of State, Willie Ross, in his continuous efforts to gain enhanced financial support for Scotland during the halcyon years for government expenditure in the UK. Then there was the national question. Despite the failure of the Scottish Assembly legislation in 1979, a substantial proportion of the electorate had still voted for the proposition, not least in the industrial districts of the west of Scotland. Devolution had certainly been temporarily sidelined as an issue in Scottish politics for some years afterwards, but the constitutional question had not gone away.

It is abundantly clear, therefore, that there was considerable potential for deep conflict between the Prime Minister's beliefs, the likely future shape of the policies of her government, and the realities of contemporary Scottish society. The battle lines were clearly drawn, both politically and ideologically, from the start of Mrs Thatcher's premiership. Yet few could have predicted the scale, bitterness and duration of the hostilities that eventually broke out.

At first, surprisingly, relative peace reigned on all fronts. The Conservatives made a modest recovery in Scotland in the 1979 general election by increasing their share of the vote from 24.7 per cent in October 1974 to 31.3 per cent, a better result than the SNP had achieved five years earlier. Throughout the UK there was also the feeling that something, perhaps even drastic in nature, had to be done about the endemic problems of high inflation, perennial balance of payments crises, and the effects of trade union militancy. If the decline of Britain was ever to be reversed, resolute action by the government might be imperative. Rising unemployment and the first evidence of de-industrialization were already apparent before Mrs Thatcher set foot in 10 Downing Street. They did not begin with the new Conservative administration. In her address to the Scottish Conservative Party Conference of May 1979, she made reassuring noises and acknowledged that government had a duty to ease the harsher effects of economic change, while noting that Scotland indeed had its own special problems of a decline in manufacturing and a rise in unemployment. There was, however, an important qualification:

> While we see no benefit in pouring vast sums of taxpayers' money into
> firms or industries which have no future, or which lack the will to

adapt to the new demand of their customers, we will certainly not turn a blind eye to industries which need assistance to overcome the problems of transition – we will be prepared to help them along the way as long as there is a real prospect of success.[9]

George Younger, Secretary of State for Scotland and MP for Ayr, was a patrician Tory of the old school. Emollient in personality and conscious of the political sensitivities in Scotland, 'Gentleman George' was able to smooth out some of the harder edges of Thatcherite dogma as they affected the country. Rarely dictatorial, he and his colleagues in the Scottish Office for some years did much to protect Scottish economic and social interests from the harsher pronouncements emanating from Downing Street. For instance, when the government decided to sell its share in Ferranti, the successful Scottish electronics company, Younger and his ministerial team managed to water down the wishes of 'the true believers' in Cabinet and ensured that 50 per cent of the firm's shareholding would be placed with Scottish financial institutions and not with the highest bidder. Other early victories involved support for the engineering company Weir Group, based in Glasgow, and ensuring that the Department of Trade referred two potential takeover bids for the Royal Bank of Scotland to the Monopolies and Mergers Commission. The Scottish Office also had a key role to play in defending and protecting the historically high public-spending levels in Scotland that remained broadly unchanged by the time Mrs Thatcher left office in 1990. All this did not go down at all well, however, with the zealots in the Thatcher camp. Radical right-wing think tanks, such as the Adam Smith Institute, recommended the abolition of the Scottish Office in order to ensure that Scotland was no longer sheltered from the full impact of the 'New Realism'.

The unpopularity of the government in Scotland soon became apparent. The strict adherence to policies of 'sound money' in the early 1980s had a devastating effect on Scottish industry as interest rates spiralled to astronomical levels in a determined effort to squeeze out the evils of inflation from the system once and for all. But even this did not destroy Tory electoral credibility in the short term. Scotland like the rest of Britain was influenced by the 'Falklands factor' in the general election of 1983, which was held in the aftermath of British victory in the South Atlantic in June 1982. Some scholars doubt the impact of that war on Scottish opinion. Certainly, the Scottish press, including the tabloids, were nowhere near as jingoistic as in England. The best-selling *Daily Record*, for instance, avoided triumphalism of the *Sun* variety and instead called for UN intervention to broker a peace. However, vocal public opposition to the conflict, in contrast to the later Iraq War, was uncommon. As the Labour politician Brian Wilson recalled of that time, 'there has always been a market in Scotland for a patriotic war'.[10] The size of the audiences for radio and television programmes devoted to the conflict differed little from the interest shown south of the border. Whatever the reason, the Conservative vote held up in Scotland with the retention of 21 seats compared to 22 in 1979, while both Labour and the SNP lost support. The Nationalists still languished in electoral irrelevance with two seats. Almost certainly, however, the Thatcher government would have been in more serious trouble but for North Sea oil revenues, which helped to cover much of the costs of rising unemployment and social security benefits as the recession deepened.

II

The crucial period of Scottish alienation from the policies and persona of Mrs Thatcher and her governments were the years after 1983. Even before the next general election of 1987 the omens were not good. The Conservatives reached their lowest-ever ebb in Scotland in the regional council elections of May 1986. Even traditional areas of Tory loyalty in rural Scotland began to desert the cause. An extrapolation of the results to parliamentary constituencies showed that the vast majority of Scottish Conservative MPs would be at risk of losing their seats. Soon afterwards, one opinion poll showed four out of five Scots were dissatisfied with Mrs Thatcher as Prime Minister. Of those who had voted Tory in 1983, but did not intend to do so again, Mrs Thatcher herself was given as the third influential reason for their decision after unemployment and pensions.

In June 1987 her party won another landslide majority, especially in the south of England. Scotland, northern England and Wales were not so enthusiastic. The Conservatives lost 11 seats north of the border, leaving them with a mere 10 MPs out of the 72 in Scotland. As recently as 1970 the Conservatives had held 23 Scottish seats. Several top Tory scalps were taken, including those of the Scottish education and housing ministers. George Younger, the former Scottish Secretary and now at Defence, scraped home in Ayr after several recounts. The result was very significant because it confirmed the growing divergence between Scottish voting patterns and those elsewhere in the UK. The argument now began to be heard that the Tories had no mandate in Scotland and that the nation was suffering from a profound democratic deficit as it consistently voted Labour in large numbers but ended up with Conservative administrations in Westminster. The Conservatives' so-called 'Doomsday Scenario', whereby they increased their majority in England but were soundly defeated in Scotland, had become reality. Constitutionally, of course, as she stressed more than once, Mrs Thatcher had the authority to govern Scotland whatever the number of her MPs there. But political legitimacy is different from constitutional legitimacy and is a sine qua non for stable government. It was also becoming increasingly difficult to staff the Scottish Office with suitable numbers from the dwindling band of Scottish-based MPs.

Pundits and politicians of all parties now began to try to read the runes of the Tory humiliation in Scotland. Predictably the abrasive and controversial personality of the Prime Minister was at the top of the list. One historian who was sympathetic to nationalism, Christopher Harvie, exclaimed of 'that bloody woman': 'Thatcher seemed to be hated so intensely north of the border because she personified every quality we have always disliked in the English: snobbery, bossiness, selfishness and, by our lights, stupidity.'[11] The use of such non-academic language highlighted the anger and frustrations of the times. It was clear that given her popularity in many parts of England, the Prime Minister was unlikely to depart the scene in the near future. Her dominance of the Conservative Party was complete. She had delivered three successful general election victories and had become a veritable icon for most of the Tory voting electorate south of the border. For many Scots the problem was that not only had she been going on for so long, but there seemed little hope that her premiership would come to an end any time soon. A year after the election, an opinion poll showed that only one in ten Scottish voters agreed with the statement 'the Prime Minister had the best interests of Scotland at heart', whereas three-quarters of those polled thought she treated 'the Scots as second-class citizens'. The Tory brand was becoming toxic and the party increasingly beyond the pale in Scotland. The country first became in part 'a Tory-free zone' in June 1989 when the party lost its remaining MEPs in the elections to the European Parliament, polling even below the SNP. Tactical voting was now popular, though with debatable results, in order to remove all Scottish Tories from their seats at future UK general elections as well as those for Europe.

Despite the assertions of her many critics, then and since, the historical record demonstrates that Margaret Thatcher was capable of some compromises in relation to Scottish issues. She did not rein in the Scottish Office under George Younger when some of her policies were softened for Scottish appetites. She was prepared to provide a temporary subsidy for the Invergordon aluminium smelter, though the offer was not taken up and the works closed in 1981. Thatcher spared the mighty Ravenscraig steelworks in Motherwell, which could produce 3 million tonnes of steel a year in an economy where demand never exceeded 2 million. In Thatcherite dogma, such an archetypal lame duck was an obvious candidate for closure. Nevertheless, she accepted the argument that estimated job losses of more than 10,000 were unacceptable. The labour force did decline in number but it fell to another Conservative government, under John Major, to finally wield the axe of execution. Other red lines that Mrs Thatcher did not cross included Mortgage Interest Tax Relief, rail privatization and the NHS. Also, despite some initial enthusiasm, she shelved the so-called *Omega Report* that called for replacement of the NHS by a system of private health insurance, an end to state funding of universities, and much more in the same vein, in what can only be described as a free marketeer's ultimate wish list.

But by the later 1980s even Thatcher's colleagues observed more inflexibility in her approach, which ultimately led to her downfall. Her response to the Scottish vote in 1987 was brazen defiance, a confidence that was hardly surprising. She had seen off both General Galtieri of Argentina and the once invincible National Union of Mineworkers, and had achieved landslide victories in England. There may have been more than a sense that elections could be won in the UK without bothering to think about the support of the troublesome Scots. Anyway, north of the border the forces of opposition to the Thatcher administrations were impotent. Labour and the SNP hated one another. Support for the SNP was also becalmed, while no matter the number of seats that Labour managed to win, it could do little within the law to halt or even constrain the Tory juggernaut.

For the Prime Minister, the onset of hubris had now become more of a probability than a possibility. She was in disbelief that Scots could take advantage of her 'right to buy' council house policies and yet at the same time turn against the party that had delivered them. Equally perplexing was that Scottish economic recovery, evident from the end of 1987, was not garnering votes for the Tories: 'Judged by cold statistics,' she observed at the Scottish Conservative Party Conference in May 1988, 'Scots enjoy greater prosperity than anywhere in the United Kingdom outside the crowded, high-priced South East.'[12] There was little awareness that her policies had alienated other sections of Scottish society well beyond her trade union enemies, including staff in the health services, the Educational Institute of Scotland and the universities. Now the latter began to have second thoughts about their opposition to devolution in 1989. Universities became subject to a new regime of vigorous external accountability, research assessment and reductions in grants. Student numbers rose by a quarter between 1978–9 and 1988–9 while staff to student ratios fell to 14:1 from 8:1. Some institutions suffered grievously. The 500-year-old University of Aberdeen endured a savage round of cuts under a vice-chancellor whose academic profession, ironically, was surgery. More than 200 redundancies were the result as well as the closure of six arts-faculty departments. Not surprisingly, the Scottish principals, who had been overwhelmingly against devolution of university financial control from London to Edinburgh in 1979, now became eager and enthusiastic converts to the idea when it was mooted again in 1991.

Mrs Thatcher became more abrasive, patronizing, defiant and even cocky in equal measure as she chided the recalcitrant Scots. She regularly invoked the stars of the Scottish Enlightenment, such as Adam Smith and David Hume, as the original progenitors of the free-market ideas that the Tories had then embraced in the late twentieth century. The 'Claim of Right' published by the Campaign for a Scottish Assembly in July 1988, was summarily dismissed as devolutionary 'mumbo jumbo'. The perception of the Conservatives as 'an English party' strengthened. A future Scottish Conservative leader, David McLetchie, spoke for many of his colleagues when he expressed insightfully in 1989:

> I believe that the perception of the Conservatives as an English-based and English-run party is the biggest single factor in our current standing in Scotland. In my experience, all Scots are nationalists with a small 'n' at heart and we have ignored this at our peril.[13]

A new conventional wisdom was now embraced by some of the Prime Minister's more radical supporters. The answer to the paradox of rising living standards and rising opposition to the Conservative Party was that the Scots, inured to decades of socialism, were still locked in a dependency culture from which they awaited liberation. In January 1986 the emollient George Younger in the Scottish Office was replaced by Malcolm Rifkind and Michael Forsyth, a junior minister. Forsyth was known as a zealot, a 'true believer' in Thatcherism, who was once described as 'Thatcher in drag'. Brian Wilson, from the Labour perspective, scorned the Scottish Tory Party. It was:

> ageing and disorganised in the constituencies, took on the air of a political freak show in its public demeanour – and an increasingly hard-hearted right-wing one at that. Mrs Thatcher's anointment of Michael Forsyth as the true face of her government in Scotland was one of her biggest provocations.[14]

When Forsyth became Minister for Education and Health in 1987, he vigorously pursued a strategy of appointing ideological supporters of the government to the committees and quangos of the Scottish Office, which advised on a range of important matters and which had hitherto jealously guarded their professional autonomy. Forsyth saw this as essential to the success of the free-market revolution and the destruction of the corporatist consensus. But his opponents saw the strategy as an intolerable undermining of independent bodies for reasons of party-political advantage and a sinister confirmation of the inexorable centralization of power taking place under the Tories.

Increasingly, the problem of governance in Scotland began to be seen not simply as rooted in Thatcherism but instead derived from the very nature of the British constitutional system itself. Mrs Thatcher, far from accepting her rejection at the Scottish polls and adjusting her policies, concluded that only a further dose of market reforms would finally wean the Scots away from bad habits grounded in 'a dependency culture'. This message was driven home by her Chancellor, Nigel Lawson, on a visit to Scotland. He argued that whole areas of Scottish life were 'sheltered from market forces and exhibit a culture of dependence rather than that of enterprise'. The Scottish edition of the *Sun* put over Lawson's point of view in its own inimitable style: 'Will you stop your snivelling, Jock?' At the same time a number of English Conservative backbenchers started to attend Scottish debates in Parliament and took the opportunity to criticize vociferously the scale of public expenditure in Scotland doled out through what one MP termed the 'slush fund' of the Scottish Office, which, of course, at that time, was controlled by the government that they supported.

A fascinating and revealing insight into the views about Scotland held by some of Mrs Thatcher's intimate circle at this time was given in a hard-hitting interview to the journalist Kenneth Roy by Sir John Junor. Junor was the Scots-born editor of the *Sunday Express*, a 'true believer', a friend of both Margaret and Denis Thatcher and a regular guest at Downing Street. He did not mince his words:

> If there is a dislike of Mrs Thatcher among the Scots, it's for two or three reasons. One is that the Scots are a male chauvinist race, and not any longer particularly intelligent, because most of the best people have left Scotland. They are also a whingeing people, which they never used to be . . . they have made a mess of industry. They've buggered up shipbuilding, they've buggered up the motor car industry . . . Margaret Thatcher's too damned good for you all. And you resent her because she's got this upper class or simulated upper class Edinburgh accent [*sic*]. And you resent also the fact that she's pulling you out of the shit that you've put yourself into over so many years.[15]

And then there was the introduction of the poll tax . . .

III

The Community Charge, better known as the 'Poll Tax', became law in Scotland on April Fool's Day, 1989. It was designed to replace the rates as a funding source for local government. The change would be a flat-rate levy, payable by all adults in a local-authority area for services provided. The government argued that it would ensure spendthrift councils could be held in check by being made accountable to a much wider section of the community. The Prime Minister christened it 'the flagship of the Thatcher fleet' and it was expected to be a sure-fire vote winner. Instead, it ignited a political firestorm, provoking widespread anger and protest in Scotland and then serious rioting south of the border. The fear of a Conservative electoral meltdown in England eventually killed off the poll tax. But the disaster took place on Mrs Thatcher's watch and became a major factor in her own eventual demise. Sir Malcolm Rifkind, Secretary of State for Scotland in her government, later judged the poll tax as 'the greatest political mistake of her premiership'.[16]

The introduction of the poll tax in Scotland was the policy more than any other which convinced many Scots that they were being ruled by an alien government. Before it even became law, the leaders of the three largest Scottish Churches condemned the tax unequivocally as 'undemocratic, unjust, socially divisive and destructive of community and family life'.[17] Its unfairness was transparent as the tax took no account of the ability to pay. Even the poll taxes in Scotland of the later seventeenth century at least did that. Moreover, it seemed that yet again the popular will north of the border had been treated with contempt, as the measure was imposed by an English Tory majority in Westminster in the teeth of bitter opposition from all other parties, local government and professional opinion. Yet, irony of ironies, this was not an example of Tory Scotophobia. Instead, the poll tax was a Scottish invention and fully deserved the description 'made in Scotland' both in its design and early introduction by Scottish local authorities.

Much of the original idea came from academics and former students of the University of St Andrews, some of whom came together to form the Adam Smith Institute, the free-market think tank. A former lecturer there and leader of the Tory group on Kirkcaldy town council, Douglas Mason, became the self-styled 'father of the poll tax'. Moreover, its introduction was triggered by a looming crisis in Scottish local-authority finance. The last revaluation of the domestic rates had been in 1978 and another could not be long delayed since it was a legal obligation to hold one every four years. This duly went ahead in 1984 and the results were published the following year. It was clear that the average rateable value of Scottish households would increase by a spectacular 260 per cent. This news led to an almighty explosion of anger among Tory ratepayers who soon vented their fury on local associations, MPs and ministers. This outcry convinced Mrs Thatcher that 'her people' had had enough. The rates had long been a bête noire of the Conservatives in Scotland. The government had progressively cut the block grant to local authorities and introduced 'capping'. In response, however, some councils simply put up the rates to balance the books. Inevitably, this hit property owners hardest, who were believed to be Tory voters to a man and woman, not least because the proportion of homeowners north of the border was much smaller than in England. Hence, the burden on the few was all the greater. The view also was that Labour authorities used income from the rates to subsidize the rents of council-house tenants in order to buttress their loyalties to the Labour Party.

The usual suspects, such as *Radical Scotland*, railed against the decision to implement the poll tax as an alternative to the rates as another 'alien' imposition from the Thatcher government in London. The fact that the tax was to be introduced in Scotland a year earlier than the rest of the country was thought to confirm that the Scots were to be used as 'guinea pigs' for a Tory policy imposed by an uncaring and anti-Scottish government. Nothing could be further from the truth. Not only was the idea of the tax incubated in Scotland, but it was Scottish ministers who were desperate to enforce it as soon as was possible in order to avoid a ferocious electoral backlash from their own supporters who were nearing a state of insurrection. Even the Chancellor of the Exchequer, Nigel Lawson, urged caution, but his voice was drowned out amid the panic-stricken pleadings from the Scottish Office. As Sir Malcolm Rifkind, the then Scottish Secretary, later admitted:

The Poll Tax was a quite different matter. The policy was hers [Margaret Thatcher's] but the political misjudgements about the timing of the introduction of the legislation in Scotland, a year ahead of England, were not her responsibility but that of George Younger and, subsequently mine when I succeeded him at the Scottish Office.[18]

The Prime Minister was able to triumphantly announce the poll tax as a replacement for the rates at the Scottish Conservative Party Conference in May 1987. The announcement was greeted with ecstatic applause. The revolt had been defused. Mrs Thatcher proudly declared: 'It was in response to your needs in Scotland that we finally decided on the introduction of the community charge.'[19]

The Scottish people as a whole gave her no credit for responding to their 'needs'. Quite the contrary. The poll tax came to be regarded, despite its history, as the most infamous act of the Thatcher governments, further cementing her now established reputation as an anti-Scottish, uncaring and a divisive leader who looked after the interests of the rich rather than of the population as a whole. Looking back on the affair, the Labour MP and a future minister Brian Wilson recalled the reactions of the opposition:

At first, the 'abolition of rates' was hailed as a political masterstroke. But it did not take long before the full horrors of the Poll Tax with all its administrative absurdities and gross inequities became apparent. For the Tories' opponents in Scotland, it was manna from heaven. It conveniently encapsulated the contempt in which the Thatcher regime held any remotely egalitarian principle such as 'ability to pay'. Its introduction was an act of political triumphalism in which an all-powerful government would steam-roller over all rational arguments in order to create a system which revelled in its own inherent unfairness.[20]

IV

One Scottish political commentator several years later identified what he saw as 'the first cardinal rule of Scottish politics' post-Thatcher, 'namely to vilify, degrade and denounce Thatcher and Thatcherism with every word in your vocabulary, while being influenced, shaped and following in her footsteps'.[21] As it was during her premiership, the Thatcher legacy in Scotland continues to provoke controversy and debate.

Some things, however, seem reasonably clear. The old industrial economy of Scotland was dying before Mrs Thatcher became Prime Minister and would have come to an end if her governments had never existed, though perhaps more slowly and with less pain. Whether Margaret Thatcher can be regarded as the midwife of the Scottish Parliament is a moot point because devolution had been on the political agenda for a decade before she entered Downing Street. The SNP might have been an electoral irrelevance during the Thatcher years, but nationalism had not gone away. The experience of Thatcherism, however, undoubtedly put more steel into the movement for home rule and ensured that its achievement would come sooner rather than later.

The de-industrialization over which Mrs Thatcher presided was not unique to Scotland. The north of England, Midlands and Wales also experienced its many ravages, as did other parts of the developed world. Yet opposition to Thatcherism did not trigger much increased enthusiasm for home rule among the Welsh. The distinctive factor in Scotland was probably that her policies were increasingly regarded as a threat to Scottish identity. The centralizing approach of her governments and their refusal to compromise on key issues treated Scotland like any other region in the UK rather than as a nation. Virtually all the political traditions that had been built up over many generations and rendered the Union stable and secure were abandoned: sensitivity to Scottish interests, consultation on Scottish issues, and respect for Scotland's semi-autonomy with the Union state. Never since the aftermath of the last Jacobite rising in 1745 had an all-powerful Westminster intervened in Scottish affairs to such an extent. For many Scots this caused a deep crisis in the governance of the country.

Thus, Mrs Thatcher may not have begun the movement towards devolution, which would probably have grown anyway in due course if she had never existed, but her policies and the hostility they engendered guaranteed the creation of a Scottish Parliament. Many came around to the view that some form of constitutional protection had to be embedded for Scotland in domestic policy if the experience of the

1980s was not to be repeated by a future Westminster government with an equally massive majority. Crucially, the Labour Party, the only political force that could deliver devolution, now embraced it in a way that the party had not done in the 1970s. As an editorial in *Radical Scotland* put it in 1985, 'The case for an Assembly is also the case against Thatcher.'[22] Also of considerable political and constitutional significance was the impact of Thatcherism in hastening the long-term decline of the Conservative vote in Scotland. After the Labour landslide victory in 1997 under Tony Blair, the demise of the Conservatives was complete as the party was erased from the electoral map of the country. Not a single seat was held by a Scottish Tory MP after that general election, throughout the length and breadth of Scotland. Since the Conservatives were by tradition the most ardent and committed supporters of the Union, the annihilation of all their candidates in 1997 inevitably helped to further weaken political support for the Union state. As Michael Gove, the Scottish-born Conservative and government minister, noted that, by 1988 'You could only be a good Scot if you were pro-Parliament and anti-Thatcher; the three became one.'[23] There was, however, one aspect of the national question that was little mentioned in the public discourse outside the ranks of the SNP at this time – namely, independence for Scotland.

13

'There shall be a Scottish Parliament'*

I

The political scientist W. L. Miller concluded after a large-scale system-atic study had been completed at Glasgow University: 'The myth of a peculiarly Scottish political culture is just that, a myth.'[1] The research found that living in Scotland or England had no significant effect on issues of equality or liberty, especially when account was taken of social background. Scots *believed* themselves to be more egalitarian than the English, but their responses to questions on taxation and wel-fare suggested that this was not the case in reality.

What did distinguish the Scottish people, however, were identities not values. Since the early 1970s, the majority of Scots have identified themselves as Scottish not British or mainly Scottish rather than Brit-ish. The figure was as high as two-thirds in 1974, fell back to just over a half after the failure of the devolution proposals in 1979, but returned to a new peak in 1997 when the referendum of that year resulted in an overwhelming vote to establish a Scottish Parliament. In electoral terms the Thatcher years, when there was a sharp erosion of the unionist vote, were a crucial influence. The old Scottish Union-ist Party had always combined loyalty to Britain with a concern for Scottish heritage and interests. The 18 years of Thatcherite policies, however, redefined that 'unionist nationalism' as British nationalism, which despite being decisively rejected at the polls in Scotland, was consistently imposed north of the border. As Miller argued:

---

* The first clause of the Scotland Bill to establish a Scottish Parliament (1998). It was later embossed on the mace of the new legislature.

This allowed the SNP to depict unionist nationalism as not merely 'British nationalist' but as essentially 'English nationalist'. At least in party terms that was the 'death of unionism' in its historic form; and the assassin was Thatcher, not the Scottish public.[2]

Nevertheless, though the Conservatives may be seen as the principal villains of the piece, influences were running in parallel that also helped erode Britishness in Scotland over the long run as several of its old bastions and symbols began to lose some of their former authority and power.

The decline of Protestantism has already been described as a factor earlier in this book. But by the 1980s even the weakened Church of Scotland could no longer be relied upon to uncritically support the British state. By that decade, the leadership of the Church and many ministers had adopted left-wing sympathies and were appalled by the ravages caused by Thatcherism to some of the poorest communities. The tensions between government and Church were made manifest at the time of the famous 'Sermon on the Mound' when Margaret Thatcher addressed the General Assembly in Edinburgh in May 1988. She also attended the Scottish Cup Final between Celtic and Dundee United at Hampden Park. There she was literally shown the red card from the stands, which had been distributed before the match, and booed to the echo by the serried ranks of fans of both teams. Her visit to the Kirk had not been popular either. When news of it was released, the letter pages of several newspapers were crammed with missives denouncing the invitation. After she had delivered her speech in the Assembly Hall, the ministers and brethren clapped courteously but the general feeling was that the Prime Minister had tried to highjack Christian scripture for her own ideological purposes. A traditional bastion of unionism and Britishness was mortally offended.

Scottish loyalty to another major support of Britishness, the monarchy, had endured strongly after 1945. The coronation of Elizabeth II in 1953 was followed just as avidly on television in Scotland as in the rest of the UK. Public interest in the royal family, who always attended zealously and with an admirable sense of responsibility to their duties in Scotland, was still considerable when Prince Charles wed Lady Diana Spencer in 1981. But as in the rest of Britain, though there remains enormous respect for the current monarch, a noticeable decline in support for the institution itself has taken place. Some evidence suggests the fall has been steeper in Scotland than in the rest of the UK. When asked by *British Future* 'Are you very proud of the Queen?', 50 per cent of English respondents said 'Yes', compared with 15 per cent in Scotland. A total of 55 per cent of Scots compared with only 17 per cent of English answered that they were 'not proud'. The decline in deference across society since the 1960s, a series of royal scandals and press and media intrusion, have all affected the standing of the House of Windsor during this period.

The armed forces had helped to bind Scotland to the British nation since the later eighteenth century. The two world wars of the twentieth century were especially powerful engines buttressing Britishness. Even after 1945 a quarter of a million Scots continued to serve in the army. Respect and reverence for the dead of both world wars, the Korean War of the 1950s and subsequent conflicts, remain strong in Scottish society. The campaign to save the Argyll and Sutherland Highlanders in 2006 had huge public support and showed that the old traditions of Scottish militarism in the service of the British state had not disappeared. But the bonds have loosened. The end of conscription in 1963 was an important watershed but so too were mergers and suppressions of the famous old Scottish regiments. There were 11 of them in 1957. Today in 2015 only one survives, the Royal Regiment of Scotland, and its battalions. An authentically Scottish but also highly visible British institution has dramatically contracted as the UK has shed international responsibilities. The reach of the British armed forces into Scottish society has fallen to little more than around one in every hundred families, probably fewer than at any period in history since the Napoleonic Wars.

The UK Parliament, the very heart of the British political system, also came in for much criticism long before the reputational damage of the expenses scandals. The authority of Westminster was affected in the eyes of some because it came to be seen as the source of the obnoxious legislation of the 1980s that the majority of the electorate in Scotland firmly opposed. The Scots had continuously and overwhelmingly rejected the policies of the majority party in Parliament, but these votes seemed to count for little. For the first time since the early eighteenth century, questions were raised about the legitimacy of the institution. The notion of

the so-called 'democratic deficit', the impotence of the official opposition, and the apparent capacity of the governing party to pass deeply
unpopular legislation with its huge majority whenever it saw fit, were
very damaging. Pro-devolutionist rhetoric began to talk about the 'sovereignty of the Scottish people' that was being undermined by the
'absolute authority' of the 'Crown-in-Parliament'. One survey held in
Scotland in 1999 showed that the House of Commons was judged to be
'very important' by only around one-third of the electorate. Parliamentary authority was also likely to ebb as the European Union extended its
power, with some of the traditional attributes of a sovereign parliament
transferred to Brussels. European integration was much more advanced
by the later 1980s, with sovereignty shared far more than had been
imagined when Britain joined the European Economic Community in
1973. Globalization also proved a threat to the authority of all national
governments as the formidable resources of multinational companies,
some more powerful than nation states, grew ever more evident.

Some argue also that a potent Scottish cultural dynamic emerged in
the 1970s and 1980s which may also have accelerated the erosion of
Britishness. A simple roll call of celebrated names confirms the cultural exuberance of the period: in literature, Iain M. Banks, Willie
McIlvanney, Alasdair Gray and Liz Lochhead, to name but a few; in
art, Peter Howson, Ken Currie and Steven Campbell established international reputations; and pop music flourished with leading-edge
bands such as Simple Minds and Nazareth.

But despite the overall richness not much of this outpouring of
creativity had a direct bearing on the political sphere. Obvious excep-
tions to this generalization included The Proclaimers' 'Letter from
America' (1987), with its evocative memorialization of the sites of
de-industrialization linked to the Highland Clearances of the past;
the folk-song revival, which conveyed a deep and lyrical sense of
traditional Scottishness; the political theatre of John McGrath's 7:84
Company, especially The Cheviot, the Stag and the Black, Black Oil
(1973); and the novels of James Kelman and Irvine Welsh, particularly The Busconductor Hines (1984) and Trainspotting (1993),
depicting the alienation of youth, the drug culture, and lives broken
by economic transformation.

There were also refreshingly new perspectives on the Scottish past, which for the first time gave many Scots an awareness of the history of their country in the modern era. Not until the early years of the twenty-first century did the teaching of Scottish history start to become anything more than episodic and superficial in the nation's schools. Those educated before than had had to be mainly content with a diet of British, aka mainly English, and European history, and a mere sprinkling of Scottish topics. The fact that there was a large potential audience for a distinctive Scottish history was first confirmed by the runaway publishing success of the books by the journalist and screenwriter John Prebble. He was born in England in 1915 but emigrated to Canada for several years when he was a boy and grew up with tales of Scotland's history derived from his time living in a mainly Scottish township in rural Saskatchewan. His series of books included *Culloden* (1962), *The Highland Clearances* (1963), *Glencoe: The Story of the Massacre* (1966), *Darien: The Scottish Dream of Empire* (1968) and *Mutiny: Highland Regiments in Revolt* (1975). The then Historiographer Royal, Professor Gordon Donaldson of the University of Edinburgh, dismissed them contemptuously as 'utter rubbish'. Prebble himself admitted later that he never claimed to be a historian but rather a writer on themes and issues of the past.

Nonetheless, he did touch a chord in the reading public. His stories of the exploitation of the common man (he was a former Communist) chimed well with Scotland's move to the left in the post-imperial era of the 1960s. Prebble's Scotland was not a nation proudly associated with the glories of empire but rather a land of suffering, tragedy, loss and victimhood. By focusing on the tortured drama of Gaeldom during the era of Culloden and the Clearances he was also able to tap into the Highlandist tradition that had exerted such a grip on the Scottish psyche since the writings of Sir Walter Scott in the early nineteenth century. The first signs of SNP electoral success became apparent in the 1960s and 1970s and there was more than a hint of anglophobia in Prebble's oeuvre that did little to affect his sales adversely. It also helped that there was little competition in the popular modern Scottish history market at the time. Most earlier academic works had a unionist bias and were mainly designed for a scholarly readership. William Ferguson's more nuanced account of the modern nation from the late seventeenth century to the present, *Scotland: 1689 to the Present*, was only published in 1968. Above all, perhaps, Prebble could write in fluent and engaging prose that ensured a wide appeal. Not until 1969, and the appearance of Christopher Smout's *History of the Scottish People* in that year, was a university-based scholar able to achieve a similar impact with a readable text combining scholarship with accessibility.

The truth was that Scotland at that time did not possess a proper narrative of its historical development since the Union. Most high-quality academic research until the 1960s had tended to concentrate on the history of the independent nation before 1707. Little in the way of an alternative to the master narrative of British (English) historiography existed for later centuries. Indeed, in his inaugural lecture as the new Burnett-Fletcher Professor of History at Aberdeen University in 1962, John Hargreaves claimed that the history of modern Scotland was less studied than the history of Yorkshire.

But that neglect was soon and rapidly to come to an end. Later in the 1960s and 1970s, scholars of the calibre of Roy Campbell, Bill Ferguson, Malcolm Gray, Rowy Mitchison, Chris Smout, and several others, laid the foundations for what became a remarkable outpouring of monographs, textbooks and learned articles, all meticulously researched and presented. It was suggested that never since the Enlightenment of the eighteenth century had historical study in Scotland been so vibrant. By the end of the twentieth century, then, the country possessed a proper narrative of its modern past that could compete with that of any in Europe. The American political scientist Rogers Smith has argued that all political communities rely for their sense of identity on what he describes as a 'constitutive story', which explains what they are and where they came from. Only in the last quarter of the twentieth century was that constitutive story of modern Scotland being researched and written.

Of course, it would be absurd to suggest, for all the reasons noted above, that Britishness faced extinction by the turn of the new millennium. Scotland's dual identity within the Union state had been fashioned over centuries and was hardly likely to implode in the space of a few decades. That duality was inherently flexible, supple and pliant. At different times the pendulum would swing from Scottishness to Britishness and vice versa. In this period, too, independence was never seriously on the political agenda, and with the single exception of the SNP, the opposition parties were resolutely unionist. Indeed, devolution was seen not as an attempt to end the union relationship but rather a way of cementing the position of Scotland within the UK by recalibrating the terms of the Union in the changed political circumstances of the later twentieth century.

Yet it was a time when some of the traditional markers of the hybrid identity were being reinvented. Tartanry enjoyed a new vogue but in a different manner from the past and for a new audience. The 'Tartan Army' of Scottish football supporters became renowned for their wit and humour, the ability to laugh at themselves as the performance of the national team hit a new low, good behaviour on overseas trips, coupled with a capacity to consume alcohol in large quantities. The regimental prevention of any trouble-making within the ranks of 'the Army' was in part a ploy to differentiate themselves from English supporters who at the time were committing much-publicized mayhem and thuggery in European capitals when their national team were visitors. The national anthem of 'the Army' was no longer 'God Save the Queen' but rather the patriotic lament 'Flower of Scotland', which harked back to the medieval Wars of Independence against England. It was soon to become the song of choice at all Scottish national football and rugby matches.

Full tartan regalia, formerly sported mainly by toffs and gentry on occasion, was popularly reinvented as the badge of sartorial small 'n' nationalism. Soon there were few weddings, graduation ceremonies or other public celebrations in the land where men were not dressed in kilt, plaid and sporran. Alex Salmond, then leader of the SNP, recalled being the guest of honour at the final sixth-year dinner and dance at his old school, Linlithgow High. He observed that virtually all the boys were rigged out like Bonnie Prince Charlie. Salmond commented that if anyone turned up like that in his day they would have been taken to the boys' toilet and 'disciplined'.

While government buildings continued to fly the Union Jack, a transition to displaying the Scottish Saltire was already under way on other sites. Gordon Brown, the former Prime Minister and robustly effective champion of the Union during the referendum campaign of 2014, noted in his book *My Scotland, Our Britain* that 'Today it is hard to find Union Jacks flying in Scotland other than at UK government offices.' Indeed, by then probably one of the few non-governmental places in Scotland where the flag was widely displayed was on match days at Ibrox Park, Glasgow, home of Rangers FC, many of whose supporters remained ardent supporters of the Union, Queen and Protestantism. Gordon Brown also recalled attending a gala day in his Fife constituency:

> Waiting for the procession at the top of the hill, I could see the Saltire and Lion Rampant on display but not one Union Jack was in sight. This, a big change from a few years ago, is part of a pattern, not too dissimilar to the pictures I saw of a recent visit by the Queen to Edinburgh. A few years ago the flags on display in the Royal Mile would have been . . . Union Jacks mingling with the Saltire or the Lion Rampa[n]t. But not this time.

He was also a guest at a school prize-giving in Fife, where he was piped in to the tune of 'Highland Cathedral' and escorted by pupils resplendent in kilts and tartan. Brown observed that a casual visitor from the outside would have been struck by how there was nothing that could be considered remotely British about the occasion; no UK national anthem, no reference to the Queen and none to the UK Parliament. He concluded: 'We could easily have been living in a post-independence Scotland.'

II

A standing political joke of these years was that devolution was like evolution, only it takes longer. Certainly, at the end of 1979, the prospects for Home Rule for Scotland seemed as bleak as the future of the nation's traditional industries. Despite the fact that a narrow majority had voted in favour of devolution in the referendum, there was a sense of defeat and disillusion that a historic opportunity had not been embraced with more enthusiasm. But the Conservative victory in the 1987 general election gave galvanic new impetus to a still relatively moribund home-rule movement. After 1979 the torch for devolution had been kept alight by the Campaign for a Scottish Assembly (CSA), which aimed to deliver home rule by bringing together Labour, Liberal

Democrats, the SNP and representatives of Scottish civil society to plan a way forward. For most of the 1980s it was virtually a voice crying in the wilderness. After 1987, however, the CSA appointed a steering committee chaired by the distinguished academic, town planner and public servant Sir Robert Grieve, and composed of notables drawn from the Churches, trade unions, business and the universities. They were to consider the setting up of a Scottish Constitutional Convention to examine the case for an assembly and outline the measures that should be taken to achieve it. Labour was increasingly sympathetic. The 'doomsday scenario' of a mammoth Labour triumph in Scotland coinciding with another Tory victory in the UK in 1987 once again inspired the party with a new enthusiasm for devolution, not least because of fear that without it the voters would soon lose patience with the 'feeble fifty' Labour MPs and start to move their allegiance in a 'nationalist' direction. In addition, the 'modernization' of the Labour Party under Neil Kinnock was diluting the traditional commitment to central economic planning and nationalization, which in turn opened the door for a new approach to political devolution. The SNP had also recovered from the internal turmoil of the early 1980s. At its conference in 1988 the party unveiled the new flagship policy of 'Independence in Europe' and adopted the identity of a left-of-centre party through advocating a mass campaign of non-payment of the poll tax. By arguing for Scottish independence in Europe, the SNP sought to destroy the charge of separatism usually levelled against the Nationalists, while, by moving to the left, the party gave notice that it intended to take the fight into Labour's traditional heartlands and engage directly on its own political terrain. The party claimed an early success with this strategy in November 1988, when Jim Sillars took Govan from Labour in a by-election.

The CSA committee of 'prominent Scots' issued *A Claim of Right for Scotland* in 1988. The title of the document was intended to echo previous Scottish acts of resistance to the state when such 'claims' had been used to articulate opposition to the arbitrary monarchy of James II and VII in the 1680s and government interference in the Kirk in 1842 before the Disruption. The *Claim of Right*, published on 6 July 1988, was drafted by Jim Ross, a retired civil servant with long experience of the framing of devolution legislation in the 1970s. It combined historical analysis with a statement of the intellectual case for a Scottish assembly, together with the recommendation that a 210-strong constitutional convention should be established, consisting of MPs, representatives of councils, trade unions and the Churches, to discuss how home rule should be achieved. Perhaps the most striking feature of the document was its nationalist content with a small 'n'. It asserted, for instance, that 'The Union has always been, and remains, a threat to the survival of a distinctive culture in Scotland.' The *Claim of Right* went on to argue that, contrary to much received scholarly opinion at the time, the Scottish Enlightenment of the eighteenth century was not founded on the Union of 1707 but on indigenous Scottish roots and relationships with Europe.

Mrs Thatcher inevitably came in for scathing criticism and was accused of wielding more arbitrary power than virtually any English or Scottish monarch of the past. The key sections of the *Claim of Right* summarized the arguments why constitutional change was now both necessary and urgent. Scotland faced a crisis of identity and survival. It was now being governed without consent and subject to the declared intention of having imposed upon it a radical change of outlook and patterns of behaviour that it showed no sign of wanting. All questions as to whether consent should be a part of government decision-making were brushed aside. The comments of the Scottish economic sage Adam Smith were put to uses that would have astonished the great man. Scottish history was selectively distorted and the Scots were told that their votes were effectively lies – that they secretly loved the Tory policies against which they voted. The *Claim of Right* went on:

> Scotland is not alone in suffering from the absence of consent in government. The problem afflicts the United Kingdom as a whole. We have a government which openly boasts its contempt for consensus and a constitution which allows it to demonstrate that contempt in practice. But Scotland is unique both in its title to complain and in its awareness of what is being done to it.
>
> None of this has anything to do with the merits or demerits of particular policies at particular times, or with the degree of conviction with which people believe in these policies. Many a conviction politician contemptuous of democracy has done some marginal good in passing. Mussolini allegedly made the Italian trains run on time. The crucial questions are power and consent: making power accountable and setting limits to what can be done without general consent.

These questions will not be adequately answered in the United Kingdom until the concentration of power that masquerades as 'the Crown-in-Parliament' has been broken up. Government can be carried on with consent only through a system of checks and balances capable of restraining those who lack a sense of restraint. Stripping away the power of politicians outside Whitehall (and incidentally increasing the powers of Ministers inside Whitehall) restores power not to the people but to the powerful. The choice we are promised in consequence will in practice be the choice the powerful choose to offer us. Through effectively answerable representative institutions we can edit the choices for ourselves.

. . .

It is a sign of both the fraudulence and the fragility of the English constitution that representative bodies and their activities, the life-blood of government by consent, can be systematically closed down by a minority Westminster Government without there being any constitutional means of even giving them pause for thought. It is the ultimate condemnation of that constitution that so many people, in Scotland and beyond, have recently been searching in the House of Lords for the last remnants of British democracy.

Scotland, if it is to remain Scotland, can no longer live with such a constitution and has nothing to hope for from it. Scots have shown it more tolerance than it deserves. They must now show enterprise by starting the reform of their own government. They have the opportunity, in the process, to start the reform of the English constitution, to serve as the grit in the oyster which produces the pearl . . .

We are under no illusions about the seriousness of what we recommend. Contesting the authority of established government is not a light matter. We could not recommend it if we did not feel that British government has so decayed that there is little hope of its being reformed within the framework of its traditional procedures. Setting up a Scottish Constitutional Convention and subsequently a Scottish Assembly cannot by themselves achieve the essential reforms of British government, but they are essential if any remnant of distinctive Scottish government is to be saved, and they could create the ground-swell necessary to set the British reform process on its way. [3]

The Conservatives unsurprisingly declined to join the proposed Convention. However, Labour, the Liberal Democrats, 59 of Scotland's 65 regional, island and district councils, the STUC, the Scottish Churches, representatives of ethnic minorities, the Green and Communist parties and the Scottish Convention of Women did so. The crucial signatory was the Labour Party, as only it could deliver the majority in a UK election that alone could form the basis of legislation for devolution. The SNP, though at first interested, eventually did not take part. Many on the fundamentalist wing of the party feared the Convention would be dominated by Labour and also took the view that devolution would impede the movement to independence rather than facilitate it, especially since the by-election victory at Govan suggested that the SNP bandwagon was rolling once again. The absence of the SNP, however, may have made Labour more willing to make concessions than might otherwise have been the case. Under the joint chairmen, Sir David Steel, former Liberal leader, Harry Ewing, a former Labour devolution minister, and Canon Kenyon Wright, the chair of the executive committee, the Convention drew up a blueprint for a Scottish parliament. Malcolm Rifkind, then Secretary of State for Scotland, was reported to have said that 'if the disparate parties reached a common conclusion he would jump off the roof of the Scottish Office'. He was not held to his promise when, on St Andrew's Day 1990, the Convention unveiled its report that proposed a legislature elected under proportional representation, financed through 'assigned revenues' from taxes raised in Scotland.

In some ways the recommendations were vague and inconclusive. For instance, the principle of equal representation for women in the new parliament was agreed but the method of implementing it was not. Equally, the vexed question of Scottish representation at Westminster after devolution was not considered. Above all, the proposals could not be implemented until the robustly unionist Conservative administration was removed from office. Nevertheless, the work of the Convention was still important because by bringing Labour, the dominant party in Scotland, into the heart of the home-rule movement, the proposals made it politically difficult for any future Labour government to deny the Scots devolution. Equally, the vital concession of proportional representation was likely to make areas outside the Labour empire of the central Lowlands look more favourably on the concept of an Edinburgh parliament than had been the case in 1979. Finally, the political advances made in the Convention gave a further impetus to the whole movement for home rule. Its ideas may have engaged the interest of no more than a minority of the Scottish population (though there was considerable press comment), but even some of the silent majority were drawn to the defiant words of Kenyon Wright in response to the expected disapproval of the Iron Lady: 'What happens if that other voice we all know so well responds by saying, we say no. We say no and we are the state. Well we say yes and we are the people.' It was wonderful rhetoric, but only the success by the Labour Party in a UK general election could deliver the new parliament.

Ironically, in the same month in 1990 that the blueprint was produced by the Convention, Mrs Thatcher was forced to resign after the Conservative Party became increasingly split over Europe and its popularity plummeted as a result of the poll tax. A Tory defeat in a future UK general election looked more likely than at any period since the 1970s. By the time the new Prime Minister, John Major, called the election in the spring of 1992, devolution was once again a significant factor in Scottish political debate. Media expectations became almost frenzied after a *Scotsman* opinion poll in January 1992 suggested that 50 per cent of Scots actually favoured independence. Distinguished journalists predicted that there would be a Tory-free Scotland after polling day and the SNP released yet another over-optimistic slogan, 'Free by 1993'. The *Sun* thought it commercially worthwhile to back the SNP in its battle for readers with the other mass-circulation paper, the *Daily Record*. On 23 January the *Sun* unveiled its new-found nationalist enthusiasm to a bemused readership with the words 'Arise and be a Nation again' alongside a huge saltire. Even John Major made the defence of the Union the central theme of the last week of the election campaign. It seemed to the home-rule movement that at long last Scotland might indeed be approaching a historic watershed.

However, it was not to be. Major held on with a reduced majority and, far from the Tory vote collapsing in Scotland, there was a marginal increase in its share from 24 per cent to 25.6 per cent. Yet the fact remained that those parties advocating home rule or independence had won the support of 75 per cent of the electorate and 85 per cent of the seats in Scotland. This was not enough, however, for disenchanted nationalists like Jim Sillars, who, in his frustration at losing again, vented spleen on his fellow Scots by denouncing them as 'ninety-minute patriots' who had 'bottled out' at the crucial moment of decision. Sillars left politics and public life soon afterwards. The year 1992 was certainly not, as the SNP had hoped, the independence election and, while devolution remained unfinished business, the result was a major setback for the constitutional cause that had seen such progress since the late 1980s. As Andrew Marr commented, 'Those who live by the hype shall die by the hype.'[4] In retrospect, however, there had clearly been an overwhelming vote for those parties committed to constitutional change, and the Conservative performance seemed meritorious only when judged against earlier disastrous election results and the inflated expectations of nationalist politicians and some journalists. The party held its ground because John Major aroused less hostility in Scotland than Margaret Thatcher and because the menace of nationalism might well have stirred supporters of the Union to turn out in large numbers.

In the aftermath of the election, groups such as Scotland United, Common Cause and Democracy for Scotland tried to keep the spirit of home rule alive. The last of these was the most enduring and maintained a vigil outside the parliament building on Calton Hill until the referendum result in 1997. Common Cause brought some Scottish intellectuals together, while Scotland United, an alliance of politicians, novelists and pop stars, held two successful rallies and proposed a multi-option referendum on the constitution. These two organizations soon withered on the vine. But 'people power' was far from dead. It was demonstrated in December 1992 when 25,000 marched in Edinburgh during the summit meeting of European Community leaders, demanding democracy in Scotland, and even more emphatically when over 1 million people in the Strathclyde region, or 97 per cent of those who took part in the postal ballot, rejected the government's plans for water privatization in a postal ballot. This was not rioting in the streets, but it plainly articulated the strong opposition that still existed in Scotland to key aspects of Tory policy. The event that above all others was eventually to seal the fate of John Major's government and prepare the way for a landslide Labour victory in 1997 had already taken place in the first year of his term of office. This was Black Wednesday, 16 September 1992, when the UK had to withdraw from the European Exchange Rate Mechanism despite throwing many millions of pounds sterling into an abortive attempt to protect its position within it. This disaster was both a humiliation and an indictment of gross economic incompetence from which the Conservative government never recovered.

Yet in material terms Scotland was doing relatively well in this period. In 1993 and 1994 it had a marginally lower unemployment rate than the rest of Britain. In 1996 personal disposable income per head in Scotland was £9,100, only slightly lower than England's £9,140. By the early 1990s the Scottish economy, particularly in manufacturing output, was growing faster than the UK average. But the Tories were given little credit for any of these achievements. When the two-tier local-authority structure of regions and districts was dissolved in 1995, they failed to win control of a single local council. The government's problems seemed set to increase in Scotland in 1995 when Michael Forsyth was controversially appointed to succeed Ian Lang as Scottish Secretary after the latter had been promoted to a senior Cabinet position. However, before the eyes of an astonished nation, Forsyth metamorphosed from Thatcherite attack dog to Scottish patriot. He remained resolutely opposed to constitutional change, for that would imperil the Union, but all other assertions of Scottishness were to be embraced with enthusiasm. Forsyth wrapped himself in tartan – on one occasion literally, when he became perhaps the first Secretary of State for Scotland to appear in full Highland dress as he attended the premiere of the Holywood film *Braveheart*. The Tories introduced a new slogan, 'Fighting for Scotland', and Forsyth proceeded to carry off a spectacular coup of 'gesture politics' when he secured the return of the Stone of Destiny from Westminster Abbey in a ceremony that ranked as an especially fine and theatrical example of the invention of tradition. Plans were laid to boost the Scottish film industry and the Secretary of State even called for a Standard Grade course in Scottish history to remedy the deficiencies in the teaching of the subject in schools. But the real impact of all this flag-waving may be doubted because in the real world the government had still pressed ahead with the unpopular reform of local government and the extension of market principles in the health service. However, in one particular area Michael Forsyth did hit the target when he subjected Labour's new financial plans for a Scottish parliament to sustained attack.

The death in May 1994 of John Smith, MP for North Lanarkshire, the Labour leader who had succeeded Neil Kinnock in 1992, put a question mark against Labour's commitment to home rule. Smith's popularity in Scotland and elsewhere was unquestioned. Since the 1970s he had been a fervent advocate of devolution and in the Callaghan government was given responsibility for the legislative process to achieve it. His devolution credentials were therefore impeccable and when elected leader of the Labour Party he was fond of the assertion that the establishment of a parliament was now 'the settled will of the Scottish people'. It remained to be seen, however, whether home rule would survive the radical review of Labour policy undertaken by his successor, Tony Blair. In the event it did, though Blair's personal view of devolution always remained obscure. Labour gave support to the Constitutional Convention's proposal that the new parliament should be able to vary the basic rate of income tax by up to 3p in the pound. Michael Forsyth relentlessly targeted and attacked this arrangement. He recognized that the Labour Party was exposed on the taxation issue and was absolutely determined to rid itself of the old 'tax and spend' reputation if it was ever to return to office. For Forsyth and other Tory spokespersons, the revenue-varying powers were nothing other than a 'tartan tax' imposed on the Scottish people simply for being Scottish. The attack struck home and the Labour response sent tremors through the ranks of those who had long campaigned for home rule. To the outrage of its partners in the Convention and the fury of many of its own supporters in Scotland, the Shadow Cabinet decided in June 1996 that a general election victory was not in itself sufficient for such a momentous constitutional reform. Instead, a referendum should also be held to secure the creation and continuation of a parliament. Moreover, two separate questions would be posed, one on the principle of a parliament and another on its tax-raising powers. Critics saw this as an attempt to dilute the essential but limited financial powers without which the parliament would be stripped of all economic authority. Suspicion abounded that Blair was now intent on ditching the whole devolution project.

In the event, all this mistrust proved unfounded. Labour's landslide victory in May 1997 was soon followed by the promise of a referendum on 11 September. The omens for a successful outcome looked good, though the tragic death of Diana, Princess of Wales, in a car accident in Paris on 31 August meant that effective campaigning had to be confined to a short and hectic period of about one hundred hours. But the pro-home rule camp was united as never before. Under its pragmatic leader, Alex Salmond, the SNP campaigned as vigorously as did Labour and the Liberal Democrats, under Donald Dewar and Jim Wallace respectively. The opposing camp was weak by comparison. Scottish business, which had vociferously condemned devolution in 1979, was mainly silent. The one high-profile critic, Sir Bruce Pattullo, Governor of the Bank of Scotland, was vigorously condemned from several quarters and some of his customers threatened to move their accounts elsewhere. On the other hand, other major Scottish companies, such as the insurance giants Standard Life and Scottish Widows, declared they were comfortable with the proposals. 'Think Twice', the anti-devolution campaign, had few of the financial resources or personalities of the organizations that had opposed devolution in 1979. Then, when Mrs Thatcher decided to intervene and give 'Think Twice' her public support, the fate of the 'No' campaigners was effectively sealed.

When the results were declared, 74.3 per cent of those who voted supported a Scottish parliament and 63.5 per cent agreed that it should have tax-varying powers. Unlike in 1979, there was clear support in all regions, though Orkney and Shetland voted against the tax powers and the majorities were lowest in those regions that had been hostile in the 1979 referendum. Nevertheless, it seemed that the result was indeed the 'settled will' of the Scottish people. The parliament that had now been resoundingly approved would have power over all matters apart from foreign policy, defence, macro-economic policy, social security, abortion and broadcasting. It could raise or lower the basic rate of tax by 3p, or £450 million in total. Although Westminster would continue to have responsibility for relations with Europe, there would also be a Scottish representative office in Brussels and Scottish ministers could be expected to take part in the UK delegation to the EU Council of Ministers. The elections in May 1999 were by a form of proportional representation and, because the legislation only specified the powers to be reserved to Westminster, it enabled the new body to develop a potentially wider role in support of Scottish interests.

III

Delivering the White Paper on devolution and the subsequent parliamentary bill was the work of many hands. But a central figure in the process was Donald Dewar. Dewar was exactly the right man in the right place at the right time. When appointed he was Secretary of State for Scotland in the new Blair government of 1997. It is difficult to think of any other senior Labour politician who had the same commitment, background, stature or aptitude to deliver devolution. Dewar's pro-devolution credentials were well known and went back as far as his student days at Glasgow University, much longer even than his friend and close colleague, the late John Smith. Lord James Gordon recalled the Scottish Labour Party conference of 1970 that followed soon after the loss of Hamilton to the SNP in 1967 and further SNP success in the local elections in 1968. These Labour defeats, in Gordon's words, 'sent shockwaves through the party which made any rational discussion of devolution seem almost traitorous'.[5] Only two Labour MPs spoke out in favour of giving some consideration to constitutional change: Dewar and the late professor of politics and charismatic politician, John P. Mackintosh. Mackintosh's early death in July 1978 left Dewar virtually alone for some years as an enthusiastic standard bearer of home rule. Too many in the Labour Party in the 1970s either opposed the whole idea of devolution or saw it merely as a tactical ploy to see off the nationalist advance.

Furthermore, Dewar was an interesting mix of loyal unionist and cultural nationalist. His interest in and knowledge of Scottish history and culture were formidable. Forging the link between the Scottish past and the Scottish present came easily to him, as he revealed in his eloquent address at the opening of the Scottish Parliament on 1 July 1999, a speech replete with historical reference and allusion. Equally important, however, was his unionism. Under Dewar, Scottish devolution could never be a nationalist project, a stepping-stone on the road to an independent future. Home rule was meant to strengthen the Union rather than weaken it. Donald Dewar's staunch unionism helped to ease the fears of those in Westminster who suspected the whole scheme was designed to appease the nationalists and might eventually threaten a break-up of the United Kingdom.

Finally, Dewar was one of the few senior Labour politicians who could work the system both in London and Scotland. Linkage between the two was essential to the rapid and effective delivery of devolution legislation after 1997. Dewar was a respected House of Commons man and his time as a Labour Whip had ensured that he was well connected at Westminster. But his knowledge of the Scottish scene and reputation there as a political 'fixer' within the Labour Party were also important assets. Dewar, above all his peers, does seem to have had a long-term commitment to home rule and a focus on its delivery. His political opponent Malcolm Rifkind noted that:

> Donald Dewar often seemed a rather lonely figure not because his colleagues in the Shadow Cabinet disagreed with him [about constitutional reform] but because they could not be bothered to spend much time on the issue. Gordon Brown, Robin Cook and John Reid were far more concerned with trying to demolish Margaret Thatcher or John Major than with the campaign for constitutional reform in Scotland. This was not just because the key to reform lay with winning power at Westminster. It also reflected their own political ambitions. As we saw when the Parliament at Holyrood was created, only Donald made the trek north. Every other of his Cabinet colleagues opted to remain at Westminster.

It was perhaps inevitable at the time of Donald Dewar's tragic and early death in October 2000 that the media would often give the impression that he had fathered the Scottish Parliament virtually alone. The distance of a few years has allowed for a more balanced perspective on this key issue in Scottish history. As Dewar himself would have been the first to admit, devolution was the product of much longer-term processes and the work of many people. A fundamental difference from 1979 was not simply the crucial advantage of a huge parliamentary majority for the pro-devolution governing party, but the political will at the highest levels of that party to achieve constitutional reform. Tony Blair may not have been an instinctive devolutionist but as Murray Elder, a senior figure in the Labour Party at the time, observed, 'the "unfinished business" legacy of John Smith, public expectation and the long-established commitment of Gordon Brown ... and others made it impossible to dilute the policy'. Critically also, Blair backed Dewar on the contentious issue of proportional representation for the new Parliament, which helped to keep the Liberal Democrats on side and was thought to make it impossible for any one party in Scotland to gain an overall majority.

The controversial idea of a two-question referendum to endorse the devolution proposals emerged not from Donald Dewar, who was initially unconvinced, but from a committee set up by Blair in 1996, whose recommendations received his full backing when he became Prime Minister. Gordon Brown's role in the process is rarely mentioned, but Dewar's task was made easier by having such a powerful ally at the heart of government who also possessed strong pro-devolution credentials.

In addition, there was the role of the Lord Chancellor, Derry Irvine. Irvine chaired the key Cabinet forum, the Devolution to Scotland, Wales and the Regions Committee (DSWR), through which both the White Paper and the subsequent bill were negotiated. The press predicted a personal conflict between Dewar and Irvine because, 25 years before, Dewar's wife, Alison, had left him for Irvine, taking with her the couple's two children. Irvine was at pains to quash the rumour that there was any disharmony. He stressed that the line-by-line scrutiny and debate in DSWR were indeed intense and demanding, but according to him it helped that 'Donald and I were equal true believers in devolution' (though that did not necessarily mean agreement on the course which devolution would take). Plainly the evidence now suggests the two men did work closely together. Irvine also made an important contribution by drafting the chapter in the Devolution White Paper describing the proposed Scottish Executive's relationship with Europe. It was important, too, that Irvine was close to Blair and that the former apparently had the personal ambition to leave behind him the legacy of a Lord Chancellor who had successfully partially reformed the UK constitution.

Nor should the role of the Civil Service be forgotten. A team of the 'brightest and best in Whitehall', the Constitution Secretariat, was put together to piece together the complex legislation and prepare the detailed briefing papers for discussions inside the DSWR. It paralleled a similar high-powered group of civil servants drawn from the Scottish Office.

Yet, despite the many hands involved and the favourable political context, the Dewar influence on events remained important. This was the case in at least four respects. First, his decision to encourage Labour participation in the Scottish Constitutional Convention was crucial to the establishment of a wider political consensus for a parliament. Since the debacle of 1979, Dewar was conscious of the need to widen the appeal of a new settlement, to avoid the perception that had helped to wreck the earlier attempt – that of the new parliament as 'a central-belt Labour council writ large', in Murray Elder's words. Dewar's decision flew in the face of much Scottish Labour opinion at the time, as did his commitment to support proportional representation for the new parliament. Both initiatives demonstrated that this intrinsically cautious man was capable of decisive action.

Second, Dewar's personal credibility and the widespread respect for him among the general public helped to achieve a clear winning result in the referendum campaign. Even political opponents such as Alex Salmond agreed that the Dewar factor was influential in this respect.

Third, Dewar put his own personal stamp on the White Paper, which contained the basic formula for devolution and differed not only from the blueprint of the Scottish Constitutional Convention but also from the first drafts proposed by the Civil Service teams. These were rapidly restructured by Dewar and his special advisers, Murray Elder and Wendy Alexander, over a few days of intensive work. The subsequent draft went far beyond the timid proposals of 1979 by suggesting that every area was to be devolved other than those specifically reserved, a complete reversal of the earlier idea that had spelt out the devolved areas on a case-by-case basis.

Fourth, all this then had to be argued through the DSWR and the result achieved speedily in order to prevent any rearguard action by the 'Whitehall Warriors' and their departments, who might start to oppose any diminution in their own powers and responsibilities. Those discussions in that committee, which contained some pretty sceptical ministerial voices, were taxing. Equally, however, at the end of the day, Dewar and his team achieved virtually all their objectives.

14

The Modern SNP

The Queen formally opened the new Parliament at Holyrood on 1 July 1999. The first First Minister, Donald Dewar, responded by giving what many consider to be the greatest speech of his life, with its eloquent evocations of the Scottish past and hopes for the future of the nation:

> The shout of the welder in the din of the great Clyde shipyards;
> The speak of the Mearns, with its soul in the land;
> The discourse of the Enlightenment, when Edinburgh and Glasgow were a light held to the intellectual life of Europe;
> The wild cry of the Great Pipes;
> And back to the distant cries of the battles of Bruce and Wallace.
>
> The past is part of us. But today there is a new voice in the land, the voice of a democratic Parliament. A voice to shape Scotland, a voice for the future.
>
> . . .
>
> I look forward to the days ahead when this Chamber will sound with debate, argument and passion. When men and women from all over Scotland will meet to work together for a future built from the first principles of social justice.

The establishment of the Parliament was indeed a historic watershed, even if ultimate sovereignty was retained by Westminster. The nature of the Union of England and Scotland framed in 1707 had now changed irrevocably. That fact was recognized at the time. Less evident in 1999, and only to become clear later, was that devolution also built a platform which might enable the SNP to play a much more central role in Scottish politics. There was no certainty that this might be the outcome. Whether the Nationalists prospered or not depended on events, personalities, accidents of the future, as well as their own capacities. Without devolution, however, the SNP would probably have been condemned to oppositionism, with no hope at all of sharing power or achieving power for itself. They had no possibility of doing so by being elected in trivial numbers to the UK Parliament. The Scottish Conservatives' long-term decline and electoral destruction in the 1997 general election also opened up opportunities for the SNP to become the second most popular party in Scotland and enable a head-to-head contest with Labour in Holyrood.

I

The SNP had come to regard itself as a significant political force after the famous by-election victory at Hamilton in 1967 by Winnie Ewing. In part that belief was correct. At times during the following three decades the nationalist vote seriously worried the other parties. Also, without the threat of the SNP, there would probably not have been a referendum on Scottish devolution in 1979. The party enjoyed a significant media profile as the rogue card of Scottish politics. Although often quiescent, it could occasionally deliver a dramatic electoral surprise, which was then widely reported and its significance often exaggerated by the press.

Overall, however, the three decades between 1967 and the referendum of 1997 could be regarded as years of failure for the SNP. Its vote ebbed and flowed between the extremes of modest success and abysmal failure. No nationalist breakthrough was achieved, the party became mired in fratricidal dispute for a time in the 1980s, and it remained outside the national debate on Scotland's future under the auspices of the Constitutional Convention. Yet the party and particularly Alex Salmond, the leader, then worked hard and successfully alongside its Labour and Liberal Democratic partners to deliver the overwhelming 'Yes' vote in the devolution referendum. Within the UK political context, the SNP seemed doomed to be a party of eternal opposition. The modern SNP's raison d'être of independence for Scotland was given short shrift by the British political parties, which were all robust defenders of the Union.

For that reason the coming of the Scottish Parliament in 1999 was a godsend for the SNP. Ironically, delivered by its mortal enemy, the Labour Party, devolution gave the Nationalists the opportunity, in theory at least, to achieve real political influence of the kind that would have been virtually impossible under the Westminster system at that time. George Robertson, the former Shadow Labour Secretary of State for Scotland, could not have been more wrong when he confidently and famously predicted that 'devolution would kill nationalism stone dead'.

In October 1974 the SNP had won just over 30 per cent of the Scottish vote, in the process displacing the Conservatives from second place in Scotland. That level of performance was never achieved by the Nationalists again in the twentieth century. These results, however, were never reflected in the number of seats won. Even when the SNP had more votes than the Conservatives, as in October 1974, the party gained only 11 of the 71 Scottish seats compared to their rivals with 16. There was a broadly similar pattern in later general elections – a creditable number of votes cast in favour of the SNP, but few seats won. The reason for this paradox was the even spread of nationalist votes across the country, a key disadvantage in a first-past-the-post electoral system. Labour and the Tories, on the other hand, had a strikingly uneven pattern. They may have attracted few votes in some constituencies, but in others their support was so concentrated as to achieve victory. The nationalist support varied little between social classes and occupational groups, which, of course, are not uniform across Scotland. In 1997, for instance, the Labour vote varied from 46 per cent among owner-occupiers to 64 per cent for those who lived in council and other forms of social housing. In some areas this meant the Labour vote was weak, whereas in others it was formidable: 'prior to devolution the SNP struggled to secure representation because, so long at least as it did not come first in votes, the single-member plurality voting system discriminated against its socially and thus geographically evenly spread vote.'[1] Little wonder that the SNP only ever achieved minuscule representation in the House of Commons.

This was to change within the electoral system for the Scottish Parliament. Labour's future partners in the new Scottish Executive, the Liberal Democrats, had long demanded a more proportional approach.

Within the forum of the Constitutional Convention, the two parties agreed that the existing 72 constituencies would be supported by 56 'party list' seats within the eight regions of the country. The objective was to ensure fair division not only by seats but by the overall vote. This 'Additional Member System' would reflect the distribution of votes between the parties. The new system came as an 'electoral life-line' to the SNP. As shown in the data below (Table 4), the party's advance in the Parliament relied heavily down to 2007 on these list seats and they were also crucial to the SNP's ability to achieve power in Holyrood that year. Of itself, the system did not guarantee success for the party but in the long term it was the essential precondition. Nevertheless, there was one large cloud on the sunny nationalist horizon. Even if the SNP came first at some future election in votes, the intention was that no party could achieve an overall majority in terms of seats. The structure had been carefully designed to ensure that nationalism could never threaten the Union through achieving power in Holyrood. Labour was willing to concede not having a majority itself in order to ensure the Nationalists would never have one either. Later events showed that there was an additional obstacle for the Nationalists. Liberal Democrats would not enter a coalition with the SNP unless its core policy of an independence referendum for Scotland was abandoned.

Table 4. Scottish Parliament Election Results in Votes and Seats, 1999–2007

% Constituency vote (no. of seats)

	1999		2003		2007	
SNP	28.7	(7)	23.8	(9)	32.9	(21)
Labour	38.8	(53)	34.6	(46)	32.2	(37)
Conservatives	15.6	(0)	16.6	(3)	16.6	(4)
Liberal Democrats	14.2	(12)	15.4	(13)	16.2	(11)
Greens	–	–	–	–	0.1	(0)
Scottish Socialists	1.0	(0)	6.2	(0)	0.0	(0)
Others	1.7	(1)	3.5	(2)	2.0	(0)

% Regional list vote (no. of seats)

	1999		2003		2007	
SNP	27.3	(28)	20.9	(18)	31.0	(26)
Labour	33.6	(3)	29.3	(4)	29.2	(9)
Conservatives	15.4	(18)	15.5	(15)	13.9	(13)
Liberal Democrats	12.4	(5)	11.8	(4)	11.3	(5)
Greens	3.6	(1)	6.9	(7)	4.0	(2)
Scottish Socialists	2.0	(1)	6.7	(6)	0.6	(0)
Others	5.7	(0)	8.9	(2)	10.0	(1)

Note: The Greens did not fight any constituencies in 1999 or 2003.

Source: John Curtice, 'Devolution, the SNP and the Electorate', in G. Hassan, ed., *The Modern SNP* (Edinburgh, 2009), p. 59.

In the immediate aftermath of devolution there seemed little danger that independence would become a realistic vote winner. Indeed, in the first four years after devolution some thought that home rule had indeed killed the nationalist fox. There was no evidence, even down to the SNP's narrow election victory in 2007, of a rising tide of public support for independence. In that year less than a quarter of those questioned in the *Scottish Social Attitudes Survey* backed independence, even though the SNP was then in power. That figure was slightly below the 27 per cent recorded in 1999, the year of devolution. Again, before that, though well established as the opposition in the Scottish Parliament, the SNP found it difficult for several years to close the gap on Labour. In 1999 the Nationalists won an apparently creditable 35 seats, but only seven of these were won in constituencies, the others being from the list. The SNP's overall result in 2003 was even worse, with its seats falling from 35 to 27 in number. Despite the electoral advantages of proportional representation at Holyrood elections, there was little evidence of a surge, far less a breakthrough for the Nationalists. The defeat in 2003 triggered growing opposition to the party's leader, John Swinney, who had succeeded Alex Salmond in 2000. An almost unknown activist challenged him in a leadership contest in 2003. Swinney had a crushing victory but the discontent did not vanish. The SNP sustained another disappointment in the 2005 general election when its vote fell from 20.1 per cent to 17.7 per cent, a mere two points ahead of the Conservatives. Swinney had little option but to resign.

One expert asserted that 'Devolution ha[d] provided the SNP with an unparalleled political opportunity.'[2] The reasons why it proved unable to grasp this, at least before 2007, were several in number. A party whose raison d'être was the single issue of independence for Scotland was bound to have difficulty adjusting in the short run to achieving victory in the Scottish Parliament. That required the formulation of a range of policies in addition to its central aspiration of Scottish sovereignty. As these were worked out and published, the party remained vulnerable to attacks from political opponents claiming that the 'separatist' agenda was being downplayed because it had little appeal to the electorate. This was in a sense the key paradox for a party of independence but one that had also opted for gradualism by the achievement of a majority in Parliament which would allow a referendum.

There were also external problems. The SNP faced a universally hostile press at a time when the print media, as ever, still influenced the formation of opinion. Indeed, it was not only the Nationalists who suffered in this respect. The entire devolution project and the Parliament drew invective, ridicule and venom from several journalists and the tabloid press in particular. The opinion polls suggested at the beginning of the new millennium that Scots were in fact becoming weary of constitutional issues and, like others in the Western world, were less likely to vote in elections. The Union had never been so secure since the years before the Thatcher era of substantial political instability. There was sustained economic expansion in Britain, which not only generated material improvement directly but yielded for the Scottish Executive much more revenue through the 'Barnett formula' of resource allocation to Northern Ireland, Wales and Scotland as central UK government expenditure increased. In 2005 it was reported that the job market in Scotland had improved consecutively for two and a half years, with Glasgow offering one in three of the new positions. The housing and employment markets not only remained vigorous over the same period, but were more buoyant than those south of the border, where economic growth slowed after 2004. The predicted post-devolution financial tensions between London and Edinburgh did not materialize.

Administrative devices developed since 1999 helped to lend flexibility and pragmatism to the devolution arrangements. The best known were the so-called 'Sewel Conventions', named after Lord Sewel, the UK government minister who introduced them. Under these, it might be agreed that Westminster could legislate in areas that were in formal terms devolved to Scotland. The Conventions were enacted on 41 occasions from 1999 to 2003, leading to criticism that Holyrood was surrendering too many responsibilities to Westminster. Most crucially, however, devolution had a fair wind in the UK because Labour was the main party of government in both London and Edinburgh. Potential problems could therefore usually be dealt with through party channels and personal connections. What all this meant, however, is that the settlement itself had yet to be fully tested. That scenario would only come about when there were two different dominant parties in Holyrood and Westminster respectively, and/or when UK financial circumstances (and hence the value of the block grant to Scotland) became more problematic.

Yet the mediocrity of the SNP's political performance before 2007 is only one aspect of the story. Below the surface of public events, the party was building a much more professional structure that in time would reap electoral dividends. This process had begun in the 1990s under Alex Salmond's leadership. Key decisions were taken on future policy. The objective was to achieve independence by gradualism through becoming the majority party in a future Scottish Parliament. Again, unusually for a nationalist movement in Europe, the SNP remained committed to a left-of-centre agenda, even as New Labour moved in a different political direction, albeit with a dash of what became known as 'Neo-Liberalism with a Heart'. In 1995 the full extent of the SNP's commitment to 'civic nationalism' also became apparent. The existing policy for an independent Scotland had envisaged a bill of rights that guaranteed fundamental freedoms and outlawed discrimination in terms of race, gender and religion. The approach now went further. Citizenship in an independent Scotland was to be founded not on race or heritage but on residence in Scotland alone. Few nationalist parties are associated with this degree of protection and assured status for ethnic minorities within a nation state. As part of this agreement, attempts were made to develop more rapprochement with the so-called 'New Scots', particularly Asians and Catholics of Irish descent, where in the west of Scotland the

Nationalists were already winning more support among ethnicities traditionally associated with Labour. A group called New Scots for Independence was formed, consisting of SNP members and supporters who were not Scots by birth or descent but by residence. The links that were built to the Catholic community included discussion of the abolition of the centuries-old Act of Settlement by which an heir of the Catholic faith could not succeed to the monarchy of Britain.

The programme of modernization of the SNP happened in two phases, first under Salmond, and second during the short tenure of Swinney in the new millennium. In the former case, much of the drive was to establish an effective fund-raising strategy to support research, political communications, candidate training and IT. Between 1991 and 1999 annual party funds rose from a meagre £91,327 to £680,132. John Swinney later had many problems as leader but behind the scenes he was responsible for transforming the SNP into a modern and potentially effective electoral machine. He introduced inter alia 'one member, one vote' both for leadership elections and list rankings (which had long caused controversy and many personal hostilities). The fruits of Swinney's efforts would be reaped in the next Holyrood elections in 2007.

II

While the SNP was becalmed electorally but trying to prepare for future contests, the entire devolution project was falling into difficulty. There was much ill fortune, beginning with the premature death of Donald Dewar in 2000. He served as first First Minister for less than eighteen months, and for six months of that period he was battling ill health. In addition, after the high hopes and euphoria of the referendum campaign, his administration was dogged by problems and mishaps. Dewar and his ministerial team seemed in a constant state of crisis. Sections of the print media that had long opposed devolution relished denouncing the new Parliament for some of its first decisions in 'voting itself huge salaries, allowances, a three-day week with short hours, 17 weeks' holiday a year and a medal'.[3] Every little peccadillo was picked over and the tabloid newspapers in particular fuelled public scepticism by their exposures. The Executive and MSPs had to become used to such relentless and often hostile scrutiny and did not always handle it well. There was, however, plenty of meat to throw to the press wolves. Inaccurate Higher Grade results were sent out by the Scottish Qualifications Agency in the summer of 2000, causing a national furore and a long period of uncertainty for school pupils seeking university entrance. Two of Dewar's senior advisers had to resign, one of whom, John Rafferty, was his chief of staff. The national fuel protests of September 2000 then threatened to bring the country to a halt. Although a UK-wide phenomenon, the bitter dispute still conveyed the impression of a devolved administration lurching from crisis to crisis. One astringent commentator, though sympathetic to devolution, called it a 'catalogue of calamity'.[4]

But these events were nothing compared to the gathering storm over the escalating costs of the building of the new Parliament at Holyrood, followed by the controversy over the legal provision, Section 28 (2A). Dewar had wished for an iconic building to house the new Parliament, and the choice of site opposite the royal palace of Holyroodhouse in Edinburgh was very much his decision. Criticism started to mount that the costs of the project had been drastically underestimated and many feared the nation was to be landed with a huge bill. Again, it was easy to portray the Executive as incompetent, though, in fact, the project had been started before the first sitting of Parliament. Donald Dewar's short period in office spared him, however, from the full ferocity of the media backlash as the enormous scale of the Holyrood fiasco only really became clear at a later date.

More serious was the furore over Section 28 (2A). The decision was taken to abolish this legal provision, which prohibited local authorities (and hence local-authority schools) from 'promoting' homosexuality. Dewar told the Parliament that Clause 2A had to go because it 'singles out a minority in our community for stigma, isolation and fear'. The decision to legislate was announced in the autumn of 2000 by Wendy Alexander, the Communities Minister. It was not long before fierce opposition began to emerge. An unlikely alliance of the *Daily Record*, Scotland's biggest-selling tabloid, the Catholic Church, led by the high-profile Cardinal Tom Winning, and the millionaire bus tycoon, Brian Souter, an evangelical Christian, orchestrated a massive protest. This included a postal vote, funded by Souter, in which 87 per cent of respondents voted to keep the Clause. Opponents voiced a clear message: abolition was in their view merely the thin end of the wedge, the essential preliminary to gay lessons being made available in schools. Amid the hysteria, the Executive stuck to its guns and the Clause was abolished.

The episode showed that, whatever one's point of view, a Scottish Parliament could indeed make a difference and that Dewar himself was not always the cautious politician so often portrayed. His social liberal credentials were obvious for all to see, even if many others sincerely regarded this legislation as a sinister and unacceptable attack on 'family values'. Dewar proudly proclaimed at the Labour Party Conference in September 2000: 'We stood firm in the blizzard . . . section 28 is no more.'[5] But the reform was achieved at the expense of much electoral unpopularity. The First Minister's poll ratings fell to even lower levels. Cardinal Winning, a previously influential enthusiast for devolution, now proclaimed the Parliament an 'utter failure' and added that he was ashamed of Scotland's politicians. There was a general sense among the hierarchy of the Catholic Church in Scotland that the Executive was more interested in addressing a politically correct agenda than in defending traditional moral principles.

Perhaps even more significant politically, however, was Dewar's apparent inability to control his Cabinet. Infighting and leaks to the press by the opposing camps occurred on almost a daily basis. The First Minister confided to close colleagues that he ought to have had more of 'the killer instinct' and should have sacked the offenders. After his heart operation in May 2000 there was, of course, near certainty that Dewar would retire before too long. The jostling for position intensified among the main contenders for the succession – Henry McLeish, Jack McConnell and Susan Deacon.

In the event, Donald Dewar died suddenly in October 2000. The Enterprise Minister, Henry McLeish, was selected as First Minister by Labour MSPs over the rival candidate Jack McConnell. But his victory hardly amounted to a ringing endorsement. Despite being strongly backed by heavyweight London politicians such as Gordon Brown, McLeish was elected by only 44 votes to 36. However, one clear and very popular policy advance did emerge during his term of office. Free personal care for the elderly, an idea strongly opposed by the Blair government in London, became law, partly because of the enthusiastic support of Labour's coalition partners in the Scottish Parliament, the Liberal Democrats, and also of the SNP and Conservatives. At the very least, the controversy over personal care demonstrated that the new Parliament was not always prepared to toe the London Labour line. McLeish should be given considerable credit for resisting the pressures that came his way over this issue from the Treasury and the UK Department of Social Security, headed at that time by the Scottish lawyer Alistair Darling.

This success apart, however, the McLeish administration was mainly distinguished by its mediocrity. The new First Minister lacked personal authority or even confidence in his own ability. In his previous role as Enterprise Minister, McLeish had performed creditably. Now the top job seemed to overwhelm him. He was prone to verbal mishaps, which became known as 'McLeishés', and these were widely and amusingly reported by an unsympathetic press. Scotland's First Minister was soon in danger of becoming a comic figure. Insiders interviewed by the respected journalist Brian Taylor bluntly told him that McLeish had been over-promoted and was simply not up to the job. In the end he did not hold it for very long. A year after his election, he resigned on 8 November 2001 over a failure to end speculation over office cash allowances when he had been a Westminster MP. The writing had been on the wall since his appearance on the BBC's *Question Time* when he comprehensively failed to provide satisfactory answers to the issues raised before a national television audience.

This was for many pro-devolutionists a worrying and depressing time. For those who had devoted many years to promoting the cause of the Parliament the loss of two First Ministers in as many years, the public fiasco over the relentless cost increases in the Holyrood building project, and the widespread cynicism about the quality of MSPs, all seemed to put the entire devolution project in jeopardy. The Queen herself noted as much when she addressed the Parliament in its temporary home in Aberdeen in May 2002. She also added some wise words of encouragement: 'After what might be considered a Parliamentary adjournment of almost three hundred years that process [of building a new political culture] will inevitably take time. In an age which tends to instant judgements, this is something we would all do well to remember.'[6]

The monarch's supportive words were well received. There is little doubt that circumstances had indeed worked against the Parliament's early success. Expectations were certainly too high, the departure of two First Ministers in quick succession was very bad luck and, unfortunately, devolution came at a time when, throughout Western Europe, politics and politicians had fallen into a degree of disrepute. But the Executive had also scored some truly spectacular own goals, of which the most damaging remained the series of blunders over the Holyrood building project. The former Tory minister Lord Fraser of Carmyllie was appointed to find out why an unrealistic initial budget of £40 million had spiralled to a colossal £431 million. After hearings lasting for 49 days and a million words of evidence, he concluded in a damning report that there was no single villain of the piece but that the civil service in Scotland should bear most of the blame for allowing enormous cost overshoots and not keeping ministers and MSPs informed about the emerging disaster.

After 'Officegate', which ended McLeish's career, only two likely successors as First Minister were available: Jack McConnell, who had been narrowly defeated a year earlier in the last election, and Wendy Alexander, a protégée of Donald Dewar's and a young politician widely respected for her intellectual ability and work rate. After much soul-searching, Alexander pulled out of the race, leaving McConnell as the sole candidate to claim the spoils of victory. He was soon criticized for his lack of vision and commitment to 'doing less better', which sometimes tended to reduce Scottish politics to a mind-numbing condition of boredom. He was even likened by some to the 'grey' former Tory Prime Minister, John Major. After the immediate post-devolution traumas, however, there was perhaps some sense in 'bedding down' the new institutions, avoiding potential crises and going for stability. Certainly, to a greater extent than either Dewar or McLeish, McConnell was in command of his Cabinet, not least because he removed virtually all personal opposition to him on the Labour side soon after becoming First Minister. The McConnell years were not entirely devoid of policies. The attack on Scotland's age-old sectarian culture, the attempts to grapple with anti-social behaviour, the ban on smoking in public places that became law in spring 2006, and the so-called Fresh Talent Initiative, which tried to help address the problem of Scotland's then shrinking population, were all relevant to the contemporary needs of the nation. Above all, perhaps, was the decision to seek to introduce proportional representation in local government. The legislation was implemented in 2007 and at a stroke ended the hegemony of the Labour Party at the local level, ushered in coalition politics, awarded the SNP a major increase in representation in every town hall and, in the view of its supporters, stimulated much more vitality in some semi-moribund councils and 'rotten burghs'.

III

The 2007 Scottish Parliament election was significant not only because the SNP won a narrow victory over Labour for the first time since devolution but also because it allowed the party to establish the first ever nationalist administration in Scottish history. Labour had 46 seats and the SNP 47. Talks with the Liberal Democrats to form a coalition predictably soon broke down as the SNP leadership was unwilling to give up its commitment to an independence referendum. It was SNP policy not to deal with the Tories. The decision was therefore made to go it alone. Alex Salmond became First Minister and leader of a minority administration, having secured the support of the two Green MPs with the Independent, Margo MacDonald, abstaining. In an act of symbolic intent the 'Scottish Executive' name was changed to 'Scottish Government'. On the same day as the Holyrood elections, the SNP became the largest party in local government under the single transferable vote system that was used for the first time in council elections. It won 361 seats to Labour's 348, including achieving considerable success in Labour's traditional citadel of Glasgow and the west of Scotland.

Several aspects of the 2007 election require comment. First, the SNP's victory mirrored reverses for Labour in English local elections and in the Welsh Assembly. The Scottish result was therefore undeniably influenced by the Labour government's unpopularity during its third term in office. Second, the SNP success was not a vote for independence but for more competent government in Holyrood after the mediocrity of previous administrations. Opinion polls confirmed anti-independence scepticism while two-thirds of the electorate had voted for unionist parties and over 60 per cent of MSPs were from the same background. Third, the SNP made some advances in central Scotland but won only one seat in Glasgow, with Nicola Sturgeon taking Govan at the third attempt. Nevertheless, the fact was that the SNP came a close second to Labour in several constituencies in the west of Scotland.

There were also longer-term implications following the events of 2007. Manifestly, either for reasons in Scotland or because of the performance of the UK government, or a combination of both, Labour had suffered a historic defeat. The SNP boasted that this was the first time Labour had lost an election in Scotland for nearly half a century. But worryingly for the party that had dominated Scottish politics for so long, its decline both nationally and locally pre-dated 2007. Moreover, the achievement in that election was to prove much more than another flash in the pan for the SNP. Support now seemed far more deeply embedded than in the years of its electoral volatility in the later twentieth century.

15

Breakthrough of the Nationalists

The result of the 2011 Scottish Parliament election proved to be the most significant in modern Scottish history since Labour's victory in 1945 inaugurated radical welfare reforms in the UK. The Westminster general election of 2010 had given no clues to the dramatic developments that would take place in Scotland only a year later. As usual, the Scots swung heavily behind Labour, with the SNP in its wake. Labour held all of the 41 seats it had won in 2005 and, against the UK trend, increased its share of the vote. The SNP performance was much poorer than in 2005 because, although advancing by 2 per cent of the vote, it only narrowly avoided defeat for second place by the Liberal Democrats. After devolution the Scots had established the electoral habit of voting differently in Holyrood and Westminster elections, but there was little inkling of the political earthquake that was to follow.

The journalist Iain Macwhirter was present in the BBC's studios on election night in 2011 as the results started to come in. He recalled the reactions:

> Commentators and politicians ... could scarcely believe what they were hearing as [Labour] seats such as Glasgow Cathcart, Kelvin, Shettleston, Southside were gained by the Nationalists. Even Glasgow Anniesland, Donald Dewar's old seat, fell to the SNP candidate, Bill Kidd. May 2011 was Labour's worst result in Scotland since 1931 – when Labour were split over Ramsay MacDonald's national government. The Scottish system of proportional representation was supposed to prevent any party gaining an absolute majority in the Holyrood Parliament. The SNP blew that theory by winning 69 seats out of 129.[1]

Two consecutive electoral victories in 2007 and 2011 had in themselves been an achievement in the light of the historic volatility of the SNP vote. But a landslide on the scale of 2011 could not have been anticipated. The extent of the SNP triumph is recorded in the numbers in Table 5.

Table 5. Result of the Scottish Parliament Election in 2011

	First Vote		Second Vote		Total Seats
	% Vote	Seats	% Vote	Seats	
Conservatives	13.9	3	12.4	12	15
Labour	31.7	15	26.3	22	37
Liberal Democrats	7.9	2	5.2	3	5
SNP	45.4	53	44.0	16	69
Others	1.1	0	7.7	3	3

Source: Peter Lynch, *SNP: The History of the Scottish National Party* (Cardiff, 2013 edn), p. 277.

All three opposition leaders, Labour's Iain Gray, Tavish Scott of the Liberal Democrats and Annabel Goldie of the Conservatives, resigned before election night was over. When the new Parliament assembled at Holyrood, the Chamber had lost many old faces while a phalanx of beaming new SNP members cheered to the echo every word of their leader, Alex Salmond. As one observer of the proceedings put it, 'The Scottish Parliament had turned into an Alex Salmond fan club.'[2] The result also had potentially momentous consequences for the rest of the UK. By winning a majority, the Nationalists had secured a mandate to hold a referendum on Scottish independence to be put before the British government. After considerable negotiation, it was announced that this would take place in the autumn of 2014. The unionists were puzzled at first about the time lag. They might have expected a snap referendum on the back of the unprecedented SNP victory. The gap in time, however, was an eloquent acknowledgement that much had to be done to convince the Scottish people of the merits of independence. Around election day, opinion polls revealed that only 29 per cent of the electorate supported that radical option.

The Nationalists had therefore a mountain to climb if they hoped to achieve a credible result in 2014. In 2010 the Scots were not voting on the constitution but on what they thought was the most able Holyrood administration and the one best suited to defend the interests of Scotland.

An explanation of the SNP victory, therefore, must discount to a considerable extent the appeal of independence to their army of new voters. Rather the roots of victory lay in the long-term difficulties of its arch-rival, the Labour Party, and the emergence of the Nationalists as an effective election-winning machine.

To some extent, Labour's defeats in both 2007 and 2011 could be laid at the door of mediocre leadership in the past. Jack McConnell, the First Minister from 2001, who had previously presided over Labour's failure in 2007, has been roundly criticized for timidity, dependence on London Labour, and an inability to establish a distinctive Scottish agenda. One distinguished political scientist described him as 'the embodiment of conservative devolution', as he led by 'doing less better . . . the John Major of Scottish politics, in office but not quite in power'.[3] The policy cupboard was not entirely bare, however, as indicated in the previous chapter. McConnell's administration radically changed the voting system for local authorities, ironically ending the grip of Labour on several councils, introduced a ban on smoking in public places and pursued an anti-sectarian strategy. Yet, the overall verdict on his leadership of Labour rings true. McConnell had complete control of his party and was also fortunate to be First Minister when the coffers of the Executive were overflowing. Through the Barnett formula, the Scottish grant more than doubled in cash terms between 1999 and 2010, but little in the way of targeted policies for Scotland's social ills of poverty, ill health and inequality came from this unprecedented largesse. McConnell resigned as leader in 2007 (and went to the House of Lords in 2010). He was succeeded by Wendy Alexander, who had established a reputation as a sharp mind and someone with a combative (not to say abrasive) approach. Intellectually, especially in economics, she was at least the equal of Alex Salmond. In spring 2008 she decided to call the First Minister's bluff on an independence referendum by demanding in a television interview, 'Bring it on!' It was the beginning of the banking crisis, which very soon would threaten the very existence of the Royal Bank of Scotland (RBS) and Halifax Bank of Scotland (HBOS), and the SNP was at a low ebb in the opinion polls. It was to some extent an inspired move that might well have put the Nationalists on the back foot. However, Alexander had not obtained the consent of her boss, the new Labour Prime Minister, Gordon Brown, before she acted. Her sponsorship of the Commission on Devolution, set up under the chairmanship of Sir Kenneth Calman, Chancellor of Glasgow University, and former Chief Medical Officer for Scotland, had already put pressure on the SNP, which originally opposed the idea in Parliament. Calman's Report, when eventually published, advocated increased tax-raising powers for Holyrood. But by that time Wendy Alexander had gone, ostensibly over a minor case of failing to register some donations made to her leadership campaign. Many suspected, however, skullduggery and the employment of the black arts at the higher levels of the Labour Party. The departure of yet another Labour leader in Scotland in such circumstances did little for the internal morale or public standing of the party.

Alexander was replaced by Labour's finance spokesman, the well-named Iain Gray, who combined dour competence with lack of charismatic appeal. His strategy for the 2011 Holyrood election was disastrous. Confident of victory because of Scotland's loyal support for his party in the 2010 general election, he adopted a low-profile approach with few new ideas in the manifesto. Only latterly was this seen to be a catastrophic approach as the opinion polls showed considerable SNP advances. The credibility of Labour was undermined further by patently last-minute attempts to put together a more ambitious set of offerings to the electorate, with predictable results in the election. Gray and his colleagues had made the terrible mistake of assuming that the general election results meant that Scotland was likely to remain rock-solid for Labour. They failed to realize that the Scottish response then had been designed to forestall a UK Conservative victory and was not necessarily an endorsement of Labour in Scotland.

To conclude, however, that the decline of Scotland's most popular political force was a result only of poor leadership and misguided tactics would be mistaken. The problems of Labour were much more profound and reached back well into the past. Further, the humiliation of 2011 was not the end of the party's woes. Labour strongholds in Glasgow, West Dunbartonshire and North Lanarkshire voted against the unionist Labour line in the Referendum of 2014. In other areas of west-central Scotland, such as North Ayrshire and Renfrewshire, there were also substantial minority votes for independence. Then came the cataclysm of the general election of May 2015.

When Johann Lamont succeeded Iain Gray as leader of Scottish Labour, her first speech claimed the party came across to people in the Holyrood election as 'a tired old politics machine which was more about itself than it was about them'. She went on, 'If anyone has ever deluded ourselves into thinking that Scotland was really a Labour country – last May must have finally shaken us out of that delusion.'[4] The statement was an explicit admission that for Scottish Labour the age of hubris was over and the era of nemesis might well lie on the horizon. The party's omnipotence had come from its many decades of power in Scotland at both the national and local level. The destruction of the old Tory enemy in the 1990s was also a factor as was the standing of the party in relation to UK Labour. Scottish Labour had never been riven by the fratricidal disputes between modernizers, Militant and the Bennite Left which had threatened to tear the party apart south of the border. Scottish Labour was seen as an island of stability in a sea of troubles, a party that had kept the faith and its head while others were losing theirs. Hubris was confirmed by the success of so many Scots achieving Cabinet rank in the first Blair government. The Prime Minister himself had a Scottish father and was educated at Fettes College in Edinburgh. Gordon Brown, Donald Dewar, George Robertson, John Reid, Robin Cook, Alistair Darling and Derry Irvine formed a phalanx of Caledonian 'big beasts' whose prominence generated more than a little Scotophobia in sections of the English press.

The end of this golden age of Scottish Labour came about because of the erosion and, in some cases, the disappearance of the historical pillars on which its power in the past had been built. These foundations were both structural and ideological in nature. Labour had originally been born out of the trade union movement, and therefore the collapse of union membership with the decay of the old mining and manufacturing industries was bound to have a negative impact on its fortunes. Over half the Scottish workforce was unionized in 1980. By 2010 that figure had fallen to less than one-third. The new service- and finance-based economy, outside the public sector, was markedly less unionized than before. The extent of council-house building in the 1950s and 1960s had created vast Labour fiefdoms in and around the Scottish cities. The Tory 'right to buy' was only one but nonetheless a very important factor causing the Labour decline. By 2005 council housing had declined to 15 per cent of the total stock. In 1981, 40 of the country's 71 constituencies had a majority of public housing. By 2010 not one of these constituencies comprised a majority of council tenants. Alongside council housing was the Labour empire in local government. The first-past-the-post system had resulted in Labour domination of many local authorities. In 1995 the party held 20 out of 32 councils in Scotland. Its rule became almost a self-perpetuating oligarchy, inevitably causing accusations of corruption, cronyism, nepotism and patronage networks:

> In some places such as Glasgow, Lanarkshire and Ayrshire, opposition councillors became at Labour's height [of power] an endangered species, developing a one-party politics where councillors and officials saw little conflict of interest, and the main debates went on behind closed doors inside the Labour Group or between senior councillors and officials.[5]

Ironically, it was the McConnell Labour administration in the Scottish Parliament that destroyed these monopolies by abandoning first-past-the-post in local elections and introducing proportional representation. A new democratic spirit became established in town halls across the land and the party that most successfully exploited the opportunities was the SNP. Since the foundation of the Irish Free State in 1922, the Catholic minority of Irish descent had changed its loyalties from the Liberals to Labour, regarding it as the party most likely to achieve social justice for a disadvantaged community. For much of the twentieth century, Catholics voted en bloc for Labour, producing in the process many Labour councillors, MPs and civic dignitaries. The value of Catholics to the party became even more important over time. The old vote for the Tories started to die out from the 1960s, but Catholic loyalty to Labour endured. Equally, Catholics proved immune to the blandishments of the SNP until at least the 1970s. The SNP was for long viewed as a Protestant-dominated party and therefore alien to a minority in a society where sectarianism remained a serious problem. In February 1974, Labour support in the Catholic community reached nearly 80 per cent. But that was the high point of loyalty. Gradually, decline set in. The Catholic community was changing. It gained from substantial upward mobility based on educational attainments in the 1960s and 1970s. By the 1990s, Catholics had achieved broad occupational and educational parity in Scotland. The old fear of the SNP was disappearing as the Nationalists started to cultivate the Catholic community and Alex Salmond publicly praised the merits of the denominational school system, though it remained controversial in the opinion of many Scots. The President of the Scottish Catholic Bishops' Conference, Cardinal Tom Winning, dismissed any threat from the SNP and even on occasion spoke positively about Scottish independence. By 2000 the levels of Scottish identity among Catholics were comparable with the rest of the nation and, strikingly, support for devolution and independence soon became higher than among churchgoing Protestants. By 1992, Catholic backing for Labour had fallen to 53 per cent of the Catholic electorate. Thereafter the haemorrhage from Labour gathered speed. In the referendum of 2014 support for independence came strongly from parts of west-central Scotland with substantial Catholic minorities.

Then there was the issue of ideology. The transformation of old Labour to New Labour in the 1990s did not appeal to the party's traditional supporters in Scotland. Surveys taken after the 1999 Holyrood election showed that only 42 per cent thought that New Labour looked after Scottish interests. Similar evidence covering the period 1997 to 2001 demonstrated declining support for the proposition that New Labour supported class and trade union interests, but rising agreement for the view that it primarily looked after business interests. The rhetoric emanating from London on public-sector reform in the NHS and education did not go down well, especially when Labour in Scotland also started to speak about possible private-sector involvement in the health service north of the border. The Iraq War attracted little support and much disapproval in Scotland. Jack McConnell conceded that 'Alex Salmond's consistent opposition to the Iraq War started to become the accepted public opinion, and left what we were doing on the inside pages of the papers rather than the front.'[6] Theoretically, McConnell might have helped his cause by distancing the Scottish Executive from New Labour's policy on Iraq, in the same way as Welsh Labour's First Secretary, Rhodri Morgan. But McConnell was too concerned that he might antagonize the Labour leadership in London and so harm party unity.

There was also a broader context to be considered. Much of the backing for Labour from working-class communities in the past had depended on its provision of public services and low-cost housing. Areas existed in west-central Scotland where at the start of the new millennium the public spend came close to 75 per cent of the local economy. This pattern was not simply confined to parts of Glasgow but stretched into the hinterland of the city in the counties of Ayrshire, Dunbartonshire and Lanarkshire. This region had once been the dynamic heart of the old industrial economy, the modern ills a result of the social consequences of de-industrialization. Its demographic weight needs also to be emphasized. Greater Glasgow has a population of 1.2 million, the largest urban conurbation in Scotland, and fifth in the UK. The three surrounding counties number 1.1 million together. In all, the region represents 46 per cent of the population of Scotland. It would, of course, be absurd to suggest that every village, town and district in it is a centre of multiple deprivation. Indeed, east Renfrewshire and towns and districts such as Bearsden, Newlands, Alloway in Ayr, Troon and many other areas can boast standards of life equalling the wealthiest parts of the UK. But alongside them are areas of deep, historic relative poverty and social disadvantage.

Because of the high expenditures from the public purse allocated to them, these areas have bred different attitudes to the state compared, for instance, to most of the population of London and the Home Counties. In many of the working-class communities of Glasgow, Dundee and parts of Edinburgh and Stirling, there is no equivocation whatever about the vital importance of state support. As one astute observer put it:

> In a society which is heavily dependent for its wellbeing on state action, the remoteness of the directing organs of the state is likely to be resented. In a society which conceives itself to be different, and in

important respects *is* different, the preference of governments for applying standard solutions across the board and their impatience of regional differences, will provoke a sense of victimhood. All of these observable tendencies in complex societies are likely to be aggravated at a time of financial stringency, when public expectations of the state are likely to be disappointed anyway. But with or without financial constraints, people are likely to respond to state control by trying to break down the organs of the state into smaller and more responsive geographical units. When some of those units correspond to ancient polities with self-conscious identities of their own, the pressure to secede is strong.[7]

In the context of identity and territorial politics the SNP also had two intrinsic advantages over Labour. First, by reason of its raison d'être, the party was accepted as the most robust defender of the Scottish interest above all others. Second, the SNP was its own political master as a disciplined and autonomous organization. Labour in Scotland, however, was an integral part of the much broader British Labour movement. The association with London party headquarters tended to blur its Scottish identity more than a little. Jack McConnell, when First Minister, had suffered from the suspicion that he kowtowed too easily to higher authority in the south and was not willing to rock the Labour boat when any conflict of interest emerged between Scotland and the UK Labour Party. The suspicions of interference from south of the border were confirmed when the party's former leader in Scotland, Johann Lamont, gave her resignation speech in October 2014. She bitterly declared that the UK Labour leadership in effect treated the Scottish party as 'a branch office'. She also made the very damaging allegation that Scottish Labour had been prevented by its masters elsewhere from introducing the kind of social democratic policies which would have appealed to the Scottish electorate and so help the party compete much more effectively with the SNP.

This problem was likely to have become more acute when the New Labour project was launched by the party hierarchy in order to respond to the changes in attitudes among some sections of the English electorate in the 1980s and 1990s. As Labour steadily moved away from left-leaning policies it faced the danger of losing touch with some Scottish working-class communities who were not in any way alienated from the old ways of collectivism and state control of public services. As the party began to concede this ground, the SNP moved in to fill the political gap. It was an opportunity it grasped with relish.

Another difference was in terms of party leadership. From devolution until 2011, Labour had five leaders, if the short tenure of Donald Dewar before his death is excluded. Over the same period the SNP had two, Alex Salmond (twice) and John Swinney, though they were described as 'Conveners' of the party until 2004. The contrast in numbers probably says it all and implies that Labour suffered much more from internal instability, differences over policy and personality conflicts than did the Nationalists. Some commentators also detected a difference in quality at the senior levels of the two parties. Labour in Scotland undeniably suffered from the decision of all their 'big beasts' of the golden generation, apart from Donald Dewar, to continue to pursue their careers in Westminster after devolution. One reason why the SNP was seen to perform more creditably before 2011, despite being a minority government, than the Labour/Lib Dem coalitions of earlier years, was that it had more talent at the top. Alex Salmond led a team that consisted of able politicians such as Nicola Sturgeon, John Swinney, Michael Russell, Fiona Hyslop and several others who were more than a match for their opponents. This author, after giving a lecture to senior civil servants in Scotland shortly after the first SNP administration took office, asked the audience off the record to comment on the administrative competence of the present and previous regimes. The clear consensus was that the nationalist performance was of a much higher calibre.

Throughout the period from the early 1990s, Alex Salmond was, of course, a huge political presence in the SNP. Polling evidence after the victory in 2011 showed him at the height of his powers with very high popularity ratings across all sections of his party. Salmond led it into government and therefore it was relatively easy for him to achieve a strong fan base in the SNP. But there was much more to his commanding position than that. In terms of political skills, no senior politician of any party at Holyrood could touch Salmond. He had a well-deserved reputation as an effective debater, a pragmatic operator, and someone with an astute political intellect who was the equal of the top British politicians of his generation.

Nevertheless, he was not universally popular across Scotland. Some among the electorate thought him smug and self-satisfied. He had less appeal to women voters and this showed in different gender responses during the 2014 referendum campaign. His critics also accused him of egocentricity and abrasiveness, a cunning Machiavel and master of the black arts, who was little more than an opportunist. True or false, several of the accusations also showed how much his opponents feared Salmond as a political operator. He made mistakes, most controversially in condemning NATO strikes against Serb forces in Kosovo during the Balkan wars. This intervention was a diplomatic own goal that earned him widespread condemnation and few plaudits. Again, at the time of the implosion of RBS and HBOS he was perhaps too quick to defend and praise the two Scottish banks, though the evidence subsequently confirmed that they had both been brought down by poor management and their own imprudent financial practices. Doubtless Salmond would also prefer to forget his support at the time for Fred Goodwin, the boss of RBS, who was later stripped of his knighthood but earned instead another accolade as 'the most hated man in Scotland'. To his detractors Salmond was 'the most dangerous man in Britain' and a polarizing personality, but to his admirers he was the nearest the Scots have had to a national leader in recent times. Whatever history's judgement, however, few could doubt that Salmond was crucial to the SNP achievement of winning power in 2007 and then retaining it in 2011.

These successes were not based on a national yearning for independence. The key to power was that the Nationalists had delivered sound governance and some popular policies. Critics later pointed out, however, that their record was less impressive on the huge social problems that confronted Scotland, such as poverty, social inequality, and communities suffering from serious disadvantage. Yet for many Scots, the SNP administrations came like a breath of fresh air compared to much of the mediocrity that had gone before. As already noted above, the Lab/Lib coalitions had indeed managed some achievement during their periods in office. But a sense remained across the land of unfulfilled expectations and a failure to exploit the potential of the Parliament after the long struggle to establish the institution.

Donald Dewar's eloquent hopes for the new legislature at its royal opening in July 1999 seemed not to have been realized. An experienced Holyrood observer at this time pulled no punches in his personal assessment:

> The Scottish voters had tried Labour coalitions, they had tried the rainbow parliament in 2003, and they were still struggling to find some political leadership that they could respect. After eight years of incompetence, scandal, vanity politics, ultra-leftism and legislative mediocrity, they wanted someone – anyone – who would make the Holyrood parliament work and justify the £400 million spent on it.[8]

When the SNP first took office in 2007 one of its first actions had been to change the title of the administration from Scottish Executive to Scottish Government. The semantic symbolism was intended to project political authority and enhanced status. But the challenges for a minority government with an ambitious set of policies were considerable. Some commentators gave the administration only a few months before it would self-destruct. Achieving an annual budget settlement without a majority in Parliament would be especially testing. Then, a year after taking office, the government was confronted with the worst global financial crisis since the 1930s, which had inevitable consequences for their existing commitments and future spending plans. The election of a new British coalition government of Conservatives and Liberal Democrats in 2010 added another problematic element to the mix. A deep crisis because of the global meltdown in the so-called 'arc of prosperity' of formerly successful small nations such as Iceland and Ireland (much lauded by the SNP) also placed a big question mark over the economics of independence. Many asked what would have happened in an independent Scotland if the nation had had to deal with the threatened collapse of its two biggest banks.

Yet the minority administration not only survived but through its governance of the nation laid the basis for the SNP landslide victory of 2011 and then the referendum of 2014. There were several reasons for this outcome. Relations with Westminster proved to be surprisingly stable. There was at first little evidence of the expected friction between Scottish nationalism and English Toryism. Salmond's government progressed by pragmatism, concession and expediency.

Policies that would have automatically led to confrontation with other parties in Holyrood were quietly dropped, most notably proposals for a local income tax and a referendum on Scottish independence to be held in the course of the Parliament. It was their good fortune that rising unemployment after the financial crisis was not laid at the door of the Scottish government but attributed to economic problems which were affecting the entire world. To some extent also opposition in Parliament was partially neutered. If the opposition brought down the government it could risk unleashing the wrath of the citizenry for causing an election, which might only be to the political benefit of the SNP.

Then there were the so-called 'Salmond's freebies', popular decisions that garnered significant electoral support. They included the phasing out of NHS prescription charges, scrapping of student tuition fees, an end to tolls on the Forth and Tay Bridges, and a freeze on council tax. Despite dallying with some aspects of neo-liberal economics, the SNP still mainly kept to its left-of-centre agenda. There was little doubt that this went down well with the majority of the people of Scotland.

The SNP faced a tough challenge in 2007. They had responded well, staying the course, providing stable governance, and making some popular decisions. The reward was a landslide victory in 2011 and majority government thereafter.

16

The Battle for Scotland is Joined

The referendum campaign of 2014 was the most extraordinary political episode in the modern history of Scotland. Never before had the nation engaged in such a long and intensive dialogue about its present and future. Animated discussions took place within families, among friends and colleagues at work, in pubs, coffee bars, restaurants, in the streets, schools, universities and churches. Most often they were friendly but some ended in disharmony and disagreement between relatives and close acquaintances. Indeed, it was not at all unusual to find families split down the middle on how they would vote as the day of reckoning approached.

Nor were the issues at stake necessarily confined to the stark Manichaean choice between independence and union. They also included the much broader questions of what kind of society Scotland was and how it might be shaped in the future. A process of politicization was in play among many who had shown little previous interest in party politics. The political meeting, thought to have expired in recent years, was rejuvenated, as town and village halls began to echo to the clash of opposing ideas.

New movements sprang from the grass roots, which often turned out to be more dynamic and alluring than the established parties. Numerous lectures and debates were organized to satisfy the hunger for information and argument. The political parties all participated in this process, but it was often those without any affiliation to them who galvanized this so-called 'festival of democracy'. Social media and the blogosphere became key channels for the exchange of robust views that could sometimes develop into acrimonious dispute.

The number who registered to vote in the referendum was unprecedented, while the size of the actual turnout on the day itself was much greater than at any time since universal suffrage was introduced to Scotland nearly a century ago. Many who had never taken part in the democratic process at any point in their lives duly recorded their votes on 18 September 2014. It was a remarkable reversal of the general electoral trend throughout the developed world of declining turnout and voter alienation.

For a few weeks, too, Scotland became the centre of unprecedented international attention. The President of the United States, the Pope, the President of the European Union and, most bizarrely of all, the Prime Minister of Australia, thought it appropriate to comment on the referendum. Like several colleagues in Scottish academe and journalism, this author was interviewed by the radio, television and print media of numerous countries on dozens of occasions, including Argentina, Australia, Brazil, Canada, Columbia, Denmark, Finland, France, Germany, Ireland, Japan, Norway, Portugal, Russia, South Africa, Spain, Turkey, the USA – to name but a few! Every interviewer voiced their amazement at what was going on. In the days before the vote, a media village mushroomed in the environs of the Scottish Parliament at Holyrood. Ordinary citizens of Edinburgh, going about their daily business, were liable to be ambushed by camera crews from exotic locations across the globe, eager to hear their opinions, no matter how mundane, on the big question confronting the Scottish people. Rarely if ever has Scotland been the focus of such international interest.

As the campaign reached a climax and the gap between 'Yes' and 'No' in the polls started to narrow, something close to panic gripped the very highest levels of the British state. The leaders of the unionist parties desperately searched for options to stem what seemed a rising tide drifting inexorably towards a vote for independence. The much greater visibility and higher media profile of the 'Yes' campaign over the previous months only intensified their fears. It did indeed seem for a few days that what had been unthinkable a mere few weeks before might actually happen and Scotland would indeed vote to become a sovereign state, so breaking a union with England that had lasted for over three centuries.

I

With its overall victory secured in the Holyrood election of 2011, the SNP was in a position for the first time to deliver on its long-term promise to hold a referendum on Scottish independence. In early 2012, however, the polls suggested that a clear majority, not far from 60 per cent of the electorate – a figure that had hardly changed over the years – still rejected that constitutional option. It was therefore not altogether surprising against that background that the Salmond government wished to see three questions in the referendum rather than a stark choice between two. Its preferences were: the status quo, independence or maximum devolution (later to become better known as 'devo-max'). By the last, Holyrood would gain full legislative and fiscal powers, but the Crown, monetary policy, defence and foreign affairs would remain under the authority of Westminster. Devo-max, according to all the evidence in 2012, was by a long way the favoured choice of the Scottish electorate. However, the SNP was not to have its way on the issue. The 1998 Scotland Act that established the Scottish Parliament had reserved all future constitutional issues for the decision of the UK Parliament. Indeed, it was possible in law for the UK government to veto any request for a Scottish referendum. In the event, in January 2012, the Conservative Prime Minister, David Cameron, accepted that the initiative should go ahead as it had already gained the support of the Scottish people by an electoral mandate in 2011.

Cameron then went on to specify Westminster's conditions for the referendum. There was to be no truck with a three-question ballot. Instead, a straight choice between the status quo and independence was the only question on offer. The Prime Minister clearly saw an opportunity to destroy the cause for 'separatism' for a generation or more. He and his advisers knew very well that for some time the option of independence had only had minority appeal among the Scottish electorate. Potentially, therefore, a crushing defeat could be inflicted on the forces of nationalism, which would destroy any political threat from them for many years to come. In addition, and crucially, the potential consolation prize of devo-max, which the Nationalists might be able to claim in the event of a vote against independence, would also be snatched from their grasp.

Cameron, however, was willing to make three important concessions to the other side, which would later come back to haunt him during the latter stages of the referendum campaign. The Scottish government was allowed to decide on the date of the referendum, its wording, with the guidance of the Electoral Commission, and the composition of the electoral franchise. The SNP was convinced that a long campaign was vital if there was to be any chance of success in light of the widespread opposition and scepticism about independence. In March 2013 the date of the referendum was set for 18 September 2014. The question to be put to voters was designed to be positive:

> 'Do you agree that Scotland should be an independent country?' – rather than, for example, 'Should Scotland remain part of the UK?' – allowed the SNP to campaign for an upbeat Yes instead of the recalcitrant No.[1]

The franchise was extended to all voters who were registered as living in Scotland, no matter their country of origin, and the voting age for the referendum was lowered to 16 years. The Electoral Commission was mandated to supervise proceedings. On 15 October 2012, David Cameron had come north to seal the 'Edinburgh Agreement' with Alex Salmond at St Andrew's House, the old headquarters of the Scottish Office in the capital. The opening political shots in the 'Battle for Scotland' had been firing since the spring of 2012. Now, however, the broad rules of the campaign were in place and agreed by each side. The campaign could begin in earnest.

The 'Yes' camp knew it had a mountain to climb. The huge challenge confronting them was confirmed later when a poll of polls covering the two years 2012 and 2013 produced the dispiriting news of a continuing 60:40 split against independence. It also started to become clearer what the SNP actually meant by 'independence'. In outline, its definition was much closer to the concept of devo-max than an absolute sovereignty principle of the nineteenth-century variety; this latter was an ideal that would have been unattainable anyway for a small country in the modern era of globalization, powerful multinational corporations and growing interdependence between nation states. It was intended that an independent Scotland would retain the monarchy, membership of NATO and sterling, through a currency union with the rest of the former UK. This last would inevitably have major implications for the economic powers of a new Scottish state. There was also much talk of a future 'social union' between Scotland and England in the event of independence, which would ease some of the trauma of 'separation'. There were not to be any customs posts at Carlisle. Some commentators saw all of this as an attempt to make 'independence' more palatable to a cautious electorate by demonstrating that any changes in the established order would be more limited than many had feared. Nevertheless, even such finessing did not disguise the fact that the primary objective was to establish an autonomous Scottish state and terminate the political union with England. The SNP's determination to ensure the removal of the UK's nuclear-armed Trident submarines from their base on the Clyde estuary after a 'Yes' vote was the most explicit symbol of that proposed new order.

The opposing forces in the campaign now lined up as 'Better Together', supporting a 'No' vote, and 'Yes Scotland'. Better Together had Alistair Darling, the former Labour Chancellor of the Exchequer, as its figurehead and was directed by another Labour activist, Blair McDougall, who had earlier organized David Miliband's failed bid for the leadership of the Labour Party. Apart from Labour, Darling also had the support of the Scottish Conservatives and the Scottish Liberal Democrats. Yes Scotland was fronted by Blair Jenkins, a former Head of News and Current Affairs at BBC Scotland, with the SNP in close support. Aligned with them were the Scottish Green Party and the Scottish Socialists. Very quickly, however, they were also joined by a remarkable variety of other groupings that appeared in the months following, which became increasingly fundamental to the social and political reach of the 'Yes' campaign at the grass-roots level.

At the start, 'Yes' campaigners focused on the message that in ideological terms England and Scotland were increasingly travelling in different directions. This idea of a divergence between north and south Britain took hold and underpinned much of the later discourse: a social democratic Scotland was said to be in inevitable conflict with a post-Thatcherite, neo-liberal, anti-welfare England. Phrased in that way, the idea was overdrawn, but it gained much traction during the coming months and came to be regarded as an article of faith by left-leaning supporters of independence. Its evidential underpinnings, however, were weak in the extreme. The findings of the authoritative *Scottish Social Attitudes Survey* hardly suggested a yawning ideological gap between Scots and their neighbours in the south, especially in relation to those who lived outside London and the Home Counties. One poll, for instance, reported in *The Herald* in May 2014, found that seven out of ten Scots agreed with the United Kingdom Independence Party (UKIP) on immigration policy, more than half wished to see budgets cut for international aid, while six out of ten of the sample interviewed agreed with the proposition that state benefits should only be made available to those who had lived in the UK for at least five years. This was hardly consistent with the narrative of 'Yes', that it was in the clear interest of social democratic Scotland to break the union with England, a country seduced by the forces of neo-liberalism, marketization and privatization.

'Yes' campaigners also anticipated a universally hostile press as the battle for votes was joined. They were not to be disappointed, though even they were perhaps surprised by the relentlessly venomous nature of many of the attacks. The *Daily Mail* headlined on the 'savage racialism' of the Nationalists while the *Daily Telegraph* condemned their 'lies, smears and intimidation'. Other choice headlines included 'thuggish nationalism', 'Forces of Darkness would love Scottish split from the UK', and 'independence a victory for the enemies of freedom' (this last a bizarre quote from Tony Abbott, Prime Minister of Australia). A veritable litany of alleged disasters that would overwhelm the nation in the event of a 'Yes' vote was reiterated on a daily basis in most of the press: a massive budget deficit leading to huge cuts in the NHS, job losses on an enormous scale as businesses fled Scotland, and an existential threat to pension provisions – all and more were predicted.

The non-aligned agency Press Data reckoned from its analyses of stories that made the news during the campaign that the ratio in favour of the unionist cause was almost 4:1. The Scottish-based *Sunday Herald* was the only newspaper in the UK that eventually came out for independence. Its sister paper, *The Herald*, did not follow suit but still managed to maintain a fairly balanced approach to the issues throughout the campaign. Voters intending to vote 'Yes' were also often deeply suspicious about the alleged unionist bias of some aspects of BBC coverage of the referendum. The most notorious episode came when Nick Robinson, the corporation's political editor, stated on the *Six O'Clock News* on 11 September 2014 that Alex Salmond had refused to answer a key question from him at a press conference held earlier that day. The problem for Robinson was that the First Minister's extended answer had already been seen by many thousands on the internet before the broadcast. The incident triggered a wave of nationalist fury and led to protests outside BBC Scotland's headquarters at Pacific Quay, Glasgow. This then allowed an unsympathetic press to wax eloquent on the disgraceful behaviour of nationalist thugs who were allegedly trying to intimidate distinguished journalists. In spite of that bitter controversy it was acknowledged, nevertheless, that several BBC Scotland-based correspondents, such as Brian Taylor, Glen Campbell and James Cook, produced impeccably impartial reports throughout the campaign.

II

By early summer 2014 the organizers of the 'No' campaign could be well satisfied with progress. The press in both Scotland and England were on their side, and they also had the immense resources of the UK state and the three major political parties behind them. In addition, if needed, they could count on the vocal support of big business, particularly from most of those firms that had substantial business and financial interests in Scotland. Some commentators criticized the 'No' organizers for being unduly negative and pedestrian. Nonetheless, the gap between 'Yes' and 'No' intentions continued to remain wide. 'Project Fear', as it came to be known by Nationalists, seemed to be working. Hammering away at the many risks of independence may not have been exciting but it appeared to be effective. Some of London's left-leaning unionist journalists now also entered the battle in support of 'No'. For Will Hutton, the 'Yes' campaign could only bring 'darkness on the land'. He predicted 'the death of the liberal enlightenment', killed off by 'the atavistic forces of nationalism and ethnicity'.[2] A striking feature of this kind of rhetoric was its apocalyptic undertones. Others, such as Seumas Milne and Philip Stephens, also joined the assault. What most of these interventions from metropolitan journalism suggested, however, was that few of their authors appeared to have any real knowledge of what was going on in Scotland at the time.

In fact, it was agreed for some months that the most devastating weapon in the unionist armoury had already been launched in February 2014. In that month the Chancellor of the Exchequer came north on a rare visit to give a special message to the people of Scotland. Its content was explosive. George Osborne declared that there was now full agreement in place between the Conservatives, Labour and Liberal Democrats that, in the event of a vote in favour of Scottish independence, the new state would not be permitted to join a currency union with sterling. The intervention was the first key moment in the entire campaign as it was a mortal threat to the centrepiece of the SNP's economic strategy for an independent Scotland. For a time it left the 'Yes' camp in some disarray. Their eventual response that the electorate should see Osborne's so-called 'Declaration on the Pound' as a gigantic bluff did apparently manage to convince over half the electorate for a time. Nonetheless, when Alex Salmond then lost the first televised debate on the referendum to Alistair Darling on 5 August, against all predictions, the currency issue was clearly revealed as his Achilles heel. The First Minister had no satisfactory answer to Darling's repeated question on what was Salmond's Plan B, since the UK government had publicly refused to agree to a currency union.

But the Osborne statement, agreed by all the unionist parties, turned out to be a much more significant development than simply helping to deliver a victory for the 'No' campaign in a TV debate. On the one hand, it may indeed have stiffened the resolve of those who already intended to vote 'No' or were attracted to doing so. However, as the implications of the intervention sunk in, for some voters at least it proved to be having a counter-productive effect. For the majority of Scots, Conservatism remained a toxic brand. They therefore did not take kindly to being lectured and threatened by a politician from that particular stable, who was not only responsible for some of the obnoxious policies of austerity but also in both persona and in educational and social background represented the very incarnation of metropolitan Toryism.

But this was not all. The Scots had long regarded the Union as a partnership agreed between two nation states. At a stroke, however, the Chancellor had disabused them of such a naive belief. England's interest was now portrayed as paramount within the association and Scotland's subordinate status confirmed. The implication was that the UK government was not prepared to lift a finger to assist an infant new Scottish state in the event of a 'Yes' vote. Indeed, the unionist parties were stating unambiguously that a nation in a partnership union with England for over three centuries was not to receive the same favourable treatment on a shared currency that had been granted in the past to Ireland and former colonial territories when they first became independent. However, as later events were to prove, it was the Labour Party in Scotland that eventually lost most from the currency controversy. Labour had publicly stood shoulder to shoulder with the hated Tories on a fundamental policy issue during a campaign that culminated in many of the party's traditional supporters voting 'Yes'. Journalists who interviewed some of them later found evidence of a deep sense of betrayal and disillusion about their party in working-class communities. A mere seven months later, Labour in Scotland was on the brink of Armageddon as the general election approached on 7 May 2015. A brutal electoral reckoning was then to be visited upon the People's Party.

III

The polls were starting to slowly narrow in the first four months of 2014. By Easter, one had the gap between 'Yes' and 'No' down to a mere 4 per cent. Not all the others agreed, but there was a palpable sense that some kind of change in the formerly stable voting patterns leading up to the referendum was now underway. Commentators noticed that the confident complacency of the 'No' campaign was developing into concern about more fluidity among the electorate than had been previously detected. Nevertheless 'No' continued to retain its dominant position in the polls for some time, though a narrowing of the gap between the two sides continued to occur. It was less than a week before the referendum that the earthquake finally erupted. A sensational *Sunday Times*/YouGov poll on 12 September had 'Yes' in front for the first time in the campaign by a margin of 51:49 per cent. The enormous 'No' lead that had endured into 2014 was effectively wiped out. This momentum for 'Yes', occurring a mere few days before polling day, shook the 'No'campaign to its very foundations. It seemed that the final dynamic of the entire referendum process was now with 'Yes'

Westminster descended into a state of panic. A run on the pound was predicted, and across the Atlantic the US State Department and the National Security Agency rushed to produce position papers on what all this might mean for America's closest ally.

The unionist fight-back took two immediate forms. First, banks and some large companies openly talked about moving their headquarters out of Scotland in the event of a 'Yes' vote. Some of the press detected the hand of the British government in general and that of Downing Street in particular behind these scare stories. Second, the unionist parties rapidly cobbled together a new deal for Scotland to try to outflank the Nationalists as the clock ticked towards the day of reckoning. A so-called VOW was printed on mock-vellum on the front page of the best-selling and Labour-supporting *Daily Record* tabloid two days before polling day. It was signed by David Cameron, Nick Clegg and Ed Miliband and promised 'extensive new powers' to Scotland if the nation voted 'No'. Gordon Brown, the former Labour Prime Minister who had done much to bring this accord about, promised in a speech 'a modern form of Scottish Home Rule within the United Kingdom'. The pledge was to be delivered within a tight time frame. The plan would be published by 30 November 2014, St Andrew's Day, and the draft legislation was to be ready by 25 January 2015, Burn's Night. This was constitutional planning on the hoof. It was a remarkable and humiliating volte-face by the Prime Minister in particular. David Cameron had strenuously opposed the third question on devo-max in the referendum. Now he had been forced to concede something just like that in THE VOW. Earlier, in an emotional speech to the staff of Scottish Widows, the Prime Minister had pleaded with Scots not to vote for independence, 'just to give the effing Tories a kicking', as he elegantly phrased it. The Labour Party also tried to help with Ed Miliband leading over a hundred of his MPs by train to Glasgow for a last-minute push to encourage the bemused citizens of the city whom they encountered in the streets to vote for the Union.

The poll of 10 September almost certainly had another crucial effect. It probably concentrated the minds of 'No' voters who became fully aware that the referendum result was now on a knife edge. Perhaps unsurprisingly, therefore, YouGov's post-poll interviews on 18 September suggested that those who voted 'No' were more determined to turn out than those who favoured 'Yes'. But how had all this come about? Why did the 'No' campaign's significant advantage disappear in the weeks before 18 September, especially given all the advantages described earlier that were possessed by Better Together?

The irony was that in its first year at least, as one seasoned observer pointed out, Yes Scotland was a 'dysfunctional organisation at war with itself . . . almost everything that could go wrong with the "Yes" campaign did go wrong'.[3] Staff sackings and departures, accusations of dictatorial managerial behaviour and poor performance, ensured that it did little of any significance in the early stages of the campaign. Later, Yes Scotland also proved unable to deal effectively with unionist attacks on the currency issue or in rebutting the endless stream of negative stories emanating from a hostile print media.

But the 'Yes' message, in stark contrast to the relentless series of negatives of the official 'No' campaign, was consistently upbeat and optimistic, and the movement soon verged on something like a quasi-evangelical mission of liberation. Anything, it seemed to say, would be possible in an independent Scotland. At the top of the agenda was the promise (vague, to be sure) of radical social change. This visionary utopianism started to resonate strongly at the grass roots. Parallel organizations to Yes Scotland grew up everywhere: Women for Independence, Generation Yes, the National Collective of artists, writers and performers, and many, many more. Before too long, over three hundred groups, some very large, others tiny in numbers, had become affiliated to 'Yes'. The Radical Independence Campaign, for instance, was a federation of left-wing and Green Party activists, autonomous from both the SNP and Yes Scotland. Its main achievement was to energize the large working-class housing estates, or 'schemes', where often only a minority had ever voted in the past but in which substantial majorities were soon found to be willing to vote for independence. In time a 'national conversation' was underway as debate and discussion took off at the local level. Although much less noticed by the media, similar groups were also being launched in favour of 'No'. In the universities, for instance, lively exchanges took place between Academics for Independence and their colleagues on the other side who were very concerned that the end of the Union might have a devastating impact on the flow of research funds into Scottish higher education.

The long campaign arguably worked to the direct advantage of 'Yes'. But of course there was always the problem that, as 'Yes' advanced in the polls, so 'No' voters became ever more determined than ever to turn out on decision day itself in order to combat the growing threat to the Union. A metamorphosis was also developing among 'Yes' activists. Their objective remained the independence of Scotland but increasingly that was seen not as an end in itself but as a means to achieve something else, the mantra of 'a more fair and just society'. It was a message that effectively connected national identity politics with social aspirations and despite its vagueness it seems to have had a potent impact, especially, but not only, in disadvantaged communities. Also attracted were voters, often from a traditional Labour background, who did not consider themselves 'nationalists' and had never been supporters of the SNP. As popular fervour continued to grow, one observer asserted that the movement was becoming 'cult-like, with zealots employing the repeated mantra of Yes as a quasi-religious chant . . . Anyone who asked hard questions about the details of post-independence policies was criticised for negativity and accused of not belonging to the faith'.[4]

This radical utopian theme was central to the writings of some pro-independence writers. One went further than most by insisting that 'the enemy of this uprising' was not simply Westminster but also, internally, 'Scotland's traditional power-holders, from the landowners and big commercial interests to the mainstream politicians, local councillors and senior public servants'. The Union had always been conditional, in this view on, 'its ability to deliver real gains, in terms of freedom, opportunity and justice'. But it was no longer capable of doing so because of 'the huge right-ward shift of Westminster politics over the past generation'.[5] This was also to be the first political campaign in Scotland where the social media of blogs, Facebook and Twitter were employed so extensively. In effect a parallel communications universe with radio, TV and newspapers came into being via the internet. New websites, such as Newsnet Scotland, Bella Caledonia, Wings over Scotland, National Collective and a host of others became primary sources of information and news, even if not all of the output was always welcome: it could be 'a platform for abuse, bullying, misinformation, malicious propaganda and political narcissism', noted one commentator.[6]

Indeed, since the referendum some have tried to pour cold water on the idea of a great 'festival of democracy' taking place in Scotland during the summer and autumn of 2014. Was it more hype than reality? Not so, said even pro-unionist journalists and bloggers who were convinced that something very unusual was going on in the country:

> Yessers and Nawers in Scotland agree on little, save perhaps this: the campaign has been a steroid injection for democracy. (Alex Massie, *The Spectator*, 6 September 2014)

> If you love politics then you have to love the referendum campaign. It has spread conversations about politics everywhere – from pubs to offices, to school gates and hen nights ... The hallmark of the debate, despite nastier notes in the margins, has been respect, and above all else seriousness. (John McTernan, *The Scotsman*, 21 August 2014)

> Don't be fooled by the ugliness you've seen on the front pages of newspapers, or the eggs, or the cybernat ghouls. Rarely can there have been a political battle with such high stakes that has been conducted so peacefully. (Hugo Rifkind, *The Times*, 4 September 2014)

> [B]ehind all that participation was passionate debate and exuberant organisation. Groups backing 'No' and 'Yes' sprang up all over the place, some marshalled by common interests and occupation, many more drawn together by ties of community. Experienced politicians were surprised by the astounding vitality that the indyref unleashed. (Peter Jones, *The Scotsman*, 23 September 2014)

This dynamic in its totality may have been one cause of the surge behind 'Yes'. Yet a return to the bigger picture is also necessary for a fuller understanding why it occurred. The Osborne intervention on currency, supported by both Labour and the Lib Dems, may have forced an unknown number of people to reconsider their attitude to the Union. Also, as previous chapters in this book have shown, various pressures for constitutional change had been building in Scotland for many years. The period between 2011 and the autumn of 2014 was arguably a turning point in this process. It was then that a number of elements for a perfect political storm for the first time came together since the establishment of the Scottish Parliament in 1999. They included an economic crisis that had unleashed unwelcome policies of austerity with attacks on welfare budgets, widely judged to be unfair as they hit the most vulnerable in society; a majority left-leaning nationalist government in Edinburgh and a Tory-led right-wing administration in Westminster with radically different policies on offer, so prompting memories of the 'democratic deficit' of the Thatcher years; the collapse of the Labour vote, the last credible party-political champion of the Union in Scotland, its implosion accelerated by the popular reaction to the notorious alliance of the party with the Conservatives over the currency issue; and the rhetoric of Scotland as a left-wing nation travelling on a different political path from England. The combination of all these factors coming together in a relatively short time frame was likely to be catalytic.

IV

Some 4,285,323 residents in Scotland registered to vote in the referendum, including 109,000 16- and 17-year-olds who had been specially enfranchised for the occasion. It was the highest voter registration in British history since the introduction of universal suffrage. The actual turnout on 18 September 2014 was 85 per cent. By way of comparison, the turnout in Scotland in the UK general election of 2010 had been 64 per cent.

Of those registered, 2,001,926 voted 'No' (or 55 per cent); 1,617,989 (or 45 per cent) voted 'Yes'. The victory margin of 10 per cent for 'No' was greater than had been anticipated and was welcomed by the British government as a decisive result that would settle the Scottish question for a very long time to come. As events were soon to prove, however, that elusive question had still not received a final answer. Despite the defeat of the 'Yes' campaign, it stubbornly refused to go away.

After the failed referendum of 1979 it had taken several years for the supporters of devolution to recover their confidence. But this time it was to be different. Of course, both activists and 'Yes' voters were inevitably dismayed and disappointed at the result. The author was a member of a panel on BBC2's *Newsnight* on the evening when all the results had been declared. A high-profile 'Yes' campaigner, the broadcaster and journalist Lesley Riddoch, revealed to viewers that she 'was gutted'. A conference on 'Bloody Scotland', or crime writing, was being held in Stirling the following day. When asked whether she was intending to go, the immediate emotional response was: 'I have had more than enough of bloody Scotland!' But such despondency did not last for very long. Soon some observers were beginning to wonder which side had lost and which had won, so convincing did they find the determination of the 'Yes' side to fight on.

Much detailed evidence is now available on the referendum result. It is therefore possible to undertake a preliminary assessment of what actually happened on 18 September 2014 as a prelude to future more rigorous research evaluation.[7]

Issues

The 'No' campaign was right to focus on the currency question and the risks and uncertainties of independence. Almost 60 per cent of 'No' voters, surveyed by Lord Ashcroft in his polls, thought the pound was very important in their decision. But currency was not the only element. For these voters all the risks associated with independence were crucial – jobs, prices, the economy, pensions and EU membership. Interestingly, these bread-and-butter issues were much more important than attachment to the UK or the promise of additional powers for the Scottish Parliament. 'Yes' voters were mainly influenced by 'disaffection with Westminster politics'. The idea that Scotland should be in charge of its own affairs also proved to be very compelling. In the last few months of the campaign, 'Yes' focused on the potential dangers to the NHS in a UK state and this had an impact, especially among women.

But there was little doubt overall that 'Yes' lost mainly because it signally failed to provide convincing answers to the many economic uncertainties that had been triggered in the minds of the majority of the electorate during the campaign.

Regional Patterns

Apart from the capital, Edinburgh (61 per cent 'No'), the core of the 'No' vote was mainly in areas away from the central belt, namely the Northern Isles, Dumfries and Galloway (66 per cent 'No'), Perthshire and Aberdeenshire (60 per cent 'No'). This pattern was in part paradoxical. The SNP had traditionally done well in the north-east and to some extent also in Perthshire, but in both areas the 'No' votes stacked up on 18 September. All these regions had relatively low levels of unemployment and higher than average incomes. Dumfries and Galloway had experienced substantial middle-class migration from England for many years. Many families in some parts of the region had close family and business connections across the border. Moreover, before the collapse of the Conservative Party in Scotland in the 1980s and 1990s, the Tory vote had been traditionally strong in both Perthshire and the north-east.

Edinburgh is an interesting case. Only one of its parliamentary constituencies came close to voting 'Yes'. This was Edinburgh East (47 per cent 'Yes'), which contained areas of significant social disadvantage. Scotland's capital has the highest gross average earnings of any city in the UK apart from London. The middle-class social component is much larger than in any of the other Scottish cities. Edinburgh is also unique in Scotland in having a substantial number of pupils in private education. Many of its citizens work in sectors such as banking, finance and higher education, which were supposedly threatened by independence.

Apart from the 'Yes' city of Dundee, the eastern Lowlands of Scotland and the Northern Isles voted 'No'. This is the nation's most prosperous region and had been so for some time, its onward material progress driven by the success of oil, gas, the financial services and a flourishing farming sector supported by the EU Common Agricultural Policy.

'Yes' had its greatest single success in Dundee, where there was a 57 per cent vote for independence. The city had been an SNP stronghold with deep roots for some time, having returned a nationalist MP to

Westminster since 2005. It had lower average earnings than Aberdeen, Edinburgh and Glasgow, and a relatively high level of unemployment. Even more striking was the result in much of the west of Scotland, the old heartland of Scottish Labour. Glasgow, North Lanarkshire and West Dunbartonshire recorded majorities for 'Yes'. Equally, South Ayrshire, Renfrewshire and Stirlingshire, all won by 'No', nevertheless returned substantial minorities of 'Yes' votes. Labour's citadel in the west had not simply been penetrated, it was overwhelmed as many thousands of formerly loyal supporters rejected the party line against independence and deserted in large numbers. This was a much more remarkable paradox of the referendum than the failure of SNP areas in the north-east to return 'Yes' majorities. Formerly the economic dynamo of Scotland, the western Lowlands had suffered more than any other region of the country from rapid de-industrialization. In parts of Glasgow and some other localities, serious levels of disadvantage, structural unemployment and ill health existed. Large numbers depended on welfare benefits, which had been hit by the austerity cuts of the UK government.

The region also had an interesting ethnic mix. Most Scottish Asians lived there and they voted virtually en bloc for independence. More significant numerically were the descendants of Irish Catholics who had migrated to Scotland in the nineteenth century. Since the 1920s no constituency had been more loyal to Labour. A party that stood for social justice was likely to attract such a disadvantaged minority in large numbers. In addition, until the early 1990s, there had been deep suspicion of the SNP within the community as a 'Protestant party'. By the time of the referendum, however, the data show that Catholics were much more likely than members of the Church of Scotland to vote for independence. It was yet another telling sign of the rapid erosion of old Labour loyalties.

The referendum result shone a powerful beam on the deep regional and local fissures within Scotland's unequal society. Did the nation therefore divide along class lines on the constitutional issue? Was the referendum essentially about the different social aspirations of rich and poor, the haves and have nots, rather than independence per se? These and related questions will be considered below, with the important health warning that future research will certainly refine and qualify these preliminary and provisional conclusions.

Class and Background

Almost as soon as the results were announced, prominent members of the 'Yes' campaign opted for class analysis to explain its failure.[8] One expressed the feeling succinctly – the vote had 'represented a victory for the comfortable over the dispossessed'.[9] That view quickly gained considerable traction and began to be asserted in different ways by other high-profile 'Yes' supporters as the response to the result was articulated. However, the data below (Table 6) taken from the reputable *Scottish Social Attitudes Survey* of 2014 tells a more complex story.

Table 6. Support for 'Yes', by Social Class, Ideology and Gender, 2014, as percentages (excluding people who had not decided)

	Working Class	Middle Class
Left	51 (190)	47 (251)
Right	33 (172)	19 (302)
All	42 (362)	32 (553)
Male		
Left	62 (96)	53 (128)
Right	35 (82)	21 (128)
All	48 (178)	37 (256)
Female		
Left	39 (94)	40 (123)
Right	31 (90)	17 (174)
All	35 (184)	27 (297)

Source: *Scottish Social Attitudes Survey*, 2014. Cited in Lindsay Paterson, 'Utopian Pragmatism: Scotland's Choice', *Scottish Affairs* 24:1 (2015), p. 42.

Notes: The responses show people choosing 'Yes' among people who had a definite view; thus the 'No' percentages are 100 minus those shown. Percentages are weighted. Unweighted sample sizes are shown in parentheses.

First, left-leaning people from both the middle and working classes were attracted to vote 'Yes'. Second, the leadership of the grass-roots independence campaign derived from middle-class male activists addressing their message mainly to left-wing, male working-class people and, to a lesser extent, to women. Third, analysis of the surveys punctures the myth that 'Yes' was not about nationalism but exclusively about a demand for radical change and social justice. Rather, the independence movement seems to have been driven *both* by identity politics and radical ideologies:

> the 'Yes' intention was strong among left-leaning middle-class people; it was strongest among those left-leaning middle-class people who identified with working-class Scots, and among left-leaning working-class people who did not show much solidarity with working-class people across the border.[10]

Nevertheless, in broad terms, responses to the referendum did reveal considerable social differences in response to independence. The analysis carried out by the psephologist John Curtice soon after the vote concluded:

> those in working class occupations [in the census categories C2DE], were rather more likely to vote Yes than those in more middle class ABC1 jobs . . . 65% of those living in one of the 20% most deprived neighbourhoods in Scotland voted Yes, compared with just 36% of those in the one-fifth most affluent. There was a similar relationship between the breakdown of the vote in localities with respectively high and low levels of unemployment. A majority voted Yes in just four areas [of the country]. Between them these four areas are amongst the top six [in Scotland] in terms of . . . the proportion living in an area of multiple deprivation, and amongst the bottom six in their proportions in professional and managerial occupations.[11]

The future of the economy was the question of paramount importance in the minds of the electorate as the decision was made whether or not to leave the UK. The poorer and those less well off under the Union were clearly more persuaded that independence would make life better for them. Crudely, in several areas those who had least to lose tended to vote 'Yes'. The affluent, on the other hand, were more impressed by the 'No' arguments about the many risks and potential costs of leaving the Union in an uncertain world.

They probably also took note of the weaknesses of the 'Yes' campaign in relation to the future of the currency, entry to the EU, and a possible flight of capital. Those who had a substantial financial stake in society were often keen to protect it. One additional factor, however, was missed by most commentators. Back in 1979, those from Glasgow and the regional hinterland of the city were among the most enthusiastic for the Scottish Assembly in the failed referendum of that year. Regional preferences for and against constitutional change went back a long way, as also suggested below.

Other aspects of class and background also came through after the votes were cast in the September 2014 referendum. Men were more likely to vote 'Yes' than women, though, in the event, the gender gap was not as wide as the polls had predicted. The approximately 430,000 first-generation migrants to Scotland from England, Northern Ireland, Wales and elsewhere could also have had a significant impact, given the relatively small, 10 per cent difference between 'Yes' and 'No' overall. In the event, 50.2 per cent of those born in Scotland voted 'Yes', compared to 29.8 per cent of those born in the rest of the UK and 43.2 per cent of those born outside the UK. In addition, political scientists for some years have described the movement from Britishness to Scottishness within the old dual or hybrid identity. But the referendum revealed the continuing appeal and political significance of British identity for many north of the border, which may have been underplayed in some previous social science writing. Only just over a quarter of those who saw themselves as 'Equally Scottish and British' voted 'Yes'.

The four highest 'No' votes were recorded in the two districts of the Northern Isles of Orkney (67 per cent) and Shetland (64 per cent), as well as the two councils on the border with England, Dumfries and Galloway (66 per cent) and Scottish Borders (67 per cent). All four regions had also voted 'No' in the first devolution referendum of 1979 and were less keen on the idea of additional tax-raising powers for the proposed Scottish Parliament than elsewhere. They also had above-average levels for income, employment and the proportion of older people. What really marked them out, however, was the number of residents born outside Scotland but in the rest of the UK, and the relatively high proportions who described themselves as British. Clearly a strong sense of national identity was not simply the preserve of those who voted 'Yes'.

The evidence of what actually happened in the referendum also destroyed a good deal of burgeoning mythology. Most importantly, the media assumptions that the passionate and high-profile interventions in the last weeks of the campaign by Gordon Brown, and the collective VOW by the major parties days before 18 September, had saved the Union were proven to be false. In fact, two-thirds of those who made up their minds in the final few days voted 'Yes'. 'No' voters were by far the more likely to say that they had made their decision some time before.

Britishness

The fact that 45 per cent of Scots voted to end the Union might suggest the waning appeal of Britishness despite a majority being opposed to independence. Certainly, as previous chapters have shown, Scottishness was becoming more dominant in recent years. Yet some caution is needed before it is concluded that Britishness might be in its death throes in Scotland. The hybrid or dual identity of the Scots within the Union, formed and built up especially since the early nineteenth century, has complex roots and meanings. It is not easy to extract the emotions of Scottishness or Britishness from this old interrelated duality and place them analytically into neat separate compartments. Moreover, feeling British in whole or in part does not always or necessarily mean that an individual is committed to supporting political unionism. Of course, Britishness does have political manifestations. But it can also be based on pride in past achievements and a continuing awareness of cultural and social connections forged between the peoples of Britain over many years, in other words, a symbol of unity for sure but not necessarily a badge of political unionism. Data collected by Edinburgh University sociologists and published in 2014–15 suggested that:

> 'Britain' remains a salient and meaningful frame of reference, even though more and more people in England and Scotland do not define

their own identity *primarily* as British . . . Being British *does* have content and meaning in terms of important symbols of British culture which are widely and normatively held.

The findings were that Scottishness was indeed very widespread, but Britishness was also claimed by substantial numbers. Many in addition continued to see themselves as both Scottish and British.[12]

17
After the Battle

The day after the referendum results became public, on 19 September 2014, Alex Salmond announced that he intended to resign as First Minister and leader of the SNP. During the campaign he had in fact told close associates that he would go if Scotland did not vote for independence. He left behind an extraordinary but divided legacy. To his many admirers he was the most consummate politician of the age in Britain. For those less sympathetic, however, he was overconfident, smug and divisive. None could deny, however, his remarkable achievements in leading the SNP into government for two consecutive periods, delivering a referendum on independence, and helping to bring the YES vote to a level of support most thought impossible at the beginning of the campaign. It soon became clear, however, that Salmond did not intend to leave the political stage forever when he stated that he would stand for a Westminster seat at the May 2015 general election. In the event, he handsomely won the seat of Gordon in the north-east, which had formerly been held by the Liberal Democrats.

He was succeeded as First Minister and leader of the SNP by his able long-term deputy, Nicola Sturgeon. She was a different personality from her former boss: intensely disciplined and hard working, a very capable administrator, and a clear and cogent, if less charismatic, speaker than Salmond. She is also more genuinely left of centre in political terms than the former First Minister. Her Tory opponent, Ruth Davidson, leader of the Scottish Conservatives, even described her as the most left-wing First Minister to have been appointed since the foundation of the Parliament. Sturgeon quickly blossomed in the job, achieving enviable levels of popularity both within and well beyond the SNP, and she developed a high media profile across the UK during the general election campaign in the spring of 2015.

Scottish Labour also had a new leader. When Johann Lamont departed the scene in a mood of bitterness and recrimination, Jim Murphy, MP, was elected to succeed her. Murphy is an experienced career politician who had shown his mettle by winning the safest Tory seat in Scotland, Eastwood, near Glasgow, in the 1997 Labour landslide. He then went on to become a Cabinet minister in the Labour government. During the referendum campaign he became a national figure with a speaking tour of 100 Scottish towns in support of NO. He famously addressed his listeners standing on an empty Irn Bru crate. In electing him, Labour had obviously gone for experience, reputation and the recognition factor. But Murphy faced very tough challenges, not simply because of the desertion of the Labour faithful in droves to the YES campaign during the referendum, but also because he represented the very incarnation of New Labour that many of the party's one-time Scottish followers had rejected. He had supported the Iraq War and the continuing possession of nuclear weapons, and he voted for both market reform of the NHS and tuition fees. This was not a record likely to have immediate appeal in the housing 'schemes' of west-central Scotland. The election to leadership of Sturgeon and Murphy, with their different political backgrounds, tended to project and underscore the stereotypical public image of the SNP as a distinctive left-of-centre party and Scottish Labour as much less committed in that direction.

NO had won the referendum by a greater margin than had been anticipated. Afterwards an all-party commission, chaired by the Scottish businessman and crossbench peer Lord Smith of Kelvin, was set up to work out the new powers for the Scottish Parliament promised in THE VOW during the final days of the campaign. With this body in place and independence decisively rejected, Westminster concluded that the Scottish constitutional question could now be settled for a long time to come. That judgement proved illusory. Scotland remained a very restless nation. The YES campaigners did not fade away or disappear into the political undergrowth. Instead, they soon recovered from their defeat, quickly regrouped and fought on. The message went out that a battle had been lost but the war was still there to be won over the long run. A month after the referendum some unionist commentators even started to complain that the losers were strutting around like winners and the winners were behaving as if they had lost the vote.

The Prime Minister did little to slow the speedy resurrection of the YES movement when he delivered his first comments after the result became clear. He declared emphatically, in a carefully crafted statement designed especially for listeners in England, that there now had to be '*English* votes for *English* laws' (EVEL) within the UK Parliament in order to compensate for the additional powers promised to the Scottish Parliament. This commitment eventually would mean, inter alia, that English MPs would be given a veto over legislation that applied only to England, including income tax rates, and that at the crucial scrutinizing committee stage with such bills the discussion would be confined solely to MPs representing English constituencies. William Hague, the Leader of the Commons, later admitted that these measures were designed to prevent the wishes of the English and Welsh from being overridden by MPs from Scotland. In effect, for the first time since 1707, two classes of members were now to sit in the Westminster Parliament, a body with legislative responsibility for the whole of the United Kingdom. One journalist, unsympathetic to the initiative, wrote:

> He [the Prime Minister] had come to a historic fork in the national road. He might have turned one way, and stretched out a magnanimous hand to Scotland. He might have said that he appreciated the passion of the Yes campaign ... He might have reassured the Scots that he would recognise this by ensuring that their voice would be heard in Westminster, and respected.
>
> The man who days before had seemed close to tears in Edinburgh when he claimed to 'love my country much more than I love my party' could have said that he would devote himself to ensuring that Scotland felt no urge to vote on independence again for a very long time.
>
> Rather than stretch out that hand in friendship, he used it to slap the Scots in the chops by taking refuge, for short-term party political gain, in crude and petty nationalism.[1]

David Cameron may, however, have felt himself boxed in by opposing forces. The more the Scots were placated, the greater the danger of a backlash from English voters when UKIP was on the march and English nationalism was becoming a force to be reckoned with. EVEL was therefore probably an inevitable consequence of the promised extension of more powers to Holyrood. Nevertheless, since this was the first statement made by the Prime Minister after the referendum, some felt he might also be about to betray the promises made in the last days of the campaign. The former leader of the Liberal Democrats, Lord Ashdown, was aghast, accusing Cameron of making 'one of the most irresponsible speeches ever made by a Prime Minister . . . [in an] ill-advised attempt to grab onto the coat-tails of Ukip by pulling an ill-thought out proposition for English votes out of the hat'.[2]

Cameron's intervention may indeed have caused irritation north of the border, but deeper forces than that were at work after the referendum. All the pro-independence political parties, the SNP, Greens and Scottish Socialists, soon reported unprecedented surges in membership. By the end of November the SNP lists had trebled in size to 84,000 (Labour in Scotland claimed 13,000 members in 2014); in early 2015 the figure was over 100,000 and rising. The opinion polls were also showing a dramatic swing of almost 30 per cent in voting intentions in Scotland from Labour to the SNP. If there was a Murphy effect, it was obviously not working in the way Labour had intended. The polling figures predicted a catastrophic Labour loss in the general election of 37 seats or more, which would leave the party with only a tiny rump of MPs. Subsequent polls and the general election result in May 2015 suggested that even this historic collapse was not to be the end of the nightmare for a party that had dominated the landscape of Scottish politics for so long. Labour had been in retreat north of the border for some time, as discussed in previous chapters, but the referendum campaign seems to have been a kind of tipping point, transforming its earlier levels of decline into a potential political rout. The party was now likely to pay a terrible price for standing shoulder to shoulder with the Conservatives in the NO campaign. The descriptor 'political earthquake' is a term much overused by the media. But on this occasion it accurately reflected what was going on in Scotland in late 2014 and early 2015.

It soon became obvious that these seismic developments north of the border were also likely to have potentially crucial implications for politics throughout the UK. In January 2015 the UK government laid out its plans for further devolution to Scotland in response to the conclusions of the Smith Commission and in an attempt to honour THE VOW made by all three main parties in the final stages of the referendum campaign. The main points were:

- the Scottish Parliament to be given power to set the rates of income tax and the bands at which these are paid
- some welfare benefits devolved, including Attendance Allowance and Disability Living Allowance
- air passenger duty devolved
- the Barnett formula, which determines Scotland's annual budget from Westminster to continue but be reduced to compensate for the additional revenues the Scottish government would receive from the new taxation arrangements
- the Crown Estate's assets (seabed, foreshore, urban, mineral and fishing rights) and the revenue generated from them to be transferred to the Scottish government.

(For more details see 'New Powers for Holyrood' below, pp. 263–7)

The Prime Minister came to Edinburgh to unveil the new powers and declared it 'a great day for Scotland and a great day for the United Kingdom too'. Later, after the May general election, David Cameron went further and stated that the proposals when made law would make the Scottish Parliament 'the most powerful devolved assembly in the world'. He hoped these measures, together with the decisive NO vote in the referendum, would spell the end of the Scottish obsession with constitutional issues and promote a return in the country to 'normal' politics. The unionist parties had certainly honoured the tight timetable they had set themselves when THE VOW was first promised. Some of the proposals were welcomed, such as the repatriation of air passenger duty, the devolved welfare benefits, and the assets and revenues of the Crown Estate. But the package of measures did not contain any real control over the key welfare budgets and, taken in the round, was some way away from the concept of 'modern home rule' articulated so eloquently by Gordon Brown in his final speeches during the last days of the referendum campaign. Nor did the proposals live up to some of the Scottish electorate's apparent understanding of the meaning of THE VOW. Many had expected the delivery of devo-max in the classic form, with Westminster retaining responsibility only for the currency, foreign affairs and defence, but with all other powers devolved to Holyrood. If that indeed was a general expectation there was likely to have been disappointment when the details of the proposed legislation were made public. The political debate that followed the Prime Minister's announcement soon developed along predictable lines, with the parties of the Union praising the measures as the promised implementation of THE VOW, and the Nationalists condemning them as being too little, too late, to save the Union. Time may change that perception but, as this is written in the summer of 2015, the legislation has stimulated little excitement among the populace. Indeed, discussion of the proposals quickly faded from the media and public interest as the national discourse began to switch to preparations for the forthcoming May general election.

As the referendum campaign was winding down, the British political parties began to focus their attention on 7 May 2015. All the signs were that the general election would be a close-run thing. Even in early May the Conservatives and Labour remained neck and neck in the polls. In this scenario the probable destruction of Labour in Scotland could have momentous consequences. The party had relied in each general election since the 1960s on a large haul of forty-plus Scottish seats, either to win power or to have a fighting chance of victory against the Conservatives buttressed by their electoral fortresses in the Home Counties and south-east. The chances of Labour holding on to that old Scottish sheet anchor were, however, now fading fast.

Furthermore, the SNP made it clear that it would welcome the opportunity to provide support for a Labour administration in a hung parliament, though only under certain specific conditions and with some key concessions expected in return. The notion of a formal pact between his party and the Nationalists was, however, rejected publicly on more than one occasion by Ed Miliband, the Labour leader.

The SNP for its part declared equally vehemently that it would not under any circumstances provide support to the Tories if they tried to form a minority administration.

During the round of television debates as the date for the election drew near, Nicola Sturgeon impressed the general UK audience by her presence and debating skills. She was reckoned to have come out as the top performer across the piece, even when up against the leaders of the UK parties. The popularity of the leader of the SNP, already high in Scotland, continued to soar. But in the days immediately before the election, Sturgeon's political honeymoon south of the border abruptly came to an end. The Tories and their media allies went on the offensive against the Nationalists in an attempt to outflank Labour, whom they accused of likely being in hock to a party that was committed to the break-up of Britain, and also to appease those voters who were threatening to desert from the Conservatives to UKIP. The former SNP leader Alex Salmond, now with his sights on a seat in Westminster, was depicted in election posters as a thief, cunningly picking the pockets of the gullible English. It was alleged that since Sturgeon was obviously more able than Miliband, the Labour leader would be under the nationalist thumb if the two parties came to an arrangement. A storm of Scotophobia was also unleashed by the Conservative-supporting press in England. Newspapers like the *Sun* and the *Daily Mail* now became almost racist and then misogynistic in their lampooning of Scotland's First Minister. Sturgeon was labelled 'the most dangerous woman in Britain', 'the Scotweiler' and 'Little Miss McHypocrite'. The SNP was relentlessly demonized in the same papers and the London mayor, Boris Johnson, went into overdrive when he merrily predicted 'Jockalypse' if Labour were ever to enter government with nationalist support. For some of the London press, it seemed that the barbarians from the north were now truly at the gates. All this was unlikely to help to fortify a union relationship that had already been sorely battered during the referendum campaign on Scottish independence in the previous year. Despite warnings from senior members of his own party that he was playing with fire, David Cameron did nothing to try to rein in the campaign of abuse. Many drew the conclusion that he was more interested in retaining power in Downing Street than ensuring the survival of the Union. It became apparent later, however, that the scare tactics had been successful.

Despite the furore, however, the SNP must have contemplated the post-election scenario with some equanimity if, as predicted, they did win a large number of Labour seats. If Miliband led a bigger party than the Conservatives but could only govern with the informal support of the SNP, albeit on an issue-by-issue basis, the Nationalists could hope to extract some significant concessions from him in return. On the other hand, if the Conservatives moved back into government, either alone or through a coalition with the Lib Dems and the Northern Ireland Democratic Unionists, the SNP dream of an independent Scotland might come closer to reality given the expected hostile reaction in Scotland to the return to power of the hated Tories. In the interim, the nationalist MPs in the new UK Parliament in such a scenario could continuously harry the Tory-led administration and earn warm plaudits from their fellow Scots at home by doing so.

These two scenarios, however, proved to be illusory when the real results of the general election began to trickle in during the early hours of 8 May. As more seats were declared, the predictions of the opinion polls of an SNP landslide in Scotland were confirmed. In England, however, the polls were proved wrong as the Conservatives swept to a stunning victory and a small overall majority in the House of Commons. The Liberal Democrats, their former coalition partners, were annihilated, losing many of their major figures, while in Scotland, astonishingly, the Labour Party was left with just one MP (Table 7). The leaders of the UK Labour, Lib Dem and UKIP parties quickly resigned their positions, though Nigel Farage of UKIP was quickly reinstated. The SNP captured an extraordinary 56 seats and took the political scalps of the following leading figures: Jim Murphy, the recently appointed Labour leader in Scotland; Douglas Alexander, Shadow Foreign Secretary and Labour campaign strategist; Danny Alexander, Chief Secretary to the Treasury in the Conservative/Lib Dem coalition government; and the former Lib Dem leader Charles Kennedy. Only three Scottish seats eluded the Nationalists, one apiece for the Conservatives, Labour and Liberal

Democrats. The SNP now became the third largest party in the new House of Commons after the Tories and Labour.

Table 7. UK General Election Results, May 2015

Conservatives	Labour	SNP	Lib Dems	UKIP	Others
331	232	56	8	1	22
+24	−26	+50	−49	+1	+10

The English media were astonished at the destruction visited on Labour in Scotland. But its electoral humiliation did not come like a thunderbolt from a clear sky. The opinion polls north of the border, unlike their counterparts in the south, were proven to be reasonably accurate and had long predicted the disaster, albeit they had marginally underestimated the scale of the catastrophe. As shown already in this book, Labour had been in decline in Scotland since the late 1970s. But much of that process, especially in its early stages, was invisible, a subtle and gradual fall in popularity, only to be uncovered by later historians of the era with their key advantage of hindsight vision. By 2015 the party had begun to resemble a large hollowed-out nut, with the insides extracted, so leaving only an empty shell that could be cracked open with ease. The lengthy period of declining fortunes probably also meant that any Labour recovery in Scotland might take some time.

The irony was that Labour was the only Scottish political party that could and eventually did deliver a Scottish Parliament when it won the UK general election with the landslide of 1997. Without that new Parliament the SNP could not have risen to prominence and then to political power. A former Labour minister, who had opposed the original devolution settlement, complained bitterly after the historic SNP victory in May 2015 that the Labour Party had in effect built its own electoral scaffold by promoting the foundation of Holyrood. As long as Westminster elections remained a two-horse race in Scotland between Labour and a marginalized Conservative Party, the hegemony of Labour was secure. When, however, the SNP emerged as a rival and popular third force, the game changed entirely, the goalposts were moved, and the results of the match became unpredictable. People now had another party to vote for with a proven track record, attractive policies and election-winning potential.

NEW POWERS FOR HOLYROOD *

What's In

Air Passenger Duty

The tax on air passengers leaving Scottish airports will be transferred to Holyrood. SNP ministers have already made it clear they want to reduce this in order to attract more routes to Scotland and boost the country's tourism industry.

The Scottish government would also be free to make its own arrangements with regard to the design and collection of any replacement tax if this is axed, including consideration of the environmental impact. Clause 14 of the draft legislation published yesterday says the Scottish Parliament will be given the power to tax air passengers departing from Scottish airports. It adds: 'The clause includes provision for appointing the day when APD will be switched off in relation to Scotland.'

Crown Estate

The Crown Estate's economic assets in Scotland, and the revenue generated from these assets, will be transferred to the Scottish Parliament.

This will include the Crown Estate's seabed, urban assets, rural estates, mineral and fishing rights and its Scottish foreshore.

'The transfer of responsibility for the management of the Scottish assets will include control of any revenues arising from those assets as well as responsibility for managing all liabilities relating to those assets,' the document states.

---

* Source: John Macnab, 'New Powers for Holyrood: The Main Points', *The Scotsman* (23 January 2015).

Barnett Formula

As Scotland is handed sweeping new powers over taxation and public spending, including elements of the welfare system, this will be accompanied by an updated fiscal framework for Scotland.

The Barnett formula, which determines Scotland's annual budget from Westminster, will continue, but be cut back to account for extra revenues that Scotland will get from taxation. The Scottish government and UK government budgets should be unchanged as a result of the decision to devolve further powers to the Scottish Parliament. So if a future Scottish government decides it wants to put up income tax, it should be able to gain the benefit of that extra revenue and not have its budget cut by London to compensate for any perceived extra funding.

Elections

The Scottish Parliament will have full powers over elections to the Scottish Parliament and local government elections in Scotland. The parties on the commission have called on the UK Parliament to devolve the relevant powers in sufficient time to allow the Scottish Parliament to extend the franchise to 16 and 17-year-olds for the 2016 elections, should the Scottish Parliament wish to do so. This power is being fast-tracked so that this younger group can be in place in time for the election in May next year. However, they still won't be able to vote in the forthcoming Westminster election.

Borrowing

Holyrood will also get additional borrowing powers to ensure budgetary stability and provide safeguards to smooth Scottish public spending in the event of economic shocks. Consideration will also be given to handing the Scottish government extra capital borrowing powers.

The amount will be decided on the basis of 'specific risk', the document yesterday states and this has yet to be calculated.

But it adds: 'A clear plan will be needed to repay the debt incurred in order to ensure a sustainable fiscal position. This could be in the same year in the case of small and one-off shocks, or over a longer period for deeper recessions.'

Any deal will be subject to discussion between governments.

VAT

The receipts raised in Scotland by the first 10 percentage points of the standard rate of VAT will be assigned to the Scottish government's budget. These receipts will be calculated on a verified basis, to be agreed between the UK and Scottish governments, with a corresponding adjustment to the block grant received from the UK government.

The UK government proposes to go further and also assign the first 2.5 percentage points of the revenue attributable to Scotland from the 5 per cent reduced rate. VAT rates will continue to be set at a UK-wide level.

HMRC may disclose information as part of the process of deciding what may be proposed as the basis for the calculation in any agreement and as part of the process of seeking to reach agreement or in operating the agreement.

Income Tax

The Scottish Parliament will be given the power to set the rates of income tax and the bands at which these are paid. There will be no restrictions on the thresholds or rates the Scottish Parliament can set.

All other aspects of income tax will remain reserved to the UK Parliament, including the imposition of the annual charge to income tax, the personal allowance, the taxation of savings and dividend income, the ability to introduce and amend tax reliefs and the definition of income.

The Scottish government will also be responsible for non-savings and non-dividend income, with a corresponding adjustment in the block grant it receives from the UK government. It will continue to be collected and administered by HMRC.

The changes are unlikely to be introduced for three or four years, but the Scottish Parliament is already in line to get sweeping new tax powers next year. Income tax will effectively be cut by 10p, with MSPs responsible for raising it back to the required level in line with need. This will include income from 'employment, profits from self-employment, pensions, taxable social security benefits and income from property'.

An individual is a Scottish taxpayer if they are a UK resident for tax purposes and their main place of residence is in Scotland for the majority of the year.

Welfare

The most contentious area of the latest devolution settlement. The Smith agreement did state that the Scottish government should be given a number of powers over Universal Credit payments, including varying the under-occupancy charge – the so-called 'bedroom tax'. But Nicola Sturgeon went on the warpath yesterday, insisting the welfare proposals don't allow Scottish ministers to vary Universal Credit without the permission of the UK government. That means Scottish ministers would not have the independence to take action to abolish the bedroom tax.

The document published yesterday states that Universal Credit will 'remain reserved, and be delivered by DWP [Department for Work and Pensions] across Great Britain' and the Scottish Secretary will have to be 'consulted' about any variations.

But it adds: 'Scottish ministers will be able to decide whether to apply any under-occupancy reductions, or to choose to set them at different levels.'

Other newly devolved benefits include Attendance Allowance, Carer's Allowance, Disability Living Allowance (DLA), Personal Independence Payment (PIP), along with social fund welfare such as Cold Weather Payment and Funeral Payment.

What's Not

Foreign Affairs

The UK government will continue to lead on the global stage on behalf of Scotland through its membership of international bodies such as the EU, G8 and UN. Its global network of embassies will also provide support for Scots in trouble abroad. This area was never likely to be transferred under any new devolved set-up short of independence.

Defence

The UK's armed forces will continue to provide Scotland's military defence capability, including Trident. This, along with membership of the Nato defence alliance and the permanent seat on the UN security council, means the UK is still regarded as a major military power on the global stage. Defence was never likely to be devolved.

Taxes

All aspects of National Insurance contributions, inheritance tax and capital gains tax, fuel duty and excise duties will remain reserved, as will all aspects of the taxation of oil and gas receipts. Corporation tax will also remain reserved, despite the SNP demanding control.

The commission has called on the UK and Scottish governments to work together to avoid double taxation and make administration as simple as possible for taxpayers.

Welfare

Universal Credit will remain a reserved benefit administered and delivered by the Department for Work and Pensions, despite the Scottish Parliament having some controls over areas such as frequency of payments.

Other benefits remaining at Westminster include bereavement allowance, bereavement payment, child benefit, guardian's allowance, maternity allowance, statutory maternity pay, statutory sick pay and widowed parent's allowance.

All aspects of the state pension will remain shared across the United Kingdom and reserved to the UK Parliament.

Afterword

The Regal Union that was established in 1603 when James VI of Scotland became James I and VI of the new joint kingdoms of England and Scotland has now lasted for more than four centuries. Attempts by James himself and others in subsequent decades to secure an even closer association between the two nations usually ended in indifference or acrimony, with the single unlamented exception of the short-lived Cromwellian union imposed by draconian force of arms in the 1650s.

A parliamentary union when it finally came about in 1707 was essentially a marriage of convenience born out of pragmatism and expediency on both sides rather than one of amity between the two historic polities. For nearly half a century thereafter the future of that international agreement remained in considerable doubt as repeal of the Act of Union always remained a possibility. Yet, by 1815, the Union had become an accepted fact of life by the majority of English and Scots. On the whole a state of tranquillity now reigned between the two kingdoms, not least because of Scotland's sacrifice in blood alongside England during the titanic conflict with Napoleonic France and the remarkable fruits of imperial plunder gained by Scottish elites across the world.

For two hundred years thereafter the Union achieved virtually unquestioned stability throughout the era of industrialization, empire and the two world wars of the twentieth century. The bonds between the two countries deepened profoundly during this period. Scotland indeed had the best of both worlds, global market opportunities on an unprecedented scale through the Union but also an acceptance by England of Scotland's status as a partner nation with considerable autonomy over its own domestic affairs.

Crucially, however, these connections never resulted in assimilation or even full integration. Scotland remained a nation inside a joint parliamentary association with a bigger partner, while retaining a strong sense of ancient historic identity and the continuity of distinctive institutions of religion, law and education. If tensions of governance within the Union emerged, as they did in the last quarter of the twentieth century, they were likely to rub up against Scotland's sense of nationhood and pride in a special status within the Union state. During and after the years of the Thatcher governments, the crisis within the Union became so acute that it was only relieved by the promise of devolved government by Westminster to Scotland.

Despite the hopes of its Labour Party progenitors that the new Holyrood Parliament of 1999 would restore stability within the Union by destroying separatism, it ironically became the forum through which the Scottish National Party eventually rose to power and electoral popularity. The historic consequence of the SNP's success was the referendum on Scottish independence of September 2014. Never since the turbulent years of the early eighteenth century had the Union of England and Scotland faced so grave a threat to its very existence.

This book has tried to pose, consider and answer a series of questions on the historic Anglo-Scottish connection from before 1707 until the UK general election of 2015. It is abundantly clear that the most fundamental issue of all, whether Scotland will remain within the United Kingdom or become an independent state, still awaits a final answer. Indeed, the outcome of the May 2015 general election has only made this question more compelling and intriguing. In the aftermath of the contest, *The Guardian* concluded that 'What the SNP triumph means for the long term is [now] the largest question the result poses for Britain.'[1] A whole series of related matters also came into sharp focus: What impact, if any, will the phalanx of SNP MPs have on the new House of Commons? How will the Scots react to five years of a new Conservative government with a mandate to continue the imposition of policies of austerity that will cut funding, perhaps substantially, to Scotland? Will the apparent Tory determination to reduce the welfare budget in an even more radical fashion than before have the same effect on Scottish opinion as the notorious poll tax of the 1980s? Can Scottish Labour ever fully recover in the medium term from the comprehensive electoral trouncing that it suffered in 2015? Will the election of Jeremy

Corbyn as leader of the Labour Party in England, with his more left-of-centre agenda, win back the old faithful in Scotland?

As this is being written, however, the most pressing question in the media and among the commentariat is: Will recent events bring Scottish independence closer or not?

At first glance the omens seemed favourable for those who aspire to the establishment of a sovereign Scottish state in the near future. The SNP has virtually turned Scotland into a nationalist polity. The two Scottish parties that staunchly support the Union now have only tiny representations in Westminster and are massively outnumbered by the serried ranks of 56 nationalist MPs. SNP morale has been boosted to astronomical levels by its stunning 2015 general election success in Scotland. Nor has the 'Yes' movement been killed off by the referendum defeat; on the contrary, it has continued to press for another plebiscite sooner rather than later. Some of those left-wing activists who played an important role in the organization of the pro-independence campaign outside the ranks of the SNP have now come together to form a new party in Scotland named RISE. This is an acronym for Respect, Independence, Socialism, Environmentalism, and it reflects the aspirations of the different groups involved. Whether the party will survive, only time will tell.

Much Scottish opinion has now hardened around the SNP under the leadership of Nicola Sturgeon since the referendum, and so it is very likely that the party will be returned to power at the next Holyrood elections in May 2016. Moreover, the Nationalists now have the political contest for which many in their ranks have long yearned: a straight fight with a right-wing Westminster Tory government that has promised to bring in even more measures of austerity, draconian cuts in welfare, and the shrinkage of the UK state. In addition, the very hostile Conservative campaign in the last days before the general election, against the supposed threat from the Scots in support of a minority Ed Miliband government, could hardly have helped the unionist cause north of the border.

Westminster also now seems less a Parliament of the Union than it did even a few years ago. As one political scientist has written recently, 'As an unintended consequence of devolution . . . an increasingly Anglicised polity has quietly emerged as an incubus at the heart of the UK state . . .

the Westminster parliament is gradually evolving into an English-focused one'.[2] This tendency can only increase if EVEL (English votes for English laws) reaches the statute book. A federal solution in light of today's fluid set of changing relationships between Edinburgh and London could certainly provide a formidable and possibly insurmountable roadblock for the independence bandwagon. Yet recent talk of a federal solution remains just that: talk. A potential federal settlement is immediately confronted with the major problem of the grossly imbalanced demography of the UK, with England having 85 per cent of the total population and no current interest south of the border in regional assemblies. A UK state that has struggled with little success for many years to modernize the House of Lords is hardly likely to willingly undertake a root-and-branch reform of the entire British constitution and political structure in an attempt to see off the Scottish Nationalists.

Then there is the promised Conservative plebiscite whether to be in or out of Europe, which is planned for 2017. If the English vote 'Yes' to leave but the Scots vote 'No', the SNP has resolved that this might automatically trigger another referendum on Scottish independence. However, in 2015, the likely result of that European vote remains too close to call. The polls suggest the vote for a UK exit is not quite as strong as it once was some time ago in England and, significantly, UKIP, the fundamentalist opponent of the United Kingdom remaining in the European Community, only managed to win one seat at the May 2015 election.

Yet all of this does not necessarily mean that another Scottish independence referendum is inevitable before the end of the current UK Parliament in 2020. Indeed, 2015 could well represent the high-water mark of nationalist popularity. For example, Quebec in the last Canadian referendum in 1995 came even closer to independence than the Scots in 2014. The 'No' campaign in Quebec won by only 50.6 per cent to 49.4 per cent of the vote in that year. Since then, however, though the Parti Québécois still presses for separation of the province, there has not been another independence referendum and the campaign for self-determination has lost the impetus that it possessed two decades ago.

Nicola Sturgeon will also be fully aware that another referendum will be a zero-sum game. If there is one soon and the vote is lost again, the cause of independence would be sidelined for many years to come and might indeed never surface again in the foreseeable future. An entrenched opinion-poll majority for 'Yes' of as much as 60:40 or more over a period of months might be the essential precondition for trying once again at some stage. That could be very difficult to achieve in the short run, as the current popularity of the SNP is not yet based on a majority commitment to independence among those who voted for the party in May 2015. What must also give some concern to the nationalist government is that behind its popularity lies increasing polling evidence in 2015 that the electorate are increasingly underwhelmed by the SNP performance on such core policy issues as health, education and social justice. There may be much here for an effective opposition to attack. The Nationalists have also still to get to grips with their three key weaknesses in the pro-independence campaign: the unconvincing policies on the currency, relentlessly exposed by 'No' supporters; pensions; and economic strategies in a Scottish sovereign state. The evidence confirms that older voters were especially worried about these issues. Developing more convincing plans on these matters in preparation for any future referendum is likely to take time, especially since the recent steep fall in the price of North Sea oil has hardly helped the nationalist cause.

Then there is THE VOW, or what might now be termed THE VOW PLUS, articulated in the days before the referendum in September 2015. David Cameron performed a brazen volte-face in his first speech after the Conservative election victory. Only the day before he and his acolytes were still playing the Scottish card, warning of the terrible threat posed to democracy by a Caledonian takeover of Westminster in partnership with Labour. Now he declared that his firm intention was to grant Scotland 'the strongest devolved government anywhere in the world'. What this means only time will tell; and even more time will be needed before the impact of that promise on the Scottish question can be determined.

Indeed, the tactics of the Prime Minister may well be crucial to future outcomes in the short run. According to one view, Cameron lacks 'the satanic realism to grab permanent [political] control of England by letting the Scots go'.[3] It is the case that any leader of the Conservative Party, conscious of its great unionist traditions, would prefer not to go down in history as the politician who allowed the Union to end on their watch. This could turn out to be a not unimportant factor in forthcoming events relating to the immediate future of the United Kingdom.

Notes

1: THE CONTEXT OF UNION

1. Lord Sumption, 'The Disunited Kingdom: England, Ireland and Scotland', Lecture to the Denning Society, Lincoln's Inn, 5 November 2013.
2. P. W. J. Riley, 'The Scottish Parliament of 1703', *Scottish Historical Review*, 47:143, pt. 2 (1968), pp. 129–50.

2: MAKING THE UNION

1. J. M. Gray, ed., *Memoirs of the Life of Sir John Clerk of Penicuik* (Edinburgh, 1892), p. 58.
2. D. Duncan, ed., *History of the Union of Scotland and England by Sir John Clerk of Penicuik* (Edinburgh, 1993), p. 118.
3. Ibid., p. 121.

3: A FRAGILE UNION

1. Quoted in Christopher A. Whatley with Derek J. Patrick, *The Scots and the Union* (Edinburgh, 2006), p. 336.
2. Quoted in M. E. Novak, *Daniel Defoe: Master of Fictions* (Oxford, 2001), p. 423.
3. Quoted in Jeffrey Stephen, *Defending the Revolution: The Church of Scotland, 1689–1716* (Farnham, 2013), p. 169.
4. Murray Pittock, *Jacobitism* (London, 1998), pp. 44–5.
5. Stephen, *Defending the Revolution*, p. 205.
6. Rosalind Mitchison, *A History of Scotland* (London, 1970), p. 326.
7. Quoted in John S. Shaw, *The Management of Scottish Society, 1707–1764* (Edinburgh, 1983), p. 86.
8. Ibid.

4: UNION EMBEDDED

1. Linda Colley, *Britons* (London, 1995 edn), p. 135.
2. Paul Langford, 'South Britons' Reception of North Britons, 1707–1820', in T. C. Smout, ed., *Anglo-Scottish Relations from 1603 to 1900* (Oxford, 2005), p. 264.

5: EARLY FRUITS OF EMPIRE

1. Quoted in T. M. Devine, *Scotland's Empire, 1600–1815* (London, 2003), p. 329.
2. There is an abbreviated version of Seton's speech in Christopher A. Whatley, *'Bought and Sold for English Gold'?: Explaining the Union of 1707* (Glasgow, 1994), pp. 48–50.
3. Adam Smith, *An Inquiry into the Nature and Causes of the Wealth of Nations*, ed. J. R. McCulloch (Edinburgh, 1861), Book iii, p. 181.
4. Sir John Sinclair, *General Report of the Agricultural State, and Political Circumstances, of Scotland* (Edinburgh, 1814), vol. 1, p. 27.
5. Sir John Sinclair, *The [Old] Statistical Account of Scotland* (Edinburgh, 1791–9), vol. 7, p. 379.
6. John Naismith, *Thoughts on Various Objects of Industry Pursued in Scotland* (Edinburgh, 1790), pp. 94–5.
7. John Brewer, *The Sinews of Power: War, Money and the English State, 1688–1783* (Cambridge, MA, 1990), p. xvii.
8. Quoted in Devine, *Scotland's Empire*, p. 65.
9. This and the following two paragraphs summarize the arguments in T. M. Devine, 'Scottish Élites and the Indian Empire, 1700–1815', in T. C. Smout, ed., *Anglo-Scottish Relations from 1603 to 1900* (Oxford, 2005), pp. 213–32.
10. Neal Ascherson, *Stone Voices: The Search for Scotland* (London, 2002), p. 237.
11. Sir G. Macartney, *An Account of Ireland in 1773 by a Late Chief Secretary of that Kingdom* (London, 1773), cited in Thomas Bartlett, '"This famous island set in a Virginian sea": Ireland in the British Empire, 1690–1801', in P. J. Marshall, ed., *The Oxford History of the British Empire*, vol. 2: *The Eighteenth Century* (Oxford, 1998), p. 262.
12. P. J. Marshall, *East Indian Fortunes* (Oxford, 1976), p. 234.
13. Quoted in Devine, *Scotland's Empire*, p. 259.
14. Ascherson, *Stone Voices*, p. 237.

15. Quoted in G. J. Bryant, 'Scots in India in the Eighteenth Century', *Scottish Historical Review*, 64 (1985), p. 27.

6: AULD SCOTIA OR NORTH BRITAIN?

1. Quoted in T. M. Devine, 'The Invention of Scotland', in D. Dickson, S. Duffy, C. O'Hainle and I. C. Ross, eds, *Ireland and Scotland: Nation, Region, Identity* (Durham, 2001), pp. 18–25.
2. Bruce P. Lenman, 'The Teaching of Scottish History in the Scottish Universities', *Scottish Historical Review*, 52 (October 1973), p. 174.
3. Colin Kidd and James Coleman, 'Mythical Scotland', in T. M. Devine and Jenny Wormald, eds, *The Oxford Handbook of Modern Scottish History* (Oxford, 2012), p. 68.
4. Quoted in Peter Womack, *Improvement and Romance: Constructing the Myth of the Highlands* (Basingstoke, 1989), pp. 145–6.
5. Ibid., p. 145.
6. Quoted in Bernard Cornwell, *Waterloo* (London, 2014), p. 195.
7. Quoted in H. Trevor-Roper, 'The Invention of Tradition: The Highland Tradition of Scotland', in Eric J. Hobsbawm and T. O. Ranger, eds, *The Invention of Tradition* (Cambridge, 1983), pp. 30, 31.
8. Quoted in ibid., p. 31.
9. Andrew Ross, 'Wallace's Monument and the Resumption of Scotland', *Social Text* 18:4 (2000), p. 92.
10. Quoted in Alvin Jackson, *The Two Unions* (Oxford, 2012), p. 136.

7: NO 'SCOTTISH QUESTION'

1. Colin Kidd, *Union and Unionisms* (Cambridge, 2008), p. 24.
2. Quoted in I. G. C. Hutchison, 'Anglo-Scottish Political Relations in the Nineteenth Century, c.1815–1914', in T. C. Smout, ed., *Anglo-Scottish Relations from 1603 to 1900* (Oxford, 2005), p. 247.
3. Quoted in Christopher Harvie, 'Nineteenth-Century Scotland: Political Unionism and Cultural Nationalism, 1843–1906', in R. G. Asch, ed., *Three Nations – a Common History?* (Bochum, 1993), p. 205.
4. Anon., 'Scottish Capital Abroad', *Blackwood's Edinburgh Magazine*, cxxxvi (1884), p. 468.
5. A. D. Gibb, *Scotland in Eclipse* (London, 1930), pp. 186–7.
6. Quoted in Richard J. Finlay, 'Queen Victoria and the Cult of Scottish Monarchy', in Edward J. Cowan and Richard J. Finlay, eds, *Scottish History: The Power of the Past* (Edinburgh, 2002), p. 217.

7. Ibid., p. 211.

8. Quoted in Richard J. Finlay, *A Partnership for Good?* (Edinburgh, 1997), p. 96.

9. Ibid., p. 100.

10. Michael Fry, *Patronage and Principle* (Aberdeen, 1987), pp. 184–5.

8. BRITISHNESS, 1939–1960

1. Herbert Morrison, *An Autobiography* (London, 1960), p. 199.

2. Richard Finlay, *Modern Scotland, 1914–2000* (London, 2004), p. 195.

3. 'Preamble', *Scottish Covenant*, 1949.

4. Quoted in Andrew Marr, *The Battle for Scotland* (Harmondsworth, 1992), p. 92.

5. Catriona M. M. Macdonald, *Whaur Extremes Meet: Scotland's Twentieth Century* (Edinburgh, 2009), p. 239.

6. William Ferguson, *Scotland: 1689 to the Present* (Edinburgh, 1968), p. 387.

9. NATIONALISM

1. Quoted in James Mitchell, *The Scottish Question* (Oxford, 2014), p. 129.

2. Quoted in James Mitchell, *Conservatives and the Union* (Edinburgh, 1990), p. 55.

3. Quoted in A. Clements, K. Farquarson and K. Wark, *Restless Nation* (Edinburgh, 1996), p. 66.

4. Ibid., pp. 63–4.

5. Arnold Kemp, *The Hollow Drum: Scotland since the War* (Edinburgh, 1993), p. 152.

6. Quoted in Mitchell, *Conservatives and the Union*, p. 91.

10. SEEDS OF DISCONTENT

1. Murray Pittock, *The Road to Independence?* (London, 2013 edn), p. 82.

2. All quotations in this paragraph and the preceding one come from Alan Allport, *Browned Off and Bloody-Minded: The British Soldier Goes to War, 1939–1945* (London, 2015), *passim*.

3. Gordon T. Stewart, *Jute and Empire* (Manchester, 1998), pp. 2–4.

4. Glasgow Caledonian University Research Collections, Scottish Trades Union Congress Archive, *Annual Reports of the STUC* (1953–5).

5. Quoted in Ewen A. Cameron, *Impaled upon a Thistle: Scotland since 1880* (Edinburgh, 2010), p. 283.

6. Quoted in James Mitchell, 'Scotland in the Union, 1945–95', in T. M. Devine and R. J. Finlay, eds, *Scotland in the Twentieth Century* (Edinburgh, 1996), p. 97.
7. Simon Johnson, 'North Sea Oil Gave Scotland "Massive" Budget Surplus, Say Government Records', *The Daily Telegraph* (28 September 2009).
8. Billy Wolfe, *Scotland Lives: The Quest for Independence* (Edinburgh, 1973), p. 160.

11. SCOTLAND TRANSFORMED

1. Richard Finlay, *Modern Scotland, 1914–2000* (London, 2004), pp. 342–3.
2. James Mitchell, *Conservatives and the Union* (Edinburgh, 1990).
3. Jim Sillars, *Scotland: The Case for Optimism* (Edinburgh, 1986), p. 1.
4. Quoted in Catriona M. M. Macdonald, *Whaur Extremes Meet: Scotland's Twentieth Century* (Edinburgh, 2009), p. 23.
5. Peter L. Payne, *Growth & Contraction: Scottish Industry c.1860–1990* (Glasgow, 1992).
6. Esther Breitenbach, *Radical Scotland* (October/November 1985).
7. Lindsay Paterson, Frank Bechhofer and David McCrone, *Living in Scotland: Social and Economic Change since 1980* (Edinburgh, 2004), p. 4.
8. Ibid., p. 95.
9. Sir Malcolm Rifkind, 'Foreword', in David Torrance, *'We in Scotland': Thatcherism in a Cold Climate* (Edinburgh, 2009), p. xvii.

12: 'THE GREATEST OF ALL SCOTTISH NATIONALISTS'

1. *The Herald* (28 March 2015).
2. Sir Malcolm Rifkind, 'Foreword', in David Torrance, *'We in Scotland': Thatcherism in a Cold Climate* (Edinburgh, 2009), p. xv.
3. William McIlvanney, *Surviving the Shipwreck* (Edinburgh, 1991), p. 246.
4. A. D. R. Dickson, 'The Peculiarities of the Scottish: National Culture and Political Action', *Political Quarterly*, 59 (July 1988), pp. 358–68.
5. Rifkind, 'Foreword', p. xv.
6. *Scotland on Sunday* (17 October 1993).
7. Quoted in James Naughtie, *The Rivals* (London, 2001), p. 21.
8. Margaret Thatcher's speech to the Scottish Conservative Party Conference, Perth (13 May 1988), quoted in Torrance, *'We in Scotland'*, p. 184.
9. Margaret Thatcher's speech to the Scottish Conservative Party Conference, Perth (12 May 1979).

10. Brian Wilson, 'Foreword', in Torrance, '*We in Scotland*', p. xxii.
11. *The Observer* (26 June 1988).
12. Speech to Scottish Conservative Party Conference, Perth (13 May 1988).
13. Quoted in Torrance, '*We in Scotland*', p. 222.
14. Wilson, 'Foreword', p. xxiii.
15. Kenneth Roy, *Conversations in a Small Country* (Ayr, 1989), pp. 190–1.
16. Rifkind, 'Foreword', p. xviii.
17. Quoted in Kenyon Wright, *The People Say Yes* (Glendaruel, 1997), p. 55.
18. Rifkind, 'Foreword', p. xvii.
19. Margaret Thatcher's speech to the Scottish Conservative Party Conference, Perth (15 May 1987).
20. Wilson, 'Foreword', pp. xxiii–xxiv.
21. Gerry Hassan (26 August 2008), as cited in Torrance, '*We in Scotland*', p. 262.
22. Esther Breitenbach, *Radical Scotland* (June/July 1985).
23. Quoted in Torrance, '*We in Scotland*', p. 264.

13: 'THERE SHALL BE A SCOTTISH PARLIAMENT'

1. W. L. Miller, 'The Death of Unionism?', in T. M. Devine, ed., *Scotland and the Union, 1707–2007* (Edinburgh, 2008), p. 179.
2. Ibid., pp. 184–5.
3. Owen Dudley Edwards, ed., *A Claim of Right for Scotland* (Edinburgh, 1989), pp. 51–3.
4. Andrew Marr, *The Battle for Scotland* (Harmondsworth, 1992), p. 230.
5. All quotations, including this one, come from T. M. Devine, 'History's Judgement', in Wendy Alexander, ed., *Donald Dewar: Scotland's first First Minister* (Edinburgh, 2005), pp. 196–206.

14: THE MODERN SNP

1. John Curtice, 'Devolution, the SNP and the Electorate', in G. Hassan, ed., *The Modern SNP* (Edinburgh 2009), pp. 58–9.
2. Ibid., p. 65.
3. 'Holyrood Must Raise its Game', *Scottish Daily Mail* (6 May 2000).
4. Peter Jones, 'The Modernising Radical', in Wendy Alexander, ed., *Donald Dewar: Scotland's first First Minister* (Edinburgh, 2005), p. 168.
5. Ibid., p. 91.
6. Quoted in Brian Taylor, *Scotland's Parliament: Triumph and Disaster* (Edinburgh, 2002), p. 315.

15: BREAKTHROUGH OF THE NATIONALISTS

1. Iain Macwhirter, *Road to Referendum* (Glasgow, 2013), p. 301.
2. Ibid., p. 302.
3. James Mitchell, *The Scottish Question* (Oxford, 2014), pp. 259 and 266.
4. BBC News (17 December 2011).
5. Gerry Hassan and Eric Shaw, *The Strange Death of Labour Scotland* (Edinburgh, 2012), p. 8.
6. Quoted in Macwhirter, *Road to Referendum*, p. 281.
7. Lord Sumption, 'The Disunited Kingdom: England, Ireland and Scotland', Lecture to the Denning Society Lincoln's Inn, 5 November 2013.
8. Macwhirter, *Road to Referendum*, p. 280.

16: THE BATTLE FOR SCOTLAND IS JOINED

1. Neil Davidson, 'A Scottish Watershed', *New Left Review*, 89 (September–October 2014), p. 4.
2. Quoted in ibid., p. 45.
3. Iain Macwhirter, *Disunited Kingdom* (Glasgow, 2014), p. 21.
4. Walter Humes, 'The Silent Majority Need to Play a More Active Role', *Scottish Review* (24 September 2014), p. 3.
5. Joyce McMillan, 'The Yes Campaign is Not Anti-English, it's About Promoting a Positive Future for Scotland', *The Scotsman* (17 July 2014).
6. Macwhirter, *Disunited Kingdom*, p. 89.
7. See, for example, Lord Ashcroft Polls (http://lordashcroftpolls.com), 'How Scotland Voted, and Why?' (19 September 2014); John Curtice, 'So Who Voted Yes and Who Voted No?' (http://blog.whatscotlandthinks.org/2014/09/voted); www.scottishreferendumstudy.com.
8. This section has benefited from my colleague Lindsay Paterson's 'Utopian Pragmatism: Scotland's Choice', *Scottish Affairs*, 24:1 (2015), pp. 22–46.
9. Joyce McMillan, 'Is No Vote Fear over Common Sense?', *The Scotsman* (20 September 2014).
10. Paterson, 'Utopian Pragmatism', pp. 41–2.
11. Curtice, 'So Who Voted Yes . . .', p. 1.
12. Frank Bechhofer and David McCrone, 'The End of Being British?', *Scottish Affairs*, 23:3 (2014), pp. 319–20; Michael Rosie and Eva Hepburn, '"The Essence of the Union . . .": Unionism, Nationalism and Identity on these Disconnected Islands', *Scottish Affairs*, 24:2 (2015), p. 155.

17: AFTER THE BATTLE

1. Matthew Norman, 'David Cameron May Have Won the Election, but it's for Wrecking the Union that he Will be Remembered', *The Independent* (8 May 2015).
2. *The Guardian* (11 May 2015).

AFTERWORD

1. 'Cameron Vows to Rule UK as "one nation" but the Scottish Question Looms', *The Guardian* (9 May 2015).
2. Michael Kenny, *The Politics of English Nationhood* (Oxford, 2014), cited in Neil Ascherson, 'For Scotland, Independence Day has already Dawned', *The Guardian* (11 May 2015).
3. Ibid.

Selected Further Reading

1: THE CONTEXT OF UNION

T. M. Devine, ed., *Scotland and the Union, 1707–2007* (Edinburgh, 2008)

Michael Fry, *The Union: England, Scotland and the Treaty of 1707* (Edinburgh, 2006)

Alvin Jackson, *The Two Unions* (Oxford, 2012)

Colin Kidd, *Union and Unionisms* (Cambridge, 2008)

Allan I. Macinnes, *Union and Empire: The Making of the United Kingdom in 1707* (Cambridge, 2007)

Iain McLean and Alistair McMillan, *State of the Union* (Oxford, 2005)

Christopher A. Whatley, *'Bought and Sold for English Gold'? Explaining the Union of 1707* (Glasgow, 1994)

Christopher A. Whatley with Derek J. Patrick, *The Scots and the Union* (Edinburgh, 2006)

2: MAKING THE UNION

As above

3: A FRAGILE UNION

T. M. Devine, ed., *Scotland and the Union, 1707–2007* (Edinburgh, 2008)

H. T. Dickinson and Michael Lynch, eds, *The Challenge to Westminster* (East Linton, 2000)

Roger L. Emerson, *An Enlightened Duke* (Kilkerran, 2013)

John S. Gibson, *Playing the Scottish Card: The Franco-Jacobite Invasion of 1708* (Edinburgh, 1988)

Tim Harris, *Revolution: The Great Crisis of the British Monarchy, 1685–1720* (London, 2006)

Alvin Jackson, *The Two Unions* (Oxford, 2012)

John S. Shaw, *The Management of Scottish Society, 1707-1764* (Edinburgh, 1983)

Jeffrey Stephen, *Defending the Revolution: The Church of Scotland, 1689-1716* (Farnham, 2013)

Daniel Szechi, *1715: The Great Jacobite Rebellion* (New Haven and London, 2006)

Christopher A. Whatley with Derek J. Patrick, *The Scots and the Union* (Edinburgh, 2006)

4: UNION EMBEDDED

Robert Clyde, *From Rebel to Hero: The Image of the Highlander, 1745-1830* (East Linton, 1995)

Linda Colley, *Britons* (New Haven, 1992)

T. M. Devine, *Clanship to Crofters' War: The Social Transformation of the Scottish Highlands* (Manchester, 2013)

T. M. Devine and Jenny Wormald, eds, *The Oxford Handbook of Modern Scottish History* (Oxford, 2012)

Roger L. Emerson, *An Enlightened Duke* (Kilkerran, 2013)

Michael Fry, *The Dundas Despotism* (Edinburgh, 2004 edn)

Andrew Mackillop, 'More Fruitful than the Soil': Army, Empire and the Scottish Highlands, 1715-1815* (East Linton, 2000)

Alexander Murdoch, 'The People Above' (Edinburgh, 1980)

John S. Shaw, *The Management of Scottish Society, 1707-1764* (Edinburgh, 1983)

T. C. Smout, ed., *Anglo-Scottish Relations from 1603 to 1900* (Oxford, 2005)

5: EARLY FRUITS OF EMPIRE

John Brewer, *The Sinews of Power: War, Money and the English State, 1688-1783* (Cambridge, MA, 1990)

T. M. Devine, *The Tobacco Lords* (Edinburgh, 1990 edn)

T. M. Devine, *Scotland's Empire, 1600-1815* (London, 2003)

T. M. Devine, ed., *Recovering Scotland's Slavery Past: The Caribbean Connection* (Edinburgh, 2015)

Douglas J. Hamilton, *Scotland, the Caribbean and the Atlantic World, 1750-1820* (Manchester, 2005)

Ned C. Landsman, ed., *Nation and Province in the First British Empire* (London, 2001)

George McGilvary, *East India Patronage and the British State* (London, 2008)

John M. Mackenzie and T. M. Devine, eds, *Scotland and the British Empire* (Oxford, 2011)

6: AULD SCOTIA OR NORTH BRITAIN?

Benedict Anderson, *Imagined Communities* (London, 1983)

L. Brockliss and D. Eastwood, eds, *A Union of Multiple Identities* (Manchester, 1997)

Ian Brown, ed., *From Tartan to Tartanry: Scottish Culture, History and Myth* (Edinburgh, 2010)

W. Donaldson, *The Jacobite Song* (Aberdeen, 1988)

I. L. Donnachie and C. A. Whatley, eds, *The Manufacture of Scottish History* (Edinburgh, 1992)

David Hesse, *Warrior Dreams* (Manchester, 2014)

Graeme Morton, *Unionist Nationalism* (East Linton, 1999)

Lindsay Paterson, *The Autonomy of Modern Scotland* (Edinburgh, 1994)

John Prebble, *The King's Jaunt* (London, 1988)

H. R. Trevor-Roper, *The Invention of Scotland* (New Haven, 2009 edn)

7: NO 'SCOTTISH QUESTION'

Edward J. Cowan and Richard J. Finlay, eds, *Scottish History: The Power of the Past* (Edinburgh, 2002)

T. M. Devine and R. J. Finlay, eds, *Scotland in the Twentieth Century* (Edinburgh, 1996)

T. M. Devine and Jenny Wormald, eds, *The Oxford Handbook of Modern Scottish History* (Oxford, 2012)

Richard J. Finlay, *Independent and Free: Scottish Politics and the Origins of the Scottish National Party, 1918–1945* (Edinburgh, 1994)

Christopher Harvie, *No Gods and Precious Few Heroes: Scotland 1914–1980* (Edinburgh, 1996)

I. G. C. Hutchison, *A Political History of Scotland, 1832–1924* (Edinburgh, 1986)

Colin Kidd, *Union and Unionisms* (Cambridge, 2008)

John M. Mackenzie and T. M. Devine, eds, *Scotland and the British Empire* (Oxford, 2011)

Graeme Morton, *Ourselves and Others: Scotland 1832–1914* (Edinburgh, 2012)

T. C. Smout, ed., *Anglo-Scottish Relations from 1603 to 1900* (Oxford, 2005)

8: BRITISHNESS 1939–1960

T. M. Devine and R. J. Finlay, eds, *Scotland in the Twentieth Century* (Edinburgh, 1996)

T. M. Devine, C. H. Lee and G. C. Peden, eds, *The Transformation of Scotland: The Economy since 1700* (Edinburgh, 2005)

Richard Finlay, *Modern Scotland, 1914–2000* (London, 2004)

Catriona M. M. Macdonald, *Whaur Extremes Meet: Scotland's Twentieth Century* (Edinburgh, 2009)

William L. Miller, ed., *Anglo-Scottish Relations from 1900 to Devolution and Beyond* (Oxford, 2005)

James Mitchell, *The Scottish Question* (Oxford, 2014)

Peter L. Payne, *Growth & Contraction: Scottish Industry c.1860–1990* (Glasgow, 1992)

9: NATIONALISM

J. Bochel, D. Denver and A. Macartney, *The Referendum Experience: Scotland 1979* (Aberdeen, 1981)

Jack Brand, *The National Movement in Scotland* (London, 1978)

T. M. Devine and Jenny Wormald, eds, *The Oxford Handbook of Modern Scottish History* (Oxford, 2012)

Richard Finlay, *Modern Scotland, 1914–2000* (London, 2004)

I. G. C. Hutchison, *Scottish Politics in the Twentieth Century* (Basingstoke, 2001)

James G. Kellas, *The Scottish Political System* (Cambridge, 1989 edn)

James Mitchell, *The Scottish Question* (Oxford, 2014)

Paula Somerville, *Through the Maelstrom* (Edinburgh, 2013)

10: SEEDS OF DISCONTENT

Vernon Bogdanor, *Devolution in the United Kingdom* (Oxford, 1999)

Ewen A. Cameron, *Impaled upon a Thistle: Scotland since 1880* (Edinburgh, 2010)

T. M. Devine and R. J. Finlay, eds, *Scotland in the Twentieth Century* (Edinburgh, 1996)

T. M. Devine, C. H. Lee and G. C. Peden, eds, *The Transformation of Scotland: The Economy since 1700* (Edinburgh, 2005)

Christopher Harvie, *Fool's Gold: The Story of North Sea Oil* (London, 1994)

Alex Kemp, *The Official History of North Sea Oil and Gas*, vol. 1: *The Growing Dominance of the State* (London, 2012)

Peter Lynch, *SNP: The History of the Scottish National Party* (Cardiff, 2002)

David McCrone, *Understanding Scotland* (London, 2001, 2nd edn)

Catriona M. M. Macdonald, ed., *Unionist Scotland, 1800–1997* (Edinburgh, 1998)

Iain McLean and Alistair McMillan, *State of the Union* (Oxford, 2005)

William L. Miller, *The End of British Politics?* (Oxford, 1981)

William L. Miller, ed., *Anglo-Scottish Relations from 1900 to Devolution and Beyond* (Oxford, 2005)

James Mitchell, *Conservatives and the Union* (Edinburgh, 1990)

James Mitchell, *The Scottish Question* (Oxford, 2014)

11: SCOTLAND TRANSFORMED

Alice Brown, David McCrone and Lindsay Paterson, *Politics and Society in Scotland* (Basingstoke, 1996)

T. M. Devine, ed., *Scotland and the Union, 1707–2007* (Edinburgh, 2008)

Peter Lynch, *SNP: The History of the Scottish National Party* (Cardiff, 2002)

Lindsay Paterson, Frank Bechhofer and David McCrone, *Living in Scotland: Social and Economic Change since 1980* (Edinburgh, 2004)

Graham Stewart, *Bang! A History of Britain in the 1980s* (London, 2013)

Margaret Thatcher, *The Downing Street Years* (London, 1993)

12: 'THE GREATEST OF ALL SCOTTISH NATIONALISTS'

Keith Aitken, *The Bairns o' Adam: The Story of the STUC* (Edinburgh, 1997)

John Campbell, *Margaret Thatcher*, vol. 2: *The Iron Lady* (London, 2003)

Owen Dudley Edwards, ed., *A Claim of Right for Scotland* (Edinburgh, 1989)

Ian Gilmour, *Dancing with Dogma: Britain under Thatcherism* (London, 1992)

Arnold Kemp, *The Hollow Drum: Scotland since the War* (Edinburgh, 1993)

David McCrone, *Understanding Scotland* (London, 2001, 2nd edn)

Andrew Marr, *The Battle for Scotland* (Harmondsworth, 1992)

Kenneth Roy, *Conversations in a Small Country* (Ayr, 1989)

David Seawright, *An Important Matter of Principle: The Decline of the Scottish Conservative and Unionist Party* (Aldershot, 1999)

Margaret Thatcher, *The Downing Street Years* (London, 1993)

David Torrance, '*We in Scotland': Thatcherism in a Cold Climate* (Edinburgh, 2009)

David Torrance, ed., *Whatever Happened to Tory Scotland?* (Edinburgh, 2012)

Hugo Young, *One of Us: A Biography of Margaret Thatcher* (London, 1991 edn)

13: 'THERE SHALL BE A SCOTTISH PARLIAMENT'

Wendy Alexander, ed., *Donald Dewar: Scotland's first First Minister* (Edinburgh, 2005)

Alice Brown, David McCrone and Lindsay Paterson, *Politics and Society in Scotland* (Basingstoke, 1998 edn)

Gordon Brown, *My Scotland, Our Britain* (London and New York, 2014)

Ewen A. Cameron, *Impaled upon a Thistle: Scotland since 1880* (Edinburgh, 2010)

T. M. Devine, ed., *Scotland and the Union, 1707–2007* (Edinburgh, 2008)

Owen Dudley Edwards, ed., *A Claim of Right for Scotland* (Edinburgh, 1989)

Iain Macwhirter, *Road to Referendum* (Glasgow, 2013)

James Mitchell, *Devolution in the UK* (Manchester, 2009)

James Mitchell, *The Scottish Question* (Oxford, 2014)

Murray Pittock, *The Road to Independence?* (London, 2013 edn)

Brian Taylor, *The Road to the Scottish Parliament* (Edinburgh, 2002 edn)

14: THE MODERN SNP

Linda Colley, *Acts of Union and Disunion* (London, 2014)

Gerry Hassan, ed., *The Modern SNP* (Edinburgh, 2009)

Michael Keating, *The Government of Scotland* (Edinburgh, 2010 edn)

Peter Lynch, *SNP: The History of the Scottish National Party* (Cardiff, 2013 edn)

James Mitchell, *The Scottish Question* (Oxford, 2014)

Brian Taylor, *Scotland's Parliament: Triumph and Disaster* (Edinburgh, 2002)

David Torrance, *Salmond: Against the Odds* (Edinburgh, 2010)

15: BREAKTHROUGH OF THE NATIONALISTS

Eberhard Bort, *The Annals of the Holyrood Parish: A Decade of Devolution, 2004–2014* (Ochtertyre, 2014)

J. Curtice, D. McCrone, N. McEwen, M. Marsh and R. Ormston, *Revolution or Evolution? The 2007 Scottish Elections* (Edinburgh, 2009)

Gerry Hassan and Eric Shaw, *The Strange Death of Labour Scotland* (Edinburgh, 2012)

Peter Lynch, *SNP: The History of the Scottish National Party* (Cardiff, 2013 edn)

Iain Macwhirter, *Road to Referendum* (Glasgow, 2013)

James Mitchell, Lynn Bennie and Rob Johns, *The Scottish National Party: Transition to Power* (Oxford, 2012)

David Torrance, *Salmond: Against the Odds* (Edinburgh, 2010)

16: THE BATTLE FOR SCOTLAND IS JOINED
and
17: AFTER THE BATTLE

http://blog.whatscotlandthinks.org/2014

http://www.scottishreferendumstudy.com

J. Curtice, J. Eichhorn, Rachel Ormston and L. Paterson, *The Scottish Referendum 2014* (London, 2015).

Peter Geoghegan, *The People's Referendum* (Edinburgh, 2014)

Andrew Goudie, ed., *Scotland's Future: The Economics of Constitutional Change* (Dundee, 2013)

Peter Hennessy, *The Kingdom to Come: Thoughts on the Union before and after the Scottish Referendum* (London, 2015)

Irish Times, *Scotland's Moment: The Story of the Referendum* (Dublin, 2014)

Gavin McCrone, *Scottish Independence* (Edinburgh, 2013)

Iain Macwhirter, *Disunited Kingdom* (Glasgow, 2014)

A. Moffat and A. Riach, *Arts of Independence* (Edinburgh, 2014)

Alex Salmond, *The Dream Shall Never Die: 100 Days that Changed Scotland Forever* (London, 2015)

Index

India
  British rule 70–73
  independence (1947) 136, 140
  Scots in 48, 73 (table)
  soldiers' view of 137–8
industrial relations 133, 143, 146
  see also trade unions
industrialization, Scotland 48–50,
    59–62, 78
  failure to diversify 105, 143
  specialized heavy industry 95–8,
    103, 111, 143, 144
industry
  and de-industrialization (1980s)
    156–62, 171–2, 182
  multinationals 160
  nationalization 120, 144
  origins of decline of 157–8, 182
  subsidy intervention 144
  transformation (from late 1980s)
    160–62
internationalism
  post-Second World War 111
  of Scottish Enlightenment 77
Invergordon Aluminium Smelter 154,
    175
Inverness 12
Iraq War 225–6
Ireland 6, 50, 55
  contrasted with Scotland 50, 55,
    56–7, 93–4
  Great Famine (1845–9) 50, 88
  Irish home rule (Irish question)
    92, 94
iron industry 49
Irvine, Derry, Lord Chancellor
    203, 223
Islay, Earl of 33, 37
  as 3rd Duke of Argyll 50–51
  as Secretary for Scotland 37–9

Jacobite risings
  1715 rising 10, 34–5, 36
  1745 rising 42–6
  first (1689) 7

role of Catholicism 10
Jacobites and Jacobitism 9, 10, 29, 56
  and 1703 elections 18–19
  and Cavaliers parliamentary
    grouping 23, 24
  cult of 46, 82–3
  decline of 44–6
  and possible French invasion 18, 23
  and survival of Union 42–6
James I and VI, King 4, 14, 268
James II and VII, King 5–6, 9
  forfeits Crown 6–7
Jenkins, Blair 236
Jenkins, Roy, MP 128, 155
Johnson, Boris 260
Johnson, Dr Samuel 81
Johnston, Tom, MP 105–6, 112–13
Johnstone, James, Lord Clerk Register
    24
Johnstone, Sir Patrick 22
Johnstone of Westerhall, John 73–4
Jones, Peter 244
Junior Empire League 100
Junor, Sir John 178
jute manufacture, Dundee 96, 103,
    159

Kaufmann, Gerald, MP 155
Keir Hardie, James 93, 100
Kelman, James 160, 187
Kennedy, Charles, MP 155, 261
Kenya 141
Kidd, Colin 92
Killicrankie, Pass of, battle (1689) 9
Kinnock, Neil, MP 192
knowledge economy 164
Kvaerner, shipbuilders 158

labour
  productivity 163
  shortage of skilled 49
Labour Party
  and 2007 Scottish Parliament
    election 217–18
  and 2010 election 219, 222